David Budescu

DR. DAVID BUDESCU
DEPT. OF PSYCHOLOGY
UNIVERSITY OF HAIFA
HAIFA 31999 ISRAEL

APPLICATIONS OF
ITEM RESPONSE THEORY
TO PRACTICAL TESTING PROBLEMS

FREDERIC M. LORD
Educational Testing Service

LEA LAWRENCE ERLBAUM ASSOCIATES, PUBLISHERS

1980   Hillsdale, New Jersey

Copyright is claimed until 1990. Thereafter all portions of this work
covered by this copyright will be in the public domain.
This work was developed under a contract with the National Institute of
Education, Department of Health, Education, and Welfare. However, the
content does not necessarily reflect the position or policy of that
Agency, and no official endorsement of these materials should be inferred.

Lawrence Erlbaum Associates, Inc., Publishers
365 Broadway
Hillsdale, New Jersey 07642

Library of Congress Cataloging in Publication Data

Lord, Frederic M   1912–
  Applications of item response theory to practical
testing problems.

  Bibliography: p.
  Includes index.
  1. Examinations.   2. Examinations—Evaluation.
I. Title.
LB3051.L64   371.2′6   79-24186
ISBN 0-89859-006-X

Printed in the United States of America

Contents

PART IV: ESTIMATING TRUE-SCORE DISTRIBUTIONS

Preface

The purpose of this book is to make it possible for measurement specialists to solve practical testing problems by use of item response theory. This theory expresses all the properties of the test, as a measuring instrument, in terms of the properties of the test items. Practical applications include

1. The estimation of invariant parameters describing each test item; item banking.
2. Estimating the statistical characteristics of a test for any specified group.
3. Determining how the effectiveness of a test varies across ability levels.
4. Comparing the effectiveness of different methods of scoring a test.
5. Selecting items to build a conventional test.
6. Redesigning a conventional tests.
7. Design and evaluation of mastery tests.
8. Designing and evaluating novel testing methods, such as flexilevel tests, two-stage tests, multilevel tests, tailored tests.
9. Equating and preequating.
10. Study of item bias.

The topics, organization, and presentation are those used in a 4-week seminar held each summer for the past several years. The material is organized primarily to maintain the reader's interest and to facilitate understanding; thus all related topics are not always packed into the same chapter. Some knowledge of classical test theory, mathematical statistics, and calculus is helpful in reading this material.

Chapter 1, a perspective on classical test theory, is perhaps not essential for the reader. Chapter 2, an introduction to item response theory, is easy to read. Some of Chapter 3 is important only for those who need to understand the relation of item response theory to classical item analysis. Chapter 4 is essential to any real understanding of item response theory and applications. The reader who takes the trouble to master the basic ideas of Chapter 4 will have little difficulty in learning what he wants from the rest of the book. The information functions of Chapter 5, basic to most applications of item response theory, are relatively easy to understand.

The later chapters are mostly independent of each other. The reader may choose those that interest him and ignore the others. Except in Chapter 11 on mastery testing and Chapters 16 and 17 on estimating true-score distributions, the reader can usually skip over the mathematics in the later chapters, if that suits his purpose. He will still gain a good general understanding of the applications under discussion provided he has previously understood Chapter 4.

The basic ideas of Chapters 16 and 17, on estimated true-score distributions, are important for the future development of mental test theory. These chapters are not a basic part of item response theory and may be omitted by the general reader.

Reviewers will urge the need for a book on item response theory that does not require the mathematical understanding required here. There is such a need; such books will be written soon, by other authors (see Warm, 1978).

Journal publications in the field of item response theory, including publications on the Rasch model, are already very numerous. Some of these publications are excellent; some are exceptionally poor. The reader will not find all important publications listed in this book, but he will find enough to guide him in further search (see also Cohen, 1979).

I am very much in debt to Marilyn Wingersky for her continual help in the theoretical, computational, mathematical, and instructional work underlying this book. I greatly appreciate the help of Martha Stocking, who read (and checked) a semifinal manuscript; the errors in the final publication were introduced by me subsequent to her work. I thank William H. Angoff, Charles E. Davis, Ronald K. Hambleton, and Hariharan Swaminathan and their students, Huynh Huynh, Samuel A. Livingston, Donald B. Rubin, Fumiko Samejima, Wim J. van der Linden, Wendy M. Yen, and many of my own students for their helpful comments on part or all of earlier versions of the manuscript. I am especially indebted to Donna Lembeck who typed innumerable revisions of text, formulas, and tables, drew some of the diagrams, and organized production of the manuscript. I would also like to thank Marie Davis and Sally Hagen for proofreading numerous versions of the manuscript and Ann King for editorial assistance.

Most of the developments reported in this book were made possible by the support of the Personnel and Training Branch, Office of Naval Research, in the form of contracts covering the period 1952–1972, and by grants from the Psychobiology Program of the National Science Foundation covering the period

1972–1976. This essential support was gratefully acknowledged in original journal publications; it is not detailed here. The publication of this book was made possible by a contract with the National Institute of Education. All the work in this book was made possible by the continued generous support of Educational Testing Service, starting in 1948. Data for ETS tests are published here by permission.

References

Cohen, A. S. *Bibliography of papers on latent trait assessment*. Evanston, Ill.: Region V Technical Assistance Center, Educational Testing Service Midwestern Regional Office, 1979.

Warm, T. A. *A primer of item response theory*. Technical Report 941078. Oklahoma City, Okla.: U.S. Coast Guard Institute, 1978.

FREDERIC M. LORD

INTRODUCTION TO ITEM
RESPONSE THEORY

1
Classical Test Theory— Summary and Perspective

1.1. INTRODUCTION

This chapter is not a substitute for a course in classical test theory. On the contrary, some knowledge of classical theory is presumed. The purpose of this chapter is to provide some perspective on basic ideas that are fundamental to all subsequent work.

A psychological or educational test is a device for obtaining a sample of behavior. Usually the behavior is quantified in some way to obtain a numerical score. Such scores are tabulated and counted. Their relations to other variables of interest are studied empirically.

If the necessary relationships can be established empirically, the scores may then be used to predict some future behavior of the individuals tested. This is actuarial science. It can all be done without any special theory. On this basis, it is sometimes asserted from an operationalist viewpoint that there is no need for any deeper theory of test scores.

Two or more "parallel" forms of a published test are commonly produced. We usually find that a person obtains different scores on different test forms. How shall these be viewed?

Differences between scores on parallel forms administered at about the same time are usually not of much use for describing the individual tested. If we want a single score to describe his test performance, it is natural to average his scores across the test forms taken. For usual scoring methods, the result is effectively the same as if all forms administered had been combined and treated as a single test.

The individual's average score across test forms will usually be a better measurement than his score on any single form, because the average score is based on a larger sample of behavior. Already we see that there is something of deeper significance than the individual's score on a particular test form.

1.2. TRUE SCORE

In actual practice we cannot administer very many forms of a test to a single individual so as to obtain a better sample of his behavior. Conceptually, however, it is useful to think of doing just this, the individual remaining unchanged throughout the process.

The individual's average score over a set of postulated test forms is a useful concept. This concept is formalized by a mathematical model. The individual's score X on a particular test form is considered to be a chance variable with some, usually unknown, frequency distribution. The mean (expected value) of this distribution is called the individual's *true score T*. Certain conclusions about true scores T and *observed scores X* follow automatically from this model and definition.

Denote the discrepancy between T and X by

$$E \equiv X - T; \tag{1-1}$$

E is called the *error of measurement*. Since by definition the expected value of X is T, the expectation of E is zero:

$$\mu_{E|T} \equiv \mu_{(X - T)|T} \equiv \mu_{X|T} - \mu_{T|T} = T - T = 0, \tag{1-2}$$

where μ denotes a mean and the subscripts indicate that T is fixed.

Equation (1-2) states that *the errors of measurement are unbiased*. This follows automatically from the definition of true score; it does not depend on any ad hoc assumption. By the same argument, in a group of people,

$$\mu_T \equiv \mu_X - \mu_E = \mu_X.$$

Equation (1-2) gives the regression of E on T. Since mean E is constant regardless of T, this regression has zero slope. It follows that *true score and error are uncorrelated in any group*:

$$\rho_{ET} = 0. \tag{1-3}$$

Note, again, that this follows from the definition of true score, not from any special assumption.

From Eq. (1-1) and (1-3), since T and E are uncorrelated, the observed-score variance in any group is made up of two components:

$$\sigma_X^2 = \sigma_{T+E}^2 \equiv \sigma_T^2 + \sigma_E^2. \tag{1-4}$$

The covariance of X and T is

$$\sigma_{XT} \equiv \sigma_{(T+E)T} = \sigma_T^2 + \sigma_{ET} = \sigma_T^2. \tag{1-5}$$

An important quantity is the test *reliability,* the squared correlation between X and T, by (1-5),

$$\rho_{XT}^2 \equiv \frac{\sigma_{XT}^2}{\sigma_X^2 \sigma_T^2} = \frac{\sigma_T^2}{\sigma_X^2}$$

$$= 1 - \frac{\sigma_E^2}{\sigma_X^2} . \tag{1-6}$$

If ρ_{XT} were nearly 1.00, we could safely substitute the available test score X for the unknown measurement of interest T.

Equations (1-2) through (1-6) are tautologies that follow automatically from the definition of T and E.

What has our deeper theory gained for us? The theory arises from the realizations that T, not X, is the quantity of real interest. When a job applicant leaves the room where he was tested, it is T, not X, that determines his capacity for future performance.

We cannot observe T, but we can make useful inferences about it. How this is done becomes apparent in subsequent sections (also, see Section 4.2).

An example will illustrate how true-score theory leads to different conclusions than would be reached by a simple consideration of observed scores. An achievement test is administered to a large group of children. The lowest scoring children are selected for special training. A week later the specially trained children are retested to determine the effect of the training.

True-score theory shows that a person may receive a very low test score either because his true score is low or because his error score E is low (he was unlucky), or both. The lowest scoring children in a large group most likely have not only low T but also low E. If they are retested, the odds are against their being so unlucky a second time. Thus, even if their true scores have not increased, their observed scores will probably be higher on the second testing. Without true-score theory, the probable observed-score increase would be credited to the special training. This effect has caused many educational innovations to be mistakenly labeled ''successful.''

It is true that repeated observations of test scores and retest scores could lead the actuarial scientist to the observation that in practice, other things being equal, initially low-scoring children tend to score higher on retesting. The important point is that true-score theory predicts this conclusion before any tests are given and also explains the reason for this odd occurrence. For further theoretical discussion, see Linn and Slinde (1977) and Lord (1963). In practical applications, we can determine the effects of special training for the low-scoring children by splitting them at random into two groups, comparing the experimental group that received the training with the control group that did not.

Note that we do *not* define true score as the limit of some (operationally impossible) process. The true score is a mathematical abstraction. A statistician doing an analysis of variance components does not try to define the model parameters as if they actually existed in the real world. A statistical model is chosen, expressed in mathematical terms undefined in the real world. The question of whether the real world corresponds to the model is a separate question to be answered as best we can. It is neither necessary nor appropriate to define a person's true score or other statistical parameter by real world operational procedures.

1.3. UNCORRELATED ERRORS

Equations (1-1) through (1-6) cannot be disproved by any set of data. These equations do not enable us to estimate σ_T^2, σ_E^2, or ρ_{XT}, however. To estimate these important quantities, we need to make some assumptions. Note that *no assumption about the real world has been made up to this point.*

It is usual to assume that errors of measurement are uncorrelated with true scores on different tests and with each other: For tests X and Y,

$$\rho(E_X, E_Y) = 0, \qquad \rho(E_X, T_Y) = 0 \qquad (X \neq Y). \tag{1-7}$$

Exceptions to these assumptions are considered in path analysis (Hauser & Goldberger, 1971; Milliken, 1971; Werts, Linn, & Jöreskog, 1974; Werts, Rock, Linn, & Jöreskog, 1977).

1.4. PARALLEL TEST FORMS

If a test is constructed by random sampling from a pool or "universe" of items, then σ_E^2, σ_T^2, and ρ_{XT} can be estimated without building any parallel test forms (Lord & Novick, 1968, Chapter 11). But perhaps we do not wish to assume that our test was constructed in this way. If three or more roughly parallel test forms are available, these same parameters can be estimated by the theory of *nominally parallel tests* (Lord & Novick, 1968, Chapter 8; Cronbach, Gleser, Nanda, & Rajaratnam, 1972), an application of analysis of variance components.

In contrast, classical test theory assumes that we can build *strictly parallel* test forms. By definition, every individual has (1) the same true score and (2) the same conditional error variance $\sigma^2(E|T)$ on all strictly parallel forms:

$$T = T', \qquad \sigma^2(E|T) = \sigma^2(E'|T'), \tag{1-8}$$

where the prime denotes a (strictly) parallel test. It follows that $\sigma_X^2 = \sigma_{X'}^2$.

When strictly parallel forms are available, the important parameters of the *latent variables* T and E can be estimated from the observed-score variance and from the intercorrelation between parallel test forms by the following familiar equations of classical test theory:

$$\rho_{XT}^2 \ (= \rho_{X'T'}^2) = \rho_{XX'}, \tag{1-9}$$

$$\sigma_T^2 \ (= \sigma_{T'}^2) = \sigma_X^2 \rho_{XX'}, \tag{1-10}$$

$$\sigma_E^2 \ (= \sigma_{E'}^2) = \sigma_X^2 (1 - \rho_{XX'}). \tag{1-11}$$

1.5. ENVOI

In item response theory (as discussed in the remaining chapters of this book) the expected value of the observed score is still called the *true score*. The discrepancy between observed score and true score is still called the *error of measurement*. The errors of measurement are thus necessarily unbiased and uncorrelated with true score. The assumptions of (1-7) will be satisfied also; thus all the remaining equations in this chapter, including those in the Appendix, will hold.

Nothing in this book will contradict either the assumptions or the basic conclusions of classical test theory. Additional assumptions will be made; these will allow us to answer questions that classical theory cannot answer. Although we will supplement rather than contradict classical theory, it is surprising how little we will use classical theory explicitly.

Further basic ideas and formulas of classical test theory are summarized for easy reference in an appendix to this chapter. The reader may skip to Chapter 2.

APPENDIX

Regression and Attenuation

From (1-9), (1-10), (1-11) we obtain formulas for the linear regression coefficients:

$$\beta_{XT} = 1, \qquad \beta_{TX} = \rho_{XX'}. \tag{1-12}$$

Let ξ and η be the true scores on tests X and Y, respectively. As in (1-5), $\sigma_{\xi\eta} = \sigma_{XY}$. From this and (1-10) we find the important *correction for attenuation*,

$$\rho_{\xi\eta} = \frac{\sigma_{\xi\eta}}{\sigma_\xi \sigma_\eta} = \frac{\sigma_{XY}}{\sigma_X \sigma_Y \sqrt{\rho_{XX'}\rho_{YY'}}} = \frac{\rho_{XY}}{\sqrt{\rho_{XX'}\rho_{YY'}}}. \tag{1-13}$$

From this comes a key inequality:

$$\sqrt{\rho_{XX'}} \geq \rho_{XY}. \tag{1-14}$$

This says that test validity (correlation of test score X with any criterion Y) is never greater than the square root of the test reliability.

Composite Tests

Up to this point, there has been no assumption that our test is composed of subtests or of test items. If the test score X is a sum of subtest or item scores Y_i, so that

$$X = \sum_{i=1}^{n} Y_i,$$

then certain tautologies follow:

$$\sigma_X^2 = \sum_{i=1}^{n} \sigma_i^2 + \sum_{i \neq j}^{n(n-1)} \sigma_{ij}, \tag{1-15}$$

where $\sigma_i \equiv \sigma(Y_i)$ and $\sigma_{ij} \equiv \sigma(Y_i, Y_j)$. Similarly,

$$\rho_{XX'} = \frac{\sum_i \sum_{i'} \sigma_{ii'}}{\sigma_X^2}, \tag{1-16}$$

where i' indexes the items in test X'. If all subtests are parallel,

$$\rho_{XX'} = \frac{n\rho_{YY'}}{1 + (n-1)\rho_{YY'}}, \tag{1-17}$$

the Spearman–Brown formula.

Coefficient alpha (α) is obtained from (1-15) and (1-16) and from the Cauchy–Schwartz inequality:

$$\rho_{XT}^2 = \rho_{XX'} \geqslant \frac{n}{n-1}\left(1 - \frac{\sum \sigma_i^2}{\sigma_X^2}\right) \equiv \alpha. \tag{1-18}$$

Alpha is not a reliability coefficient; it is a lower bound.

If items are scored either 0 or 1, α becomes the Kuder–Richardson formula-20 coefficient ρ_{20}: from (1-18) and (1-23),

$$\rho_{XT}^2 = \rho_{XX'} \geqslant \frac{n}{n-1}\left[1 - \frac{\sum \pi_i (1 - \pi_i)}{\sigma_X^2}\right] \equiv \rho_{20}, \tag{1-19}$$

where π_i is the proportion of correct answers ($Y_i = 1$) for item i. Also,

$$\rho_{20} \geqslant \frac{n}{n-1}\left[1 - \frac{\mu_X (n - \mu_X)}{n\sigma_X^2}\right] \equiv \rho_{21}, \tag{1-20}$$

the Kuder–Richardson formula-21 coefficient.

Item Theory

Denote the score on item i by Y_i. Classical item analysis provides various tautologies. The variance of the test scores is

$$\sigma_X^2 = \sum_i \sum_j \sigma_i \sigma_j \rho_{ij} = \sigma_X \sum_i \sigma_i \rho_{iX}, \tag{1-21}$$

where ρ_{ij} and ρ_{iX} are Pearson product moment correlation coefficients. If Y_i is always 0 or 1, then X is the number-right score, the interitem correlation ρ_{ij} is a phi coefficient, and ρ_{iX} is an item-test point biserial correlation. Classical item analysis theory may deal also with the biserial correlation between item score and test score and with the tetrachoric correlations between items (see Lord & Novick, 1968, Chapter 15). In the case of dichotomously scored items ($Y_i = 0$ or 1), we have

$$\mu_X = \sum_{i=1}^{n} \pi_i, \tag{1-22}$$

$$\sigma_i^2 = \pi_i(1 - \pi_i). \tag{1-23}$$

From (1-18) and (1-21), coefficient α is

$$\alpha = \frac{n}{n-1} \left(1 - \frac{\Sigma \sigma_i^2}{\Sigma \Sigma \sigma_i \sigma_j \rho_{ij}}\right). \tag{1-24}$$

If C is an outside criterion, the test validity coefficient is

$$\rho_{XC} = \frac{\sum_i \sigma_i \rho_{iC}}{\sqrt{\sum_i \sum_j \sigma_i \sigma_j \rho_{ij}}}. \tag{1-25}$$

These two formulas provide the two paradoxical classical rules for building a test:

1. To maximize test reliability, choose test items that correlate as high as possible with each other.
2. To maximize validity, choose test items that correlate as high as possible with the criterion and as low as possible with each other.

Overview

Classical test theory is based on the weak assumptions (1-7) plus the assumption that we can build strictly parallel tests. Most of its equations are unlikely to be contradicted by data. Equations (1-1) through (1-13) are unlikely to be falsified, since they involve the unobservable variables T and E. Equations (1-15), (1-16), and (1-20)–(1-25) cannot be falsified because they are tautologies.

The only remaining equations of those listed are (1-14) and (1-17)–(1-19). These are the best known and most widely used practical outcomes of classical test theory. Suppose when we substitute sample statistics for parameters in (1-17), the equality is not satisfied. We are likely to conclude that the discrepancies are due to sampling fluctuations or else that the subtests are not really strictly parallel.

The assumption (1-7) of uncorrelated errors is also open to question, however. Equations (1-7) can sometimes be disproved by path analysis methods. Similar comments apply to (1-14), (1-18), and (1-19).

Note that classical test theory deals exclusively with first and second moments: with means, variances, and covariances. An extension of classical test theory to higher-order moments is given in Lord and Novick (1968, Chapter 10). Without such extension, classical test theory cannot investigate the linearity or nonlinearity of a regression, nor the normality or nonnormality of a frequency distribution.

REFERENCES

Cronbach, L. J., Gleser, G. C., Nanda, H., & Rajaratnam, N. *The dependability of behavioral measurements: Theory of generalizability for scores and profiles.* New York: Wiley, 1972.

Hauser, R. M., & Goldberger, A. S. The treatment of unobservable variables in path analysis. In H. L. Costner (Ed.), *Sociological methodology, 1971.* San Francisco: Jossey-Bass, 1971.

Linn, R. L., & Slinde, J. A. The determination of the significance of change between pre- and posttesting periods. *Review of Educational Research,* 1977, *47,* 121–150.

Lord, F. M. Elementary models for measuring change. In C. W. Harris (Ed.), *Problems in measuring change.* Madison: University of Wisconsin Press, 1963.

Lord, F. M., & Novick, M. R. *Statistical theories of mental test scores.* Reading, Mass.: Addison-Wesley, 1968.

Milliken, G. A. New criteria for estimability for linear models. *The Annals of Mathematical Statistics,* 1971, *42,* 1588–1594

Werts, C. E., Linn, R. L., & Jöreskog, K. G. Intraclass reliability estimates: Testing structural assumptions. *Educational and Psychological Measurement,* 1974, *34,* 25–33.

Werts, C. E., Rock, D. A., Linn, R. L., & Jöreskog, K. G. Validating psychometric assumptions within and between several populations. *Educational and Psychological Measurement,* 1977, *37,* 863–872.

2 Item Response Theory— Introduction and Preview

2.1. INTRODUCTION

Commonly, a test consists of separate items and the test score is a (possibly weighted) sum of item scores. In this case, statistics describing the test scores of a certain group of examinees can be expressed algebraically in terms of statistics describing the individual item scores for the same group [see Eq. (1-21) to (1-25)]. As already noted, classical item theory (which is only a part of classical test theory) consists of such algebraic tautologies.

Such a theory makes no assumptions about matters that are beyond the control of the psychometrician. It cannot predict how individuals will respond to items unless the items have previously been administered to similar individuals. In practical test development work, we need to be able to predict the statistical and psychometric properties of any test that we may build when administered to any target group of examinees. We need to describe the items by item parameters and the examinees by examinee parameters in such a way that we can predict probabilistically the response of any examinee to any item, even if similar examinees have never taken similar items before. This involves making predictions about things beyond the control of the psychometrician—predictions about how people will behave in the real world.

As an especially clear illustration of the need for such a theory, consider the basic problem of tailored testing: Given an individual's response to a few items already administered, choose from an available pool one item to be administered to him next. This choice must be made so that after repeated similar choices the examinee's ability or skill can be estimated as accurately as possible from his responses. To do this even approximately, we must be able to estimate the examinee's ability from any set of items that may be given to him. We must also know how effective each item in the pool is for measuring at each ability level. Neither of these things can be done by means of classical mental test theory.

In most testing work, our main task is to infer the examinee's ability level or skill. In order to do this, we must know something about how his ability or skill determines his response to an item. Thus item response theory starts with a mathematical statement as to how response depends on level of ability or skill. This relationship is given by the *item response function* (trace line, item characteristic curve).

This book deals chiefly with dichotomously scored items. Responses will be referred to as *right* or *wrong* (but see Chapter 15 for dealing with omitted responses). Early work in this area was done by Brogden (1946), Lawley (1943), Lazarsfeld (see Lazarsfeld & Henry, 1968), Lord (1952), and Solomon (1961), among others. Some polychotomous item response models are treated by Andersen (1973a, b), Bock (1972, 1975), and Samejima (1969, 1972). Related models in bioassay are treated by Aitchison and Bennett (1970), Amemiya (1974a, b, c), Cox (1970), Finney (1971), Gurland, Ilbok, and Dahm (1960), Mantel (1966), van Strik (1960).

2.2.   ITEM RESPONSE FUNCTIONS

Let us denote by θ the trait (ability, skill, etc.) to be measured. For a dichotomous item, the item response function is simply the probability P or $P(\theta)$ of a correct response to the item. Throughout this book, it is (very reasonably) assumed that $P(\theta)$ increases as θ increases. A common assumption is that this probability can be represented by the (three-parameter) logistic function

$$P \equiv P(\theta) = c + \frac{1-c}{1 + e^{-1.7a(\theta-b)}} , \qquad (2\text{-}1)$$

where a, b, and c are parameters characterizing the item, and e is the mathematical constant $2.71828\ldots$. Logistic item response functions for 50 four-choice word-relations items are shown in Fig. 2.2.1 to illustrate the variety found in a typical published test. This logistic model was originated and developed by Allan Birnbaum.

Figure 2.2.2 illustrates the meaning of the item parameters. Parameter c is the probability that a person completely lacking in ability ($\theta = -\infty$) will answer the item correctly. It is called the *guessing parameter* or the *pseudo-chance score level*. If an item cannot be answered correctly by guessing, then $c = 0$.

Parameter b is a location parameter: It determines the position of the curve along the ability scale. It is called the *item difficulty*. The more difficult the item, the further the curve is to the right. The logistic curve has its inflexion point at $\theta = b$. When there is no guessing, b is the ability level where the probability of a

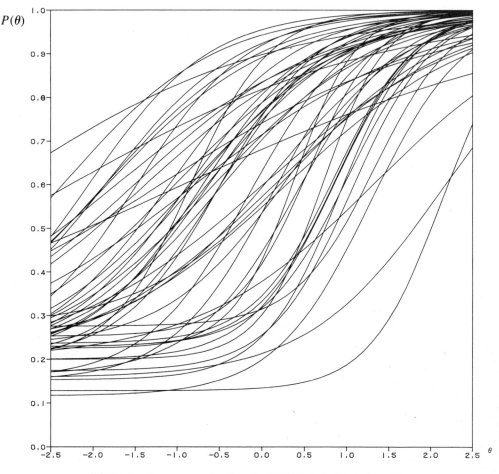

FIG. 2.2.1. Item response functions for SCAT II Verbal Test, Form 2B.

correct answer is .5. When there is guessing, b is the ability level where the probability of a correct answer is halfway between c and 1.0.

Parameter a is proportional to the slope of the curve at the inflexion point [this slope actually is $.425a(1 - c)$]. Thus a represents the *discriminating power* of the item, the degree to which item response varies with ability level.

An alternative form of item response function is also frequently used: the (three-parameter) normal ogive,

$$P \equiv P(\theta) = c + (1 - c) \int_{-\infty}^{a(\theta - b)} \frac{1}{\sqrt{2\pi}} \, e^{-t^2/2} dt. \qquad (2\text{-}2)$$

Again, c is the height of the lower asymptote; b is the ability level at the point of inflexion, where the probability of a correct answer is $(1 + c)/2$; a is propor-

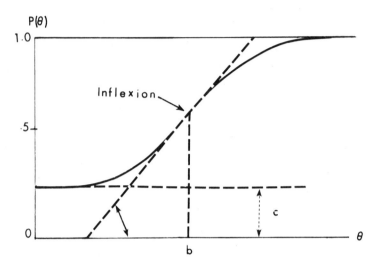

FIG. 2.2.2.   Meaning of item parameters (see text).

tional to the slope of the curve at the inflexion point [this slope actually is $a(1 - c)/\sqrt{2\pi}$].

The difference between functions (2-1) and (2-2) is less than .01 for every set of parameter values. On the other hand, for $c = 0$, the ratio of the logistic function to the normal function is 1.0 at $a(\theta - b) = 0$, .97 at $- 1$, 1.4 at $- 2$, 2.3 at $- 2.5$, 4.5 at $- 3$, and 34.8 at $- 4$. The two models (2-1) and (2-2) give very similar results for most practical work.

The reader may ask for some a priori justification of (2-1) or (2-2). No convincing a priori justification exists (however, see Chapter 3). The model must be justified on the basis of the results obtained, not on a priori grounds.

No one has yet shown that either (2-1) or (2-2) fits mental test data significantly better than the other. The following references are relevant for any statistical investigation along these lines: Chambers and Cox (1967), Cox (1961, 1962), Dyer (1973, 1974), Meeter, Pirie, and Blot (1970), Pereira (1977a, b) Quesenberry and Starbuck (1976), Stone (1977).

In principle, examinees at high ability levels should virtually never answer an easy item incorrectly. In practice, however, such an examinee will occasionally make a careless mistake. Since the logistic function approaches its asymptotes less rapidly than the normal ogive, such careless mistakes will do less violence to the logistic than to the normal ogive model. This is probably a good reason for preferring the logistic model in practical work.

Prentice (1976) has suggested a two-parameter family of functions that includes both (2-1) and (2-2) when $a = 1$, $b = 0$, and $c = 0$ and also includes a variety of skewed functions. The location, scale, and guessing parameters are easily added to obtain a five-parameter family of item response curves, each item being described by five parameters.

2.3. CHECKING THE MATHEMATICAL MODEL

Either (2-1) or (2-2) may provide a mathematical statement of the relation between the examinee's ability and his response to a test item. A more searching consideration of the practical meaning of (2-1) and (2-2) is found in Section 15.7.

Such mathematical models can be used with confidence only after repeated and extensive checking of their applicability. If ability could be measured accurately, the models could be checked directly. Since ability cannot be measured accurately, checking is much more difficult. An ideal check would be to infer from the model the small-sample frequency distribution of some observable quantity whose distribution does not depend on unknown parameters. This does not seem to be possible in the present situation.

The usual procedure is to make various tangible predictions from the model and then to check with observed data to see if these predictions are approximately correct. One substitutes estimated parameters for true parameters and hopes to obtain an approximate fit to observed data. Just how poor a fit to the data can be tolerated cannot be stated exactly because exact sampling variances are not known. Examples of this sort of check on the model are found throughout this book. See especially Fig. 3.5.1. If time after time such checks are found to be satisfactory, then one develops confidence in the practical value of the model for predicting observable results.

Several researchers have produced simulated data and have checked the fit of estimated parameters to the true parameters (which are known since they were used to generate the data). Note that this convenient procedure is not a check on the adequacy of the model for describing the real world. It is simply a check on the adequacy of whatever procedures the researcher is using for parameter estimation (see Chapter 12).

At this point, let us look at a somewhat different type of check on our item response model (2-1). The solid curves in Fig. 2.3.1 are the logistic response curves for five SAT verbal items estimated from the response data of 2862 students, using the methods of Chapter 12. The dashed curves were estimated, almost without assumption as to their mathematical form, from data on a total sample of 103,275 students, using the totally different methods of Section 16.13. The surprising closeness of agreement between the logistic and the unconstrained item response functions gives us confidence in the practical value of the logistic model, at least for verbal items like these.

The following facts may be noted, to point up the significance of this result:

1. The solid and dashed curves were obtained from totally different assumptions. The solid curve assumes the logistic function, also that the test items all measure just one psychological dimension. The dashed curve assumes only that the conditional distribution of number-right observed score for given true score is a certain approximation to a generalized binomial distribution.

2. The solid and dashed curves were obtained from different kinds of raw

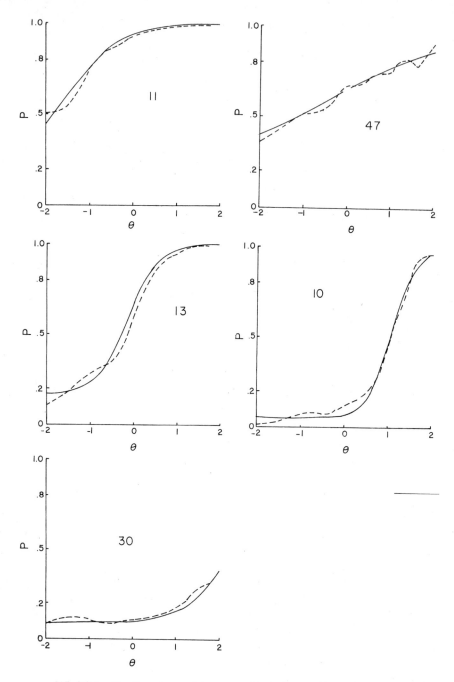

FIG. 2.3.1. Five item characteristic curves estimated by two different methods. (From F. M. Lord, Item characteristic curves estimated without knowledge of their mathematical form—a confrontation of Birnbaum's logistic model. *Psychometrika*, 1970, *35*, 43–50.)

data. The solid curve comes from an analysis of all the responses of a sample of students to all 90 SAT verbal items. The dashed curve is obtained just from frequency distributions of number-right scores on the SAT verbal test and, in a minor way, from the variance across items of the proportion of correct answers to the item.

3. The solid curve is a logistic function. The dashed curve is the ratio of two polynomials, each of degree 89.

4. The solid curve was estimated from a bimodal sample of 2862 examinees, selected by stratified sampling to include many high-ability and many low-ability students. The dashed curve was estimated from all 103,275 students tested in a regular College Board test administration.

Further details of this study are given in Sections 16.12 and 16.13.

These five items are the only items to be analyzed to date by this method. The five items were chosen solely for the variety of shapes represented. If a hundred or so items were analyzed in this way, it is likely that some poorer fits would be found.

It is too much to expect that (2-1) or (2-2) will hold exactly for every test item and for every examinee. If some examinees become tired, sick, or uncooperative partway through the testing, the mathematical model will not be strictly appropriate for them. If some test items are ambiguous, have no correct answer, or have more than one correct answer, the model will not fit such items. If examinees omit some items, skip back and forth through the test, and do not have time to finish the test, perhaps marking all unfinished items at random, the model again will not apply.

A test writer tries to provide attractive incorrect alternatives for each multiple-choice item. We may imagine examinees so completely lacking in ability that they do not even notice the attractiveness of such alternatives and so respond to the items completely at random; their probability of success on such items will be $1/A$, where A is the number of alternatives per item. We may also imagine other examinees with sufficient ability to see the attractiveness of the incorrect alternatives although still lacking any knowledge of the correct answer; their probability of success on such items is often less than $1/A$. If this occurs, the item response function is not an increasing function of ability and cannot be fitted by any of the usual mathematical models.

We might next imagine examinees who have just enough ability to eliminate one (or two, or three, . . .) of the incorrect alternatives from consideration, although still lacking any knowledge of the correct answer. Such examinees might be expected to have a chance of $1/(A - 1)$ (or $1/(A - 2)$, $1/(A - 3)$, . . .) of answering the item correctly, perhaps producing an item response function looking like a staircase.

Such anticipated difficulties deterred the writer for many years from research on item response theory. Finally, a large-scale empirical study of 150 five-choice

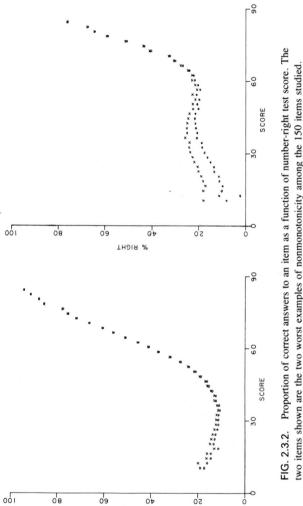

FIG. 2.3.2. Proportion of correct answers to an item as a function of number-right test score. The two items shown are the two worst examples of nonmonotonicity among the 150 items studied.

items was made to determine proportion of correct answers as a function of number-right test score. With a total of 103,275 examinees, these proportions could be determined with considerable accuracy. Out of 150 items, only six were found that clearly failed to be increasing functions of total test score, and for these the failure was so minor as to be of little practical importance. The results for the two worst items are displayed in Figure 2.3.2; the crosses show where the curve would have been if examinees omitting the item had chosen at random among the five alternative responses instead. No staircase functions or other serious difficulties were found.

2.4.   UNIDIMENSIONAL TESTS

Equation (2-1) or (2-2) asserts that probability of success on an item depends on three item parameters, on examinee ability θ, and on nothing else. If the model is true, a person's ability θ is all we need in order to determine his probability of success on a specified item. If we know the examinee's ability, any knowledge of his success or failure on other items will add nothing to this determination. (If it did add something, then performance on the items in question would depend in part on some trait other than θ; but this is contrary to our assumption.)

The principle just stated is Lazarsfeld's assumption of *local independence*. Stated formally, Prob(success on item i given θ) = Prob(success on item i given θ and given also his performance on items $j, k, \ldots$). If $u_i = 0$ or 1 denotes the score on item i, then this may be written more compactly as

$$P(u_i = 1|\theta) = P(u_i = 1|\theta, u_j, u_k, \ldots) \qquad (i \neq j, k, \ldots). \tag{2-3}$$

A mathematically equivalent statement of local independence is that the probability of success on all items is equal to the product of the separate probabilities of success. For just three items $i, j, k,$ for example,

$$P(u_i = 1, u_j = 1, u_k = 1|\theta) = P(u_i = 1|\theta)P(u_j = 1|\theta)P(u_k = 1|\theta). \tag{2-4}$$

Local independence requires that any two items be uncorrelated when θ is fixed. It definitely does *not* require that items be uncorrelated in ordinary groups, where θ varies. Note in particular that local independence follows automatically from unidimensionality. It is not an additional assumption.

If the items measure just one dimension (θ), if θ is normally distributed in the group tested, and if model (2-2) holds with $c = 0$ (there is no guessing), then the matrix of tetrachoric intercorrelations among the items will be of unit rank (see Section 3.6). In this case, we can think of θ as the common factor of the items. This gives us a clearer understanding of what is meant by θ and what is meant by unidimensionality.

Note, however, that latent trait theory is more general than factor analysis. Ability θ is probably not normally distributed for most groups of examinees. Unidimensionality, however, is a property of the items; it does not cease to exist just because we have changed the distribution of ability in the group tested. Tetrachoric correlations are inappropriate for nonnormal distributions of ability; they are also inappropriate when the item response function is not a normal ogive. Tetrachoric correlations are always inappropriate whenever there is guessing. This poses a problem for factor analysts in defining what is meant by *common factor,* but it does not disturb the unidimensionality of a pool of items.

It seems plausible that tests of spelling, vocabulary, reading comprehension, arithmetic reasoning, word analogies, number series, and various types of spatial tests should be approximately one-dimensional. We can easily imagine tests that are not. An achievement test in chemistry might in part require mathematical training or arithmetic skill and in part require knowledge of nonmathematical facts.

Item response theory can be readily formulated to cover cases where the test items measure more than one latent trait. Practical application of multidimensional item response theory is beyond the present state of the art, however,

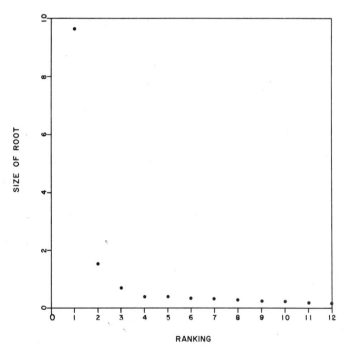

FIG. 2.4.1.   The 12 largest latent roots in order of size for the SCAT 2A Verbal Test.

except in special cases (Kolakowski & Bock, 1978; Mulaik, 1972; Samejima, 1974; Sympson, 1977).

There is great need for a statistical significance test for the unidimensionality of a set of test items. An attempt in this direction has been made by Christoffersson (1975), Indow and Samejima (1962), and Muthén (1977).

A rough procedure is to compute the latent roots of the tetrachoric item intercorrelation matrix with estimated communalities placed in the diagonal. If (1) the first root is large compared to the second and (2) the second root is not much larger than any of the others, then the items are approximately unidimensional. This procedure is probably useful even though tetrachoric correlation cannot usually be strictly justified. (Note that Jöreskog's maximum likelihood factor analysis and accompanying significance tests are not strictly applicable to tetrachoric correlation matrices.)

Figure 2.4.1 shows the first 12 latent roots obtained in this way for the SCAT II Verbal Test, Form 2A. This test consists of 50 word-relations items. The data were the responses of a sample of 3000 high school students. The plot suggests that the items are reasonably one-dimensional.

2.5. PREVIEW

In order to motivate the detailed study of item response functions in succeeding chapters, it seems worthwhile to outline briefly just a few of the practical results to be developed. At this point, the reader should expect only a preview, not a detailed explanation.

For each item there is an *item information function* $I\{\theta, u_i\}$ that can be determined from the formula

$$I\{\theta, u_i\} = \frac{P_i'^2}{P_i Q_i},\tag{2-5}$$

where $P_i \equiv P_i(\theta)$ is the item response function, $Q_i \equiv 1 - P_i$, and P_i' is the derivative of P_i with respect to θ [the formula for P_i' can be written out explicitly once a particular item response function, such as (2-1) or (2-2), is chosen]. The item information functions for the five items (10, 11, 13, 30, 47) in Fig. 2.3.1 are shown in Fig. 2.5.1.

The amount of information given by an item varies with ability level θ. The higher the curve, the more the information. Information at a given ability level varies directly as the square of the item discriminating power, a_i. If one information function is twice as high as another at some particular ability level, then it will take two items of the latter type to measure as well as one item of the former type at that ability level.

There is also a *test information function* $I\{\theta\}$, which is inversely proportional to the square of the length of the asymptotic confidence interval for estimating

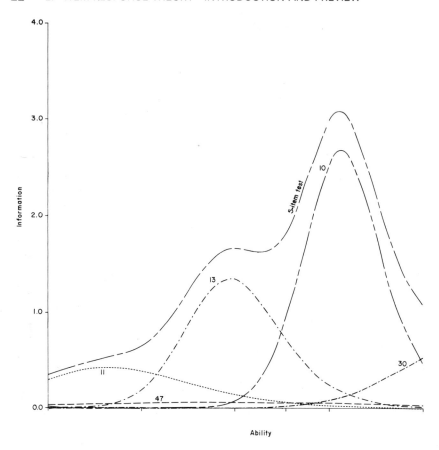

FIG. 2.5.1.   Item and test information functions. (From F. M. Lord, An analysis of the Verbal Scholastic Aptitude Test using Birnbaum's three-parameter logistic model. *Educational and Psychological Measurement*, 1968, *28*, 989–1020.)

the examinee's ability θ from his responses. It can be shown that the test information function $I\{\theta\}$ is simply the sum of the item information functions:

$$I\{\theta\} = \sum_i I\{\theta, u_i\}. \qquad (2\text{-}6)$$

The test information function for the five-item test is shown in Fig. 2.5.1.

We have in (2-6) the very important result that when item responses are optimally weighted, *the contribution of the item to the measurement effectiveness of the total test does not depend on what other items are included in the test.* This is a different situation from that in classical test theory, where the contribution of each item to test reliability or to test validity depends inextricably on what other items are included in the test.

Equation (2-6) suggests a convenient and effective procedure of test construction. The procedure operates on a pool of items that have already been calibrated, so that we have the item information curve for each item.

1. Decide on the shape desired for the test information function. The desired curve is the *target information curve.*

2. Select items with item information curves that will fill the hard-to-fill areas under the target information curve.

3. Cumulatively add the item information curves, obtaining at all times the information curve for the part-test composed of items already selected.

4. Continue (backtracking if necessary) until the area under target information curve is filled to a satisfactory approximation.

The test information function represents the maximal amount of information that can be obtained from the item responses by any kind of scoring method. The linear composite $\Sigma_i w_i^* u_i$ of item scores u_i ($= 0$ or 1) with weights

$$w_i^* = \frac{P_i'}{P_i Q_i} \tag{2-7}$$

is an optimal score yielding maximal information. The optimal score is not directly useful since the optimal weights w_i^* depend on θ, which is unknown. Very good scoring methods can be deduced from (2-7), however.

The logistic optimal weights for the five items of Fig. 2.3.1 are shown as functions of θ in Fig. 2.5.2. It is obvious that the relative weighting of different items is very different at low ability levels than at high ability levels. At high levels, optimal item weights are proportional to item discriminating power a_i. At low ability levels, on the other hand, difficult items should receive near-zero scoring weight, regardless of a_i. The reason is that when low-ability examinees guess at random on difficult items, this produces a random result that would impair effective measurement if incorporated into the examinee's score; hence the need for a near-zero scoring weight.

Two tests of the same trait can be compared very effectively in terms of their information functions. The ratio of the information function of test y to the information function of test x represents the *relative efficiency* of test y with respect to x. Figure 6.9.1 shows the relative efficiency of a STEP vocabulary test compared to a MAT vocabulary test. The STEP test is more efficient for low-ability examinees, but much less efficient at higher ability levels. The dashed horizontal line shows the efficiency that would be expected if the two tests differed only in length (number of items).

Figure 6.10.1 shows the relative efficiency of variously modified hypothetical SAT Verbal tests compared with an actual form of the test. Curve 2 shows the effect of adding five items just like the five easiest items in the actual test. Curve 3 shows the effect of omitting five items of medium difficulty from the actual test. Curve 4 shows the effect of replacing the five medium-difficulty items by

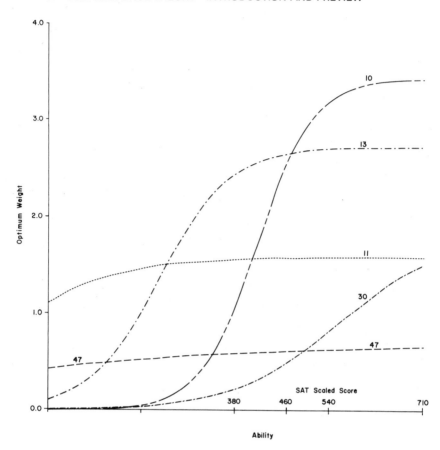

FIG. 2.5.2.   Optimal (logistic) scoring weight for five items as a function of ability level. (From F. M. Lord, An analysis of the Verbal Scholastic Aptitude Test using Birnbaum's three-parameter logistic model. *Educational and Psychological Measurement*, 1968, *28*, 989–1020.)

the five additional easy items. Curve 6 shows the effect of discarding (not scoring) the easier half of the test. Curve 7 shows the effect of discarding the harder half of the test; notice that the resulting half-length test is actually better for measuring low-ability examinees than is the regular full-length SAT. Curve 8 shows a hypothetical SAT just like the regular full-length SAT except that all items are at the same middle difficulty level.

Results such as these are useful for planning revision of an existing test, perhaps increasing its measurement effectiveness at certain specified ability levels and decreasing its effectiveness at other levels. These and other useful applications of item response theory are treated in detail in subsequent chapters.

REFERENCES

Aitchison, J., & Bennett, J. A. Polychotomous quantal response by maximum indicant. *Biometrika,* 1970, *57,* 253–262.

Amemiya, T. *Qualitative response models.* Technical Report No. 135. Stanford, Calif.: Institute for Mathematical Studies in the Social Sciences, Stanford University, 1974. (a)

Amemiya, T. *The maximum likelihood estimator vs. the minimum chi-square estimator in the general qualitative response model.* Technical Report No. 136. Stanford, Calif.: Institute for Mathematical Studies in the Social Sciences, Stanford University, 1974. (b)

Amemiya, T. *The equivalence of the nonlinear weighted least squares method and the method of scoring in the general qualitative response model.* Technical Report No. 137. Stanford, Calif.: Institute for Mathematical Studies in the Social Sciences, Stanford University, 1974. (c)

Andersen, E. B. *Conditional inference and models for measuring.* Copenhagen: Mentalhygiejnisk Forlag, 1973. (a)

Andersen, E. B. Conditional inference for multiple-choice questionnaires. *British Journal of Mathematical and Statistical Psychology,* 1973, *26,* 31–44. (b)

Bock, R. D. Estimating item parameters and latent ability when responses are scored in two or more nominal categories. *Psychometrika,* 1972, *37,* 29–51.

Bock, R. D. *Multivariate statistical methods in behavioral research.* New York: McGraw-Hill, 1975.

Brogden, H. E. Variation in test validity with variation in the distribution of item difficulties, number of items, and degree of their intercorrelation. *Psychometrika,* 1946, *11,* 197–214.

Chambers, E. A., & Cox, D. R. Discrimination between alternative binary response models. *Biometrika,* 1967, *54,* 573–578.

Christoffersson, A. Factor analysis of dichotomized variables. *Psychometrika,* 1975, *40,* 5–32.

Cox, D. R. Tests of separate families of hypotheses. In J. Neyman (Ed.), *Proceedings of the Fourth Berkeley Symposium on Mathematical Statistics and Probability* (Vol. 1). Berkeley: University of California Press, 1961.

Cox, D. R. Further results on tests of separate families of hypotheses. *Journal of the Royal Statistical Society,* 1962, *24,* 406–424.

Cox, D. R. *The analysis of binary data.* London: Methuen, 1970.

Dyer, A. R. Discrimination procedures for separate families of hypotheses. *Journal of the American Statistical Association,* 1973, *68,* 970–974.

Dyer, A. R. Hypothesis testing procedures for separate families of hypotheses. *Journal of the American Statistical Association,* 1974, *69,* 140–145.

Finney, D. J. *Probit analysis* (3rd ed.). New York: Cambridge University Press, 1971.

Gurland, J., Ilbok, J., & Dahm, P. A. Polychotomous quantal response in biological assay. *Biometrics,* 1960, *16,* 382–398.

Indow, T., & Samejima, F. *LIS measurement scale for non-verbal reasoning ability.* Tokyo: Nihon-Bunka Kagakusha, 1962. (In Japanese)

Kolakowski, D., & Bock, R. D. *Multivariate generalizations of probit analysis.* Unpublished manuscript, 1978.

Lawley, D. N. On problems connected with item selection and test construction. *Proceedings of the Royal Society of Edinburgh,* 1943, *61,* 273–287.

Lazarsfeld, P. F., & Henry, N. W. *Latent structure analysis.* Boston: Houghton-Mifflin, 1968.

Lord, F. M. A theory of test scores. *Psychometric Monograph No. 7.* Psychometric Society, 1952.

Mantel, N. Models for complex contingency tables and polychotomous dosage response curves. *Biometrics,* 1966, *22,* 83–95.

Meeter, D., Pirie, W., & Blot, W. A comparison of two model discrimination criteria. *Technometrics,* 1970, *12,* 457–470.

Mulaik, S. A. *A mathematical investigation of some multidimensional Rasch models for psychological tests.* Paper presented at the Spring meeting of the Psychometric Society, Princeton, N.J., 1972.

Muthén, B. *Statistical methodology for structural equation models involving latent variables with dichotomous indicators.* Unpublished doctoral dissertation, Uppsala University, 1977.

Pereira, B. de B. Discriminating among separate models: A bibliography. *International Statistical Review,* 1977, *45,* 163–172. (a)

Pereira, B. de B. A note on the consistency and on the finite sample comparisons of some tests of separate families of hypotheses. *Biometrika,* 1977, *64,* 109–113. (b)

Prentice, R. L. A generalization of the probit and logit methods for dose response curves. *Biometrics,* 1976, *32,* 761–768.

Quesenberry, C. P., & Starbuck, R. R. On optimal tests for separate hypotheses and conditional probability integral transformations. *Communications in Statistics,* 1976, *A5,* 507–524.

Samejima, F. Estimation of latent ability using a response pattern of graded scores. *Psychometric Monograph No. 17.* Psychometric Society, 1969.

Samejima, F. A general model for free-response data. *Psychometric Monograph Supplement, No. 18,* 1972.

Samejima, F. Normal ogive model on the continuous response level in the multidimensional latent space. *Psychometrika,* 1974, *39,* 111–121.

Solomon, H. (Ed.). *Studies in item analysis and prediction.* Stanford, Calif.: Stanford University Press, 1961.

Stone, M. An asymptotic equivalence of choice of model by cross-validation and Akaike's criterion. *Journal of the Royal Statistical Society,* Series B, 1977, *39,* 44–47.

Sympson, J. B. *A model for testing with multidimensional items.* Paper presented at the Computerized Adaptive Testing Conference, Minneapolis, 1977.

van Strik, R. A method of estimating relative potency and its precision in the case of semi-quantitative responses. *Symposium on Quantitative Methods in Pharmacology, 1960.* Amsterdam: N. Holland Publishing Company.

3 Relation of Item Response Theory to Conventional Item Analysis

3.1. ITEM-TEST REGRESSIONS

In conventional item analysis, it is common to compare high- and low-scoring students on their proportion of correct answers. Sometimes the students may be divided on test score into as many as five levels and then the levels compared on proportion of correct answers. An extension of this would be to divide the students into as many levels as there are test scores before making the comparison.

The proportion of correct answers to an (dichotomous) item is also the mean item score, the mean of the statistical variable u_i ($= 0$ or 1). Thus the curve representing proportion of correct answers as a function of test score x is also the regression of u_i on x. Such a curve is called an *item-observed score regression* (iosr). Note that for dichotomous items any item response function, as defined in Chapter 2, can be considered by the same logic to be an *item-ability regression*, the regression of u_i on θ.

Figure 3.1.1 shows sample iosr for several SAT verbal and math items. Each curve is computed from the responses of 103,275 examinees. The base line is number-right score on the verbal test or on the math test omitting the item under study. Points based on fewer than 50 examinees are not plotted.

These curves would be empirical item-response functions if the base line were θ instead of number-right score x. Thus it is common, although incorrect (as we shall see), to think that an iosr, like an item-ability regression, will have at least approximately an ogive shape, like Eq. (2-1) or (2-2).

To show that iosr cannot all be approximately normal ogives, consider a test composed of n items. Denote the iosr for item i by

$$\mu_{i|x} \equiv \mathscr{E}(u_i|x),$$

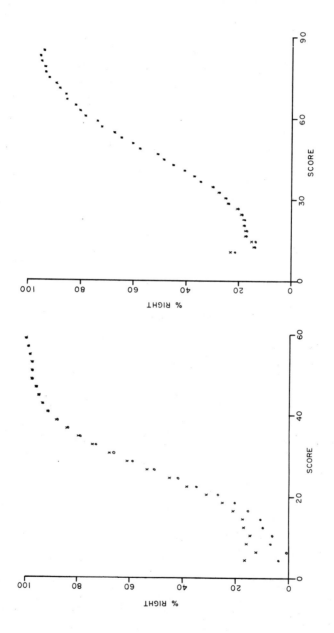

28

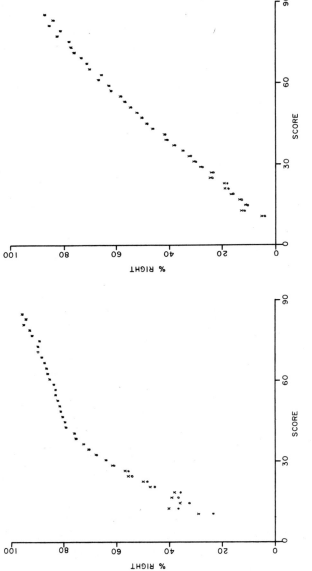

FIG. 3.1.1. Selected item-test regressions for five-choice *Scholastic Aptitude Test* items (crosses show regression when omitted responses are replaced by random responses).

29

the expectation being taken over all individuals at score level x. Now, for any individual, x is the sum (over items) of his item scores; that is

$$x = \sum_{i=1}^{n} u_i. \tag{3-1}$$

If we take the expectation of (3-1) for fixed x, we have

$$x = \mathscr{E}(x|x) = \mathscr{E}\left(\sum_{i=1}^{n} u_i|x\right) = \sum_{i=1}^{n} \mathscr{E}(u_i|x).$$

Then by definition

$$\sum_{i=1}^{n} \mu_{i|x} \equiv \sum_{i=1}^{n} \mathscr{E}(u_i|x) = x. \tag{3-2}$$

We can understand this general result most easily by considering the special case when all the items are statistically equivalent. In this case, $\mu_{i|x}$ is by definition the same for all items, so (3-2) can be written

$$\sum_{i=1}^{n} \mu_{i|x} = n\mu_{i|x} = x,$$

from which it follows that $\mu_{i|x} = x/n$ for each item. Thus the iosr of each item is a straight line through the origin with slope $1/n$. Note that for statistically equivalent items $\mu_{i|x} = x/n$ even when the items are entirely uncorrelated with each other. The iosr has a slope of $1/n$ even when the test does not measure anything! This is still true if each item is negatively correlated with every other item!

All this proves that we cannot as a general matter expect item-observed score regressions to be even approximately normal ogives. We shall not make further use of item-observed score regressions in this book. The regression of item score on true score is considered in Section 16.12.

3.2. RATIONALE FOR NORMAL OGIVE MODEL

The writer prefers to consider the choice of item response function, such as Eq. (2-1) or (2-2), as a basic assumption to be justified by methods discussed in Section 2.3 rather than by any a priori argument. This is particularly wise when there is guessing, since one assumption often used in this case to deduce Eq. (2-1) or (2-2) from a priori considerations is that examinees either know the correct answer to the item or else guess at random. This assumption is totally unacceptable and would discredit the entire theory if the theory depended on it.

The alternate, acceptable point of view is simply that Eq. (2-1) and (2-2) are useful as versatile formulas capable of adequately representing a wide variety of ogive-shaped functions that increase monotonically from a lower asymptote to 1.00. Justification of their use is to be sought in the results achieved, not in further rationalizations. In this section, a rationale is provided for Eq. (2-2) in a rather specialized situation in order to make this and similar item response models seem plausible, not with the idea of providing a firm basis for their use.

Suppose that there is a (unobservable) latent variable Y_i' that determines examinee performance on item i. If for some examinee Y_i' is greater than some constant γ_i, then he answers the item correctly, so that $u_i = 1$. Similarly, if for some examinee $Y_i' < \gamma_i$, then $u_i = 0$. (There is zero probability that $Y_i' = \gamma_i$, so we need not discuss this case.) From the point of view of the factor analyst, Y_i' is a composite of (1) the common factor θ of the test items and (2) a specific factor or error factor for item i, not found in other items.

Note that the foregoing supposition rules out guessing. If the correct answer can be obtained by a partially random process, then no attribute of the examinee can determine whether $u_i = 0$ or 1.

Assume now that

1. The regression $\mu_{i|\theta}'$ of Y_i' on θ is linear.
2. The scatter of Y_i' about this regression is homoscedastic; in other words, the conditional variance $\sigma_{i|\theta}'^2 \equiv \sigma_{i\cdot\theta}'^2$ about the regression line is the same for all θ.
3. The conditional distribution of Y_i' given θ is normal.

Conditional distributions of Y_i' for given θ are illustrated in Fig. 3.2.1. We can see from the figure that the item response function $P_i \equiv P_i(\theta) \equiv \text{Prob}(u_i = 1|\theta) \equiv \text{Prob}(Y_i' > \gamma_i|\theta)$ is equal to a standardized normal curve area. A little algebra shows that it is equal to the standardized normal curve area above $(\gamma_i - \mu_{i|\theta}')/\sigma_{i\cdot\theta}'$, which will be denoted by $-L_i$.

For convenience, let us choose (as we may) the scale of measurement for both Y_i' and θ so that for the entire bivariate population the unconditional means of both variables are 0 and their unconditional standard deviations are 1. Then the equation for the regression of Y_i' on θ is simply $\mu_{i|\theta}' = \rho_i'\theta$, where ρ_i' is the correlation between Y_i' and θ. The conditional variance about this regression is, by standard formula, $\sigma_{i\cdot\theta} = 1 - \rho_i'^2$. Making use of these last formulas, we have

$$-L_i = \frac{\gamma_i - \rho_i'\theta}{\sqrt{1 - \rho_i'^2}} \; .$$

Let

$$a_i \equiv \frac{\rho_i'}{\sqrt{1 - \rho_i'^2}} \; , \tag{3-3}$$

$$b_i \equiv \frac{\gamma_i}{\rho_i'} \; , \tag{3-4}$$

so that $-L_i = a_i(b_i - \theta)$.

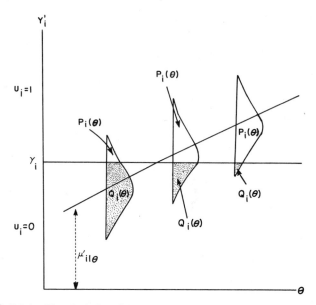

FIG. 3.2.1.   Hypothetical conditional distribution of Y_i' for three levels of ability θ, showing the regression $\mu_{i|\theta}'$ and the cutting point γ_i that separates right answers from wrong answers.

For symmetric distributions,

$$\int_{-L}^{\infty} = \int_{-\infty}^{L} \ ;$$

so, finally, the item response function is seen to be

$$P_i(\theta) = \int_{-\infty}^{a_i(\theta - b_i)} \frac{1}{\sqrt{2\pi}} e^{-t^2/2} dt. \tag{3-5}$$

This is the same as Eq. (2-2) for the normal ogive item response function when $c_i = 0$.

Note that we have *not* made any assumption about the distribution of ability θ in the total group tested. In particular, contrary to some assertions in the literature, we have *not* assumed that ability is normally distributed in the total group. Furthermore, if (3-5) holds for some group of examinees, selection on θ will not change the conditional distribution of Y_i' for fixed θ and hence will not change (3-5). Thus the shape of the distribution of ability θ in the total group tested is irrelevant to our derivation of (3-5).

Equation (3-5) has the form of a cumulative frequency distribution, as do Eq. (2-1) and (2-2) when $c = 0$. In general, however, there seems to be little reason for thinking of an item response curve as a cumulative frequency distribution.

3.3. RELATION TO CONVENTIONAL ITEM STATISTICS

Conventional item analysis deals with π_i, conventionally called the *item diffi-culty*, the proportion of examinees answering item i correctly. It also deals with ρ_{ix}, the product moment correlation between item score u_i and number-right test score x, often called the point-biserial item-test correlation, or else with ρ'_{ix}, the corresponding biserial item-test correlation. A general formula for the relation of biserial correlation (ρ') to point-biserial correlation is

$$\rho = \rho' \frac{\phi(\gamma)}{\sqrt{\pi(1 - \pi)}} ,$$
(3-6)

where $\phi(\gamma)$ is the normal curve ordinate at the point γ that cuts off area π of the standardized normal curve.

If ability θ is normally distributed and $c_i = 0$, then by definition the product-moment correlation ($\rho'_{i\theta}$ or simply ρ'_i) between Y'_i and θ is also the biserial correlation between u_i and θ. Such a relationship is just what is meant by *biserial correlation*.

There is also a product-moment or point-biserial correlation between u_i and θ, to be denoted by $\rho_{i\theta}$. To the extent that number-right score x is a measure of ability θ, ρ'_{ix} is an approximation to $\rho'_i \equiv \rho'_{i\theta}$ and ρ_{ix} is an approximation to $\rho_{i\theta}$. Combined with (3-3), this (crude) approximation yields a conceptually illuminating crude relationship between the conventional item-test correlation and the a_i parameter of item response theory, valid only for the case where θ is normally distributed and there is no guessing:

$$a_i \cong \frac{\rho'_{ix}}{\sqrt{1 - \rho'^2_{ix}}}$$
(3-7)

and

$$\rho'_{ix} \cong \frac{a_i}{\sqrt{1 + a_i^2}} ,$$
(3-8)

where $\cong$ denotes approximate equality. This shows that under the assumptions made, the item discrimination parameter a_i and the item-test biserial correlation ρ'_{ix} are approximately monotonic increasing functions of each other.

Approximations (3-7) and (3-8) hold only if the unit of measurement for θ has been chosen so that the mean of θ is 0 and the standard deviation is 1 (see Section 3.5). Approximations (3-7) and (3-8) do not hold unless θ is normally distributed in the group tested. They do not hold if there is guessing. In addition, the approximations fall short of accuracy because (1) the test score x contains errors of measurement whereas θ does not; and (2) x and θ have differently shaped distributions (the relation between x and θ is nonlinear).

Approximations (3-7) and (3-8) are given here not for practical use but rather to give an idea of the nature of the item discrimination parameter a_i. The relation of a_i to conventional item and test parameters is illustrated in Table 3.8.1.

Item i is answered correctly whenever the examinee's ability Y_i' is greater than γ_i. If ability θ is normally distributed, then Y_i' will not only be conditionally normally distributed for fixed θ but also unconditionally normally distributed in the total population. Since the unconditional mean and variance of Y_i' have been chosen to be 0 and 1, respectively, a simple relation between γ_i and π_i (proportion of correct answers to item i in the total group) can be written down: When θ is normally distributed,

$$\pi_i = \int_{\gamma_i}^{\infty} \phi(t) \, dt. \tag{3-9}$$

The parameter γ_i is the item difficulty parameter used in certain kinds of Thurstone scaling (see Fan, 1957). It is also the same as the College Entrance Examination Board *delta* (Gulliksen, 1950, pp. 368–369) except for a linear transformation.

If (3-7) and (3-8) hold approximately, then from (3-4)

$$b_i \cong \frac{\gamma_i}{\rho_{ix}'}. \tag{3-10}$$

If all items have equal discriminating power a_i, then by (3-4) all ρ_i' are equal and the difficulty parameter b_i is proportional to γ_i, the normal curve deviate corresponding to the proportion of correct answers π_i. Thus when all items are equally discriminating, there is a monotonic relation between b_i and π_i: As π_i increases, b_i and γ_i both decrease. When all items are not equally discriminating, the relation between b_i and γ_i or π_i depends on a_i. In general, arranging items in order on π_i is not the same as arranging them on b_i.

3.4. INVARIANT ITEM PARAMETERS

As pointed out earlier, an item response function can also be viewed as the regression of item score on ability. In many statistical contexts, regression functions remain unchanged when the frequency distribution of the predictor variable is changed. In the present context this should be quite clear: The probability of a correct answer to item i from examinees at a given ability level θ_0 depends only on θ_0, not on the number of people at θ_0, nor on the number of people at other ability levels $\theta_1, \theta_2, \ldots$. Since the regression is invariant, its lower asymptote, its point of inflexion, and the slope at this point all stay the same regardless of the distribution of ability in the group tested. Thus a_i, b_i, and c_i are invariant item parameters. According to the model, they remain the same regardless of the group tested.

Suppose, on the contrary, it is found that the item response curves of a set of items differ from one group to another. This means that people in group 1 (say) at ability level θ_0 have a different probability of success on the set of items than do people in group 2 at the same θ_0. This now means that the test is able to discriminate group 1 individuals from group 2 individuals of identical ability level θ_0. And this, finally, means that the test items are measuring some dimension on which the groups differ, a dimension other than θ. But our basic assumption here is that the test items have only one dimension in common. The conclusion is either that this particular test is not one-dimensional as we require or else that we should restrict our research to groups of individuals for whom the items are effectively one-dimensional.

The invariance of item parameters across groups is one of the most important characteristics of item response theory. We are so accustomed to thinking of *item difficulty* as the proportion (π_i) of correct answers that it is hard to imagine how item difficulty can be invariant across groups that differ in ability level. The following illustration may help to clarify matters.

Figure 3.4.1 shows two rather different item characteristic curves. Inverted on the baseline are the distributions of ability for two different groups of examinees. First of all, note again: The ability required for a certain probability of success on an item does not depend on the distribution of ability in some group; consequently, the item difficulty b should be the same regardless of the group from which it is determined.

Now note carefully the following. In group A, item 1 is answered correctly less often than item 2. In group B, the opposite occurs. If we use the proportion of correct answers as a measure of item difficulty, we find that item 1 is easier than item 2 for one group but harder than item 2 for the other group.

Proportion of correct answers in a group of examinees is not really a measure of item difficulty. This proportion describes not only the test item but also the group tested. This is a basic objection to conventional item analysis statistics.

Item-test correlations vary from group to group also. Like other correlations,

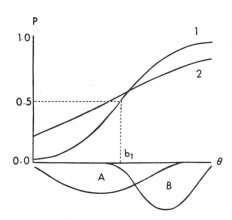

FIG. 3.4.1.   Item response curves in relation to two groups of examinees. (From F. M. Lord, A study of item bias, using item characteristic curve theory. In Y. H. Poortinga (Ed.), *Basic problems in cross-cultural psychology*. Amsterdam: Swets and Zeitlinger, 1977, pp. 19–29.)

item-test correlations tend to be high in groups that have a wide range of talent, low in groups that are homogeneous.

3.5. INDETERMINACY

Item response functions $P_i(\theta)$ like Eq. (2-1) and (2-2) ordinarily are taken to be functions of $a_i(\theta - b_i)$. If we add a constant to every θ and at the same time add the same constant to every b_i, the quantity $a_i(\theta - b_i)$ is unchanged and so is the response function $P_i(\theta)$. This means that the choice of origin for the ability scale is purely arbitrary; we can choose any origin we please for measuring ability as long as we use the same origin for measuring item difficulty b_i.

Similarly, if we multiply every θ by a constant, multiply every b_i by the same constant, and divide every a_i by the same constant, the quantity $a_i(\theta - b_i)$ remains unchanged and so does the response function $P_i(\theta)$. This means that the choice of unit for measuring ability is also purely arbitrary.

One could decide to choose the origin and unit for measuring ability in such a way that the first person tested is assigned $\theta_1 = 0$ and the second person tested is assigned $\theta_2 = 1$ or -1. Another possibility would be to choose so that for the first item $b_1 = 0$ and $a_1 = 1$. Scales chosen in this way would be meaningless to anyone unfamiliar with the first two persons tested or with the first item administered. A more common procedure is to choose the scale so that the mean and standard deviation of θ are 0 and 1 for the group at hand.

The invariance of item parameters, emphasized in Section 3.4, clearly holds only as long as the origin and unit of the ability scale is fixed. This means that if we determine the b_i for a set of items from one group of examinees and then independently from another, we should not expect the two sets of b_i to be identical. Rather we should expect them to have a linear relation to each other (like the relation between Fahrenheit and Celsius temperature scales).

Figure 3.5.1 compares estimated b_i from a group of 2250 white students with estimated b_i from a group of 2250 black students for 85 verbal items from the College Board SAT. Most of the scatter about the line is due to sampling fluctuations in the estimates; some of the scatter is due to failure of the model to hold exactly for groups as different as these (see Chapter 14).

If we determine the a_i for a set of items independently from two different groups, we expect the two sets of values to be identical except for an undetermined unit of measurement that will be different for the two groups. We expect the a_i to lie along a straight line passing through the origin (0, 0), with a slope reciprocal to the slope of the line relating the two sets of b_i. The slope represents the ratio of scale units for the two sets of parameters. The two sets of a_i are related in the same way as two sets of measurements of the same physical objects, one set expressed in inches and the other in feet.

The c_i are not affected by changes in the origin and unit of the ability scale. The c_i should be identical from one group to another.

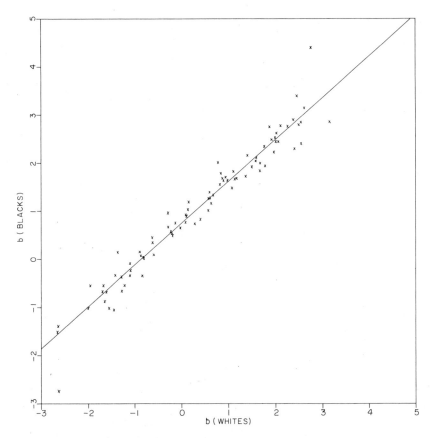

FIG. 3.5.1.   Estimated difficulty parameters (*b*) for 85 items for blacks and for whites. (From F. M. Lord, A study of item bias, using item characteristic curve theory. In Y. H. Poortinga (Ed.), *Basic problems in cross-cultural psychology.* Amsterdam: Swets and Zeitlinger, 1977, pp. 19–29.)

Ability parameters θ are also invariant from one test to another except for choice of origin and scale, assuming that the tests both measure the same ability, skill, or trait. For 1830 sixth-grade pupils, Fig. 3.5.2 compares the θ estimated from a 50-item Metropolitan vocabulary test with the θ estimated from a 42-item SRA vocabulary test. Both tests consist of four-choice items.

The scatter about a straight line is more noticeable here than in Fig. 3.5.1 because there each b_i was estimated from the responses of 2250 students, here each θ is estimated from the responses to only 42 or 50 items. Thus the estimates of θ are more subject to sampling fluctuations than the estimates of b_i. The broad scatter at low ability levels is due to guessing, random or otherwise. A more detailed evaluation of the implications of Fig. 3.5.2 is given in Section 12.6. It is shown there that after an appropriate transformation is made, the transformed

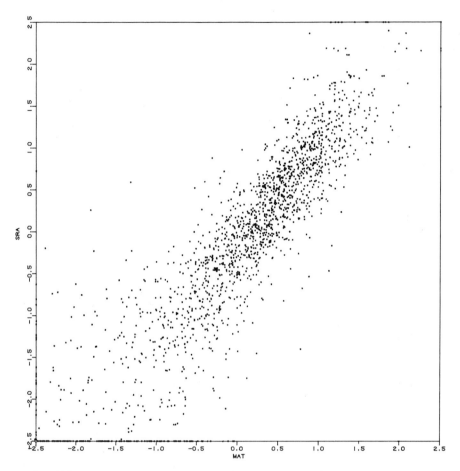

FIG. 3.5.2.   Ability estimates from a 50 item MAT vocabulary test are compared with ability estimates from a 42-item SRA vocabulary test for 1830 sixth-
grade pupils. (Ability estimates outside the range $-2.5 < \theta < 2.5$ are printed on
the border of the table.)

estimates of θ from the two tests correlate higher than do number-right scores on
the two tests.

In conclusion, in item response theory the item parameters are invariant from
group to group as long as the ability scale is not changed; in classical item
analysis, the item parameters are not invariant from group to group, although
they are unaffected by choice of ability scale. Similarly, ability θ is invariant
across tests of the same psychological dimension as long as the ability scale is not
changed; number-right test score is not invariant from test to test, although it is
unaffected by choice of scale for measuring θ.

3.6. A SUFFICIENT CONDITION FOR THE NORMAL OGIVE MODEL

In Section 3.2, we consider a variable Y_i' underlying item i. Suppose n items each have such an underlying variable, and suppose for some group of examinees all the Y_i' are jointly multinormally distributed. In this case, the joint distribution of the dichotomous item responses u_i is determined by the γ_i and by the intercorrelations ρ_{ij}' of Y_i' and Y_j' ($i \neq j$; $i, j = 1, 2, \ldots, n$). It can be shown (Lord & Novick, 1968, Section 16.8) that if the joint distribution of the observed u_i for any set of data is consistent with this multinormal model for some γ_i and ρ_{ij}' ($i \neq j$; $i, j = 1, 2, \ldots, n$), then the data are consistent with the two-parameter normal ogive response model, including the assumption of unidimensionality (local independence). Furthermore, the ρ_{ij}' will then have just one common factor, which may be considered as the ability θ measured by the n-item test.

The situation just described can only exist if there is no guessing and if θ is normally distributed in the group tested. This is a very restrictive situation; but if this situation held for some group for some free-response items, the normal ogive model would also hold for all other groups taking these same items.

The point is not that most data will fit the very restrictive conditions. They will not. The point is rather that the normal ogive model will hold in a very large variety of other, less restrictive situations. The restrictive conditions are sufficient conditions for the normal ogive model; they are very far from being necessary conditions.

3.7. ITEM INTERCORRELATIONS

Although we do not expect the restrictive model of the previous section to hold for most actual data, some useful conclusions can be drawn from it that will help us understand the relation of our latent item parameters to familiar quantities. It is clear that when Y_i' and Y_j' are normally distributed, the product-moment correlation ρ_{ij}' between them is, by definition, the same as the tetrachoric correlation between item i and item j. Under the restrictive model, the ρ_{ij}' will have just one common factor, θ, so that

$$\rho_{ij}' = \rho_i' \rho_j', \tag{3-11}$$

where ρ_i' and ρ_j' are the factor loadings of items i and j. The factor loadings are also the correlations of Y_i' and Y_j' with θ and also the biserial correlations of u_i and u_j with θ.

When there is no guessing, Eq. (3-11) will allow us to infer observable item intercorrelations from the parameters a_i and a_j: Under the restrictive model, the (observable) tetrachoric correlation between item i and item j is found from (3-3) and (3-11) to be

$$\rho'_{ij} = \frac{a_i a_j}{\sqrt{1 + a_i^2}\,\sqrt{1 + a_j^2}}.$$

Conversely, under the restrictive model the ρ'_i, and thus the a_i, can be inferred from a factor analysis of tetrachoric item intercorrelations:

$$\rho'^2_i = \frac{\rho'_{ij}\rho'_{ik}}{\rho'_{jk}} \qquad (i \neq j, i \neq k, j \neq k). \tag{3-12}$$

This is not recommended in the usual situations where there is guessing, however.

3.8.   ILLUSTRATIVE RELATIONSHIPS AMONG TEST AND ITEM PARAMETERS

Table 3.8.1 illustrates the relationship of the item discriminating power a_i to various conventional item and test statistics and also the interrelationships among them. The illustration assumes that ability θ is normally distributed with zero mean and unit variance and also that $b_i = 0$ for all items. The test statistics are for a 50-item test ($n = 50$). All quantities other than the $\rho'_{i\theta}$, including the a_i at the head of the columns, are rounded values computed from (exact) values shown for $\rho'_{i\theta}$ ($\equiv \rho'_i$). All 50 items have identical a_i and c_i.

The most familiar quantities in the table are probably the test reliabilities ($\rho_{xx'}$) in the bottom line. Most 50-item multiple-choice tests with which we are

TABLE 3.8.1

Relation of Item Discriminating Power a_i to Various Conventional Item Parameters, and to Parameters of a 50-Item Test, when Ability Is Normally Distributed ($\mu_\theta = 0$, $\sigma_\theta = 1$) and All Free-Response Items Are of 50% Difficulty ($\pi_i = .50$, $b_i = 0$)

			$a_i = 0$	.20	.44	.75	.98	1.33	2.06	Eq. no.
Free-Response Items	$c_i = 0,$ $\pi_i = .5$	$\rho'_{i\theta}$	0	.2	.4	.6	.7	.8	.9	(3-3)
		$\rho_{i\theta}$	0	.16	.32	.48	.56	.64	.72	(3-6)
		ρ'_{ij}	0	.040	.16	.36	.49	.64	.81	(3-11)
		ρ_{ij}	0	.025	.10	.23	.33	.44	.60	(3-13)
		$\rho_{i(x-i)}$	0	.12	.29	.47	.56	.66	.77	(3-14)
		$\rho_{xx'}$	0	.57	.85	.94	.96	.98	.99	(1-17)
Multiple-Choice Items	$c_i = .2,$ $\pi_i = .6$	ρ_{IJ}	0	.017	.07	.16	.22	.29	.40	(3-19)
		$\rho_{I(X-I)}$	0	.088	.23	.38	.45	.53	.62	(3-14)
		ρ_{IX}	.14	.19	.29	.42	.48	.56	.64	(3-16)
		ρ'_{IX}	.18	.24	.37	.53	.61	.70	.81	(3-6)
		σ_X	3.5	4.7	7.2	10.2	11.8	13.6	15.7	(3-15)
		$\rho_{XX'}$	0	.46	.79	.90	.93	.95	.97	(1-17)

familiar probably have reliabilities close to .90. If so, we should focus our attention on the column with $\rho_{xx'} = .90$ at the bottom and $a_i = .75$ at the top.

The top half of the table assumes that $c_i = 0$. This is referred to as the *free-response case* (although free-response items do not necessarily have $c_i = 0$). Note that by (3-4) and (3-9), under the assumptions made, free-response items with $b_i = 0$ will have exactly 50% correct answers ($\pi_i = .50$) in the total group of examinees. The parameters shown are the biserial item-ability correlation $\rho_{i\theta}'$; the point-biserial (product-moment) item-ability correlation $\rho_{i\theta}$; the tetrachoric item intercorrelation ρ_{ij}'; the product-moment item intercorrelation ρ_{ij} (phi coefficient); the item-test correlation $\rho_{i(x-i)}$, where $x - i$ is number-right score on the remaining 49 items; and the parallel-forms test reliability $\rho_{xx'}$. The equation used to calculate each parameter is referenced in the table.

The bottom half of the table deals with multiple-choice tests. The theoretical relation between the multiple-choice and the free-response case is discussed in the Appendix. For the rest of this chapter only, multiple-choice items are indexed by I and J to distinguish them from free-response items (indexed by i and j); the number-right score on a multiple-choice test will be denoted by X to distinguish it from the score x obtained from free-response items. The multiple-choice item intercorrelation ρ_{IJ} (phi coefficient) is computed by (3-19) from the free-response ρ_{ij}. All multiple-choice parameters in the table are computed from ρ_{IJ}. All numbered equations except (3-19) apply equally to multiple-choice and to free-response items.

Note in passing several things of general interest in the table:

1. A comparison of $\rho_{XX'}$ with $\rho_{xx'}$ indicates the loss in test reliability when low-ability examinees are able to get one-fifth of the items right without knowing any answers.

2. The standard deviation σ_X of number-right scores varies very sharply with item discriminating power (with item intercorrelation).

3. The usual item-test correlation ρ_{ix} or ρ_{ix}' (also ρ_{IX} or ρ_{IX}') is spuriously high because item i is included in x (or I in X). The amount of the spurious effect can be seen by comparing ρ_{IX} and $\rho_{I(X-I)}$.

4. For free-response items, the item-test correlation $\rho_{i(x-i)}$ in the last two columns of the table is higher than the item-ability correlation $\rho_{i\theta}$. This may be viewed as due to the fact (see Section 3.1) that the item observed-score regression is more nearly linear than the item-ability regression (item response function).

APPENDIX

This appendix provides those formulas not given elsewhere that are necessary for computing Table 3.8.1. In the top half of the table, the phi coefficient ρ_{ij} was obtained from the tetrachoric ρ'_{ij} by a special formula (Lord & Novick, 1968, Eq. 15.9.3) applicable only to items with 50% correct answers:

$$\rho_{ij} = \frac{2}{\pi} \arcsin \rho'_{ij} \qquad (3\text{-}13)$$

the arcsin being expressed in radians. The test reliability $\rho_{xx'}$ was obtained from ρ_{ij} by the Spearman–Brown formula (1-17) for the correlation between two parallel tests after lengthening each of them 50 times. The item-test correlation $\rho_{i(x-i)}$ was obtained from a well-known closely related formula for the correlation between one test (i) and the lengthened form (y) of a parallel test (j):

$$\rho_{iy} = \frac{m\sigma_i \rho_{ij}}{\sigma_y}, \qquad (3\text{-}14)$$

where m is the number of times j is lengthened [for $\rho_{i(x-i)}$ in Table 3.8.1, $m = 49$], y is number-right score on the lengthened test, $\sigma_i^2 = \pi_i(1 - \pi_i)$ is the variance (1-23) of the item score ($u_i = 0$ or 1), and

$$\sigma_y^2 = \sigma_i^2[m + m(m - 1)\rho_{ij}] \qquad (3\text{-}15)$$

is the variance of the y scores [see Eq. (1-21)].

The usual point-biserial *item-test correlation* ρ_{ix} is computed from $\rho_{i(x-i)}$ by a formula derived as follows:

$$\rho_{ix} \equiv \rho_{i[(x-i)+i]} = \frac{\sigma_{i(x-i)} + \sigma_i^2}{\sigma_i \sigma_x} = \frac{\sigma_i \sigma_{x-i}\, \rho_{i(x-i)} + \sigma_i^2}{\sigma_i \sigma_x}.$$

When $y \equiv x - i$, we have from (3-14) that $\sigma_{x-i}\rho_{i(x-i)} = m\sigma_i\rho_{ij}$; using these last formulas with $m = n - 1$, we have

$$\rho_{ix} = \frac{m\sigma_i^2 \rho_{ij} + \sigma_i^2}{\sigma_i \sigma_x}.$$

Finally, using Eq. (3-15) with $m \equiv n$, we find from this that

$$\rho_{ix} = \frac{(n - 1)\rho_{ij} + 1}{\sqrt{n + n(n - 1)\rho_{ij}}} = \frac{\sqrt{1 + (n - 1)\rho_{ij}}}{\sqrt{n}}. \qquad (3\text{-}16)$$

Suppose A, B, C, and D are the relative frequencies in the accompanying 2 × 2 intercorrelation table for free-response items i and j ($c_i = c_j = 0$). The general formula for the phi coefficient for any such table is

B	A	π_i
D	C	$1 - \pi_i$
$1 - \pi_j$	π_j	

$$\rho_{ij} = \frac{AD - BC}{\sqrt{\pi_i(1 - \pi_i)\pi_j(1 - \pi_j)}}. \qquad (3\text{-}17)$$

Suppose now that we change the items to multiple choice with $c_I = c_J = c >$

0. According to Eq. (2-1) or (2-2), the effect will be that of the people who got each free-response item wrong, a fraction c will now get the corresponding multiple-choice item right. Thus $\pi_I = \pi_i + c_I(1 - \pi_i)$. The new 2×2 table for multiple-choice items will therefore be

$(1 - c)B + c(1 - c)D$	$A + cB + cC + c^2D$	$\pi + c(1 - \pi)$
$(1 - c)^2D$	$(1 - c)C + c(1 - c)D$	$(1 - c)(1 - \pi_i)$
$(1 - c)(1 - \pi_j)$	$\pi + c(1 - \pi)$	

In the special free-response case where $\pi_i = \pi_j = \frac{1}{2}$, we have $B = C = \frac{1}{2} - A$ and $D = A$; also we find from (3-17) that

$$\rho_{ij} = 4A - 1. \tag{3-18}$$

In this special case, the 2×2 table for the multiple-choice items is therefore

$(1 - c)(\frac{1}{2} - A + cA)$	$A(1 - c)^2 + c$	$\frac{1}{2}(1 + c)$
$(1 - c)^2A$	$(1 - c)(\frac{1}{2} - A + cA)$	$\frac{1}{2}(1 - c)$
$\frac{1}{2}(1 - c)$	$\frac{1}{2}(1 + c)$	

When the general formula for a phi coefficient is applied to the last 2×2 table, we find that for the multiple-choice items under consideration

$$\rho_{IJ} = \frac{A^2(1 - c)^4 + cA(1 - c)^2 - (1 - c)^2(\frac{1}{2} - A + cA)^2}{\frac{1}{4}(1 - c^2)}$$

$$= \frac{1 - c}{1 + c}(4A - 1).$$

Using (3-18) we find a simple relation between the free-response ρ_{ij} and the multiple-choice ρ_{IJ} for the special case where $\pi_i = \pi_j = .5$:

$$\rho_{IJ} = \frac{1 - c}{1 + c}\rho_{ij} \tag{3-19}$$

This formula is a special case of the more general formula in Eq. (7-3).

REFERENCES

Fan, C.-T. On the applications of the method of absolute scaling. *Psychometrika*, 1957, 22, 175–183.

Gulliksen, H. *Theory of mental tests.* New York: Wiley, 1950.

Lord, F. M., & Novick, M. R. *Statistical theories of mental test scores.* Reading, Mass.: Addison-Wesley, 1968.

4

Test Scores and Ability Estimates as Functions of Item Parameters

The ideas in this chapter are essential to an understanding of subsequent chapters.

4.1. THE DISTRIBUTION OF TEST SCORES FOR GIVEN ABILITY

It is sometimes asserted that item response theory allows us to answer any question that we are entitled to ask about the characteristics of a test composed of items with known item parameters. The significance of this vague statement arises from the fact that item response theory provides us with the frequency distribution $\phi(x|\theta)$ of test scores for examinees having a specified level θ of ability or skill.

For the present, let us consider the number-right score, denoted by x. If the n items in a test all had identical item response curves $P \equiv P(\theta)$, the distribution of x for a person at ability level θ would then be the binomial distribution

$$\phi(x|\theta) = \binom{n}{x} P^x Q^{n-x},$$

where $Q \equiv 1 - P$. The expression $(Q + P)^n$ is familiar as the generating function for the binomial distribution, because the binomial expansion

$$(Q + P)^n \equiv Q^n + nPQ^{n-1} + \binom{n}{2} P^2 Q^{n-2}$$
$$+ \cdots + \binom{n}{x} P^x Q^{n-x} + \cdots + P^n$$

gives the terms of $\phi(x|\theta)$ successively for $x = 0, 1, \ldots, n$.

When the item response curves $P_i \equiv P_i(\theta)$ $(i = 1, 2, \ldots, n)$ vary from item

44

to item, as is ordinarily the case, the frequency distribution $\phi(x|\theta)$ of the number-right test score for a person with ability θ is a generalized binomial (Kendall & Stuart, 1969, Section 5.10). This distribution can be generated by the generating function

$$\prod_{i=1}^{n} (Q_i + P_i). \tag{4-1}$$

For example, if $n = 3$, the scores $x = 0, 1, 2, 3$ occur with relative frequency $Q_1Q_2Q_3$, $Q_1Q_2P_3 + Q_1P_2Q_3 + P_1Q_2Q_3$, $Q_1P_2P_3 + P_1Q_2P_3 + P_1P_2Q_3$, and $P_1P_2P_3$, respectively. The columns of Table 4.3.1 give the reader a good idea of the kinds of $\phi(x|\theta)$ encountered in practice.

Although $\phi(x|\theta)$, the conditional distribution of number-right score, cannot be written in a simple form, its mean $\mu_{x|\theta}$ and variance $\sigma_{x|\theta}^2$ for given θ are simply

$$\mu_{x|\theta} = \sum_{i=1}^{n} P_i(\theta), \tag{4-2}$$

$$\sigma_{x|\theta}^2 = \sum_{i=1}^{n} P_i Q_i. \tag{4-3}$$

The mean (4-2) can be derived from the fact that $x \equiv \Sigma_i u_i$ and the familiar fact that the mean of u_i is P_i. The variance (4-3) can be derived from the familiar binomial variance $\sigma^2(u_i) = P_i Q_i$ by noting that

$$\sigma_{x|\theta}^2 = \sigma^2(\Sigma_i u_i|\theta) = \Sigma_i \sigma^2(u_i) = \Sigma_i P_i Q_i$$

because of local independence. Note that $\phi(x|\theta)$, $\mu_{x|\theta}$, and $\sigma_{x|\theta}$ refer to the distribution of x (1) for all people at ability level θ and also (2) for any given individual whose ability level is θ.

If $\bar{P}$ is the average of the $P_i(\theta)$ taken over n items, then in practice $\phi(x|\theta)$ is usually very much like the binomial distribution $\binom{n}{x} \bar{P}^x \bar{Q}^{n-x}$ where $\bar{Q} \equiv 1 - \bar{P}$. The main difference is that the variance $\Sigma P_i Q_i$ is always less than the binomial variance $n\bar{P}\bar{Q}$ unless $P_i = \bar{P}$ for all items. The difference between the two variances is simply $n\sigma_{P|\theta}^2$, where $\sigma_{P|\theta}^2$ is the variance of the $P_i(\theta)$ for fixed θ taken over items:

$$\sigma_{x|\theta}^2 = n\bar{P}\bar{Q} - n\sigma_{P|\theta}^2. \tag{4-4}$$

4.2. TRUE SCORE

A person's number-right true score ξ (pronounced ksai or ksee) on a test is defined in Lord and Novick (1968, Chapter 2) as the expectation of his observed score x. It follows immediately from (4-2) that every person at ability level θ has the same number-right true score

$$\xi = \sum_{i=1}^{n} P_i(\theta). \tag{4-5}$$

Since each $P_i(\theta)$ is an increasing function of θ, number-right true score is an increasing function of ability.

This is the same true score denoted by T in Section 1.2. The classical notation avoids Greek letters, the present notation emphasizes that the relation of observed score x to true score ξ is the relation of a sample observation to a population parameter.

True score ξ and ability θ are the same thing expressed on different scales of measurement. The important difference is that the measurement scale for ξ depends on the items in the test; the measurement scale for θ is independent of the items in the test (Section 3.4). This makes θ more useful than ξ when we wish to compare different tests of the same ability. Such comparisons are an essential part of any search for efficient test design (Chapter 6).

4.3.   STANDARD ERROR OF MEASUREMENT

By definition, the error of measurement (e) is the discrepancy between observed score and true score: $e \equiv x - \xi$. When ξ is fixed, e and x have the same standard deviation, since in that case e and x differ only by a constant. This standard deviation is called the *standard error of measurement at ξ*, denoted here by $\sigma_{e|\xi}$. The squared standard error of measurement $s_{e\cdot\xi}^2$ of classical test theory is simply $\sigma_{e|\xi}^2$ averaged over all (N) examinees:

$$s_{e\cdot\xi}^2 = \frac{1}{N}\sum^{N} \sigma_{e|\xi}^2. \tag{4-6}$$

When ξ is fixed, so is θ and vice versa [see Eq. (4-5)]. Thus

$$\sigma_{e|\xi=\xi_0} \equiv \sigma_{e|\theta=\theta_0} \tag{4-7}$$

provided ξ_0 and θ_0 are corresponding values satisfying (4-5). By (4-3) and (4-7), finally,

$$\sigma_{e|\xi_0}^2 = \sum_{i=1}^{n} P_i(\theta_0)Q_i(\theta_0). \tag{4-8}$$

Note that the standard error of measurement approaches 0 at high ability levels, where $P_i(\theta) \to 1$. At low ability levels,

$$P_i(\theta) \to c_i \quad \text{and} \quad \sigma_{e|\xi}^2 \to \Sigma^n c_i(1 - c_i).$$

Table 4.3.1 shows the conditional frequency distribution of number-right scores at equally spaced ability levels as estimated for the 60-item Mathematics section of the Scholastic Aptitude Test. This table was computed from (4-1),

TABLE 4.3.1
Theoretical Conditional Frequency Distribution of Number-Right Scores on SAT Mathematics Test (January 1971) for Equally Spaced Fixed Values of θ (all frequencies multiplied by 100)

Selected Fixed Values of θ

Score (x)	-3.000	-2.625	-2.250	-1.875	-1.500	-1.125	-0.750	-0.375	0.000	+0.375	+0.750	+1.125	+1.500	+1.875	+2.250	+2.625	+3.000
60																28	52
59															7	37	35
58														2	20	23	11
57														6	27	9	2
56													1	12	23	3	
55													2	18	14	1	
54													5	20	7		
53													8	17	3		
52													12	12	1		
51												1	15	7			
50												1	15	4			
49												3	14	2			
48												5	11	1			
47												7	8				
46												10	5				
45											1	12	3				
44											1	14	1				
43											3	13					
42											5	11					
41											7	9					
40										1	9	6					
39										1	12	6					
38										3	13	4					
37										4	13	2					
36									1	6	11	1					
35									1	9	9						
34									2	11	7						
33									3	12	5						
32								1	5	12	3						
31								1	7	12	2						

(continued)

TABLE 4.3.1 (continued)

Selected Fixed Values of θ

Score (x)	−3.000	−2.625	−2.250	−1.875	−1.500	−1.125	−0.750	−0.375	0.000	+0.375	+0.750	+1.125	+1.500	+1.875	+2.250	+2.625	+3.000
30								2	9	10	1						
29								3	11	7							
28							1	5	12	5							
27							1	7	12	3							
26						1	2	9	11	2							
25						1	4	11	9	1							
24					1	3	6	12	7								
23				1	1	4	8	12	5								
22			1	2	2	6	10	11	3								
21		1	1	3	4	8	11	9	1								
20		1	2	4	6	10	12	7									
19	1	2	4	6	8	12	12	5									
18	2	4	6	9	10	12	10	3									
17	3	6	8	11	12	12	8	2									
16	5	9	11	12	13	10	6	1									
15	7	11	12	13	12	8	4	1									
14	10	13	13	12	11	6	2										
13	12	13	13	10	8	4	1										
12	14	13	11	7	6	2	1										
11	14	10	8	5	4	1											
10	12	8	5	3	2												
9	9	5	3	1	1												
8	6	3	1	1													
7	4	1	1														
6	2																
5	1																
4																	
3																	
2																	
1																	
0																	

using estimated item parameters. All items are five-choice items. The typical ogive shape of the regression function $\mu_{x|\theta} = \Sigma^n P_i(\theta)$ is apparent in this table and also the typical decreasing standard error of measurement and increasing skewness at high ability levels.

4.4. TYPICAL DISTORTIONS IN MENTAL MEASUREMENT

As already noted, formula (4-2) for the regression $\mu_{x|\theta}$ of number-right score on ability is the same as formula (4-5) for the relation of true score to ability. This important function $\xi \equiv \xi(\theta) \equiv \Sigma^n P_i(\theta)$ and also the function

$$\zeta \equiv \zeta(\theta) \equiv \frac{1}{n}\sum_{i=1}^{n} P_i(\theta) \tag{4-9}$$

are called *test characteristic functions*. Either of these functions specifies the distortion imposed on the ability scale when number-right score on a particular set of test items is used as a measure of ability. A typical example of a test characteristic function appears in Fig. 5.5.1.

Over ability ranges where the test characteristic curve is relatively steep, score differences are exaggerated compared to ability differences. Over ranges where the test characteristic curve is relatively flat, score differences are compressed compared to ability differences. Since number-right scores are integers, compression of a wide range of ability into one or two discrete score values necessarily results in inaccurate measurement.

If all items had the same response function, clearly the test characteristic function (4-9) would be the same function also. More generally, test characteristic curves usually have ogive shapes similar to but not identical with item response functions. Differences in difficulty among items cause a flattening of the test characteristic curve. If all items had the same response curves except that their difficulty parameters b_i were uniformly distributed, the test characteristic curve would be virtually a straight line except at its extremes. For a long test, the greater the range of the b_i, the more nearly horizontal the test characteristic curve.

If a test is composed of two sets of items, one set easy and the other set difficult, the test characteristic curve may have three relatively flat regions: It may be flat in the middle as well as at extreme ability levels. Such a test will compress the ability scale and provide poor measurement at middle ability levels, as well as at the extremes.

If the distribution of ability is assumed to have some specified shape (for example, it is bell-shaped), the effect of the distortions introduced by various types of test characteristic functions can be visualized. If a test is much too easy for the group tested, the point of inflection of the test characteristic curve may fall in the lower tail of the distribution where there are no examinees. Only the top part of the test characteristic curve may be relevant for the particular group tested. In this case, most examinees in the group may be squeezed into a few discrete score values at the top of the score range. The bottom part of the available score range is unused. Measurement is poor except for the lower ability levels of the group. An assumed bell-shaped distribution of ability is turned into a negatively skewed, in the extreme a J-shaped, distribution of number-right scores. Such a test may be very approproate if its main use is simply to weed out a few of the lowest scoring examinees.

If the test is much too hard for the group tested, an opposite situation will exist. The score distribution will be positively skewed but will not be J-shaped if there is guessing, because zero scores are then unlikely. Such a test may be very appropriate for a scholarship examination or for selecting a few individuals from a large group of applicants.

If the test is not very discriminating, the test characteristic curve will be relatively flat. If the relevant part of the characteristic curve (the part where the examinees occur) is nearly straight, the shape of the frequency distribution of ability will not be distorted by the test. However, a wide range of ability will be squeezed into a few middling number-right scores, with correspondingly poor measurement.

If the test is very discriminating, its characteristic curve will be correspondingly steep in the middle. The curve cannot be steep throughout the ability range because it is asymptotic to $\zeta = 1$ at the right and to $\zeta = \bar{c}$ at the left, where

$$\bar{c} = \frac{1}{n} \sum_{i=1}^{n} c_i. \tag{4-10}$$

Thus there will be good measurement in the middle but poor measurement at the extremes. If the test difficulty is appropriate for the group tested, the middle part of the bell-shaped distribution of ability will be spread out and the tails squeezed together. The result in this case is a platykurtic distribution of number-right scores. The more discriminating the items, the more platykurtic the number-right score distribution, other things being equal. In the extreme, a U-shaped distribution of number-right scores may be obtained.

If we wish to discriminate well among people near a particular ability level (or levels), we should build a test that has a steep characteristic curve at the point(s) where we want to discriminate. For example, if a test is to be used only to select a single individual for a scholarship or prize, then the items should be so difficult that only the top person in the group tested knows the answer to more than half of the test items. The problem of optimal test design for such a test is discussed in Chapters 5, 6, and 11.

An understanding of the role of the test characteristic curve is important in designing a test for a specific purpose. Diagrams showing graphically just how various test characteristic curves distort the ability scale, and thus the frequency distribution of ability, are given in Lord and Novick (1968, Section 16.14).

4.5. THE JOINT DISTRIBUTION OF ABILITY AND TEST SCORES

If ability had a rectangular distribution from $\theta = -3$ to $\theta = +3$, Table 4.3.1 would give a good idea of the joint distribution of ability and number-right score. Otherwise, the probabilities at each value of θ must be multiplied by its relative frequency of occurrence in order to obtain the desired joint distribution. Formally, the joint distribution is

$$\phi(x, \theta) = \phi(x|\theta)g^*(\theta), \tag{4-11}$$

where $g^*(\theta)$ is the distribution (probability density) of ability in the group tested. (The general term *distribution* rather than *probability density* or *frequency function* is used throughout this book. Where necessary to prevent confusion, *cumulative* or *noncumulative* is specified.)

Usually $g^*(\theta)$ is unknown. The observed distribution of estimated θ is an approximation to $g^*(\theta)$. A better approximation can often be obtained by the methods of Chapter 16.

Given an adequate estimate of $g^*(\theta)$, the joint distribution of ability and number-right score can be determined from (4-11) and (4-1). This joint distribution contains all relevant information for describing and evaluating the properties of the number-right score x for measuring ability θ. One such (estimated) joint distribution is shown in Table 16.11.1.

4.6. THE TOTAL-GROUP DISTRIBUTION OF NUMBER-RIGHT SCORE

Suppose we have a group of N individuals whose ability levels θ_a ($a = 1,$ $2, \ldots, N$) are known (in practice the θ_a will be replaced by estimated values $\hat{\theta}_a$). It is apparent that the total-group or marginal distribution $\phi(x)$ of number-right scores will be

$$\phi(x) = \frac{1}{N} \sum_{a=1}^{N} \phi(x|\theta_a), \tag{4-12}$$

where $\phi(x|\theta_a)$ is calculated from (4-1).

Any desired moments of the total-group distribution of test score can be calculated from the $\phi(x)$ obtained by (4-12). The expected score for the N examinees also can be found from (4-12) and (4-2):

$$\mathscr{E}x = \frac{1}{N}\sum_{a=1}^{N} \mu_{x|\theta_a} = \frac{1}{N}\sum_{a=1}^{N}\sum_{i=1}^{n} P_i(\theta_a). \qquad (4\text{-}13)$$

An estimate of the expected variance of the N scores can be found from an ANOVA identity relating total-group statistics to conditional statistics:

$$\sigma_x^2 \equiv \text{mean of } \sigma_{x|\theta_a}^2 + \text{variance of } \mu_{x|\theta_a}.$$

From this, (4-2), (4-3), and (4-13), we have the estimated total-group variance

$$\frac{1}{N}\sum_{a=1}^{N}\sum_{i=1}^{n} P_{ia}Q_{ia} + \frac{1}{N}\sum_{a=1}^{N}\left(\sum_{i=1}^{n} P_{ia}\right)^2 - \frac{1}{N^2}\left(\sum_{a=1}^{N}\sum_{i=1}^{n} P_{ia}\right)^2 \qquad (4\text{-}14)$$

where $P_{ia} \equiv P_i(\theta_a)$.

4.7.   TEST RELIABILITY

Although we shall have little use for test reliability coefficients in this book, it is reassuring to have a formula relating test reliability to item and ability parameters. A conventional definition of test reliability is given by Eq. (1-6) and (1-9): Written in our current notation, this definition is

$$\rho_{xx'} \equiv \rho_{x\xi}^2 \equiv 1 - \frac{\sigma_{e\cdot\xi}^2}{\sigma_x^2}. \qquad (4\text{-}15)$$

For a sample of examinees, (4-15), (4-6), (4-8), and (4-14) suggest an appropriate sample reliability coefficient:

$$\hat{\rho}_{xx'} = \frac{\sum_{}^{N}\left(\sum_{}^{n} P_{ia}\right)^2 - (\sum_{}^{N}\sum_{}^{n} P_{ia})^2/N}{\sum_{}^{N}\sum_{}^{n} P_{ia}Q_{ia} + \sum_{}^{N}\left(\sum_{}^{n} P_{ia}\right)^2 - (\sum_{}^{N}\sum_{}^{n} P_{ia})^2/N}. \qquad (4\text{-}16)$$

From (4-7), we see that (4-15) is the complement of the ratio of (averaged squared error about the regression of x on θ) to (variance of x). Reliability is therefore, by definition, equal to the correlation ratio of score x on ability θ.

4.8.   ESTIMATING ABILITY FROM TEST SCORE

The following procedure clarifies the construction of confidence intervals for estimating ability θ from number-right score x. Consider the score distribution in any column in Table 4.3.1. Find the highest score level below which lies no more than 2½% of the frequency. Do this for all values of θ. If x were continuous, the points would form a smooth curve; since x is an integer, the points fall on a step function. This step function cuts off 2½% or less of the frequency at every ability level θ. Repeat this process for the upper tails of the score distributions.

The two resulting step functions are shown in Fig. 4.8.1. No matter what the value of θ may be, in the long run at least 95% of all randomly chosen scores will lie in the region between these step functions.

Now consider a random examinee. His number-right score on the test is x_0, say. We are going to assert that he is in the region between the step functions. This assertion will be correct at least 95% of the time for randomly chosen examinees. But given that this examinee's test score is x_0, this assertion is in logic completely equivalent to the assertion that he lies in a certain interval on θ. In Fig. 4.8.1, the ends of an illustrative interval are denoted by $\underline{\theta}$ and $\bar{\theta}$. We shall therefore assert that his ability θ lies in the interval $(\underline{\theta}, \bar{\theta})$. Such assertions will be correct in the long run at least 95% of the time for randomly chosen examinees.

An interval with this property is called a 95% confidence interval. Such confidence intervals are basic to the very important concept of *test information*, introduced in Chapter 5. It is for this reason that we consider it in such detail here.

A point estimate of θ for given x would be provided by the regression of θ on x (see Section 12.8). Although the regression of x on θ is given by (4-2), the

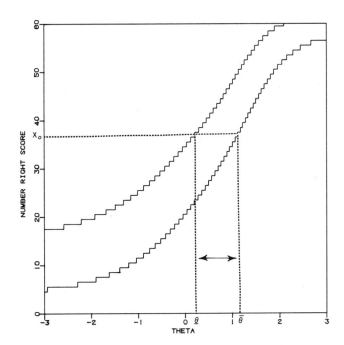

FIG. 4.8.1.   Confidence interval $(\underline{\theta}, \bar{\theta})$ for estimating ability (SAT Mathematics Test, January 1971).

regression of θ on x cannot be determined unless we know $g^*(\theta)$, the distribution of ability in the group tested. The regression of θ on x is by definition given by

$$\mu_{\theta|x} = \frac{1}{\phi(x)}\int_{-\infty}^{\infty} \theta g^*(\theta)\phi(x|\theta)d\theta \qquad (4\text{-}17)$$

[compare Eq. (4-11)]. Ordinarily it cannot be written in closed form. It can be calculated numerically if the distribution of θ is known.

4.9. JOINT DISTRIBUTION OF ITEM SCORES FOR ONE EXAMINEE

Number right is not the only way, nor the best way, to score a test. For more general results, and for other reasons, we need to know the conditional frequency distribution of the pattern of item responses—the joint distribution of all item responses u_i ($i = 1, 2, \ldots , n$) for given θ.

For item i, the conditional distribution given θ of a single item response is

$$L(u_i|\theta) = \begin{cases} P_i(\theta) & \text{if } u_i = 1, \\ Q_i(\theta) & \text{if } u_i = 0, \\ 0 & \text{otherwise.} \end{cases} \qquad (4\text{-}18)$$

This may be written more compactly in various ways. For present purposes, we shall write

$$L(u_i|\theta) = P_i^{u_i}Q_i^{1-u_i}. \qquad (4\text{-}19)$$

The reader should satisfy himself that (4-18) and (4-19) are identical for the two permissible values of u_i.

Because of local independence, which is guaranteed by unidimensionality (Section 2.4), success on one item is statistically independent of success on other items. Therefore, the joint distribution of all item responses, given θ, is the product of the distributions (4-19) for the separate items:

$$L(\mathbf{u}|\theta; \mathbf{a}, \mathbf{b}, \mathbf{c}) \equiv L(u_1, u_2, \ldots ,u_n|\theta) = \prod_{i=1}^{n} P_i^{u_i}Q_i^{1-u_i}, \qquad (4\text{-}20)$$

where $\mathbf{u} \equiv \{u_i\}$ is the column vector $\{u_1, u_2, \ldots , u_n\}'$ and $\mathbf{a}, \mathbf{b}, \mathbf{c}$ are vectors of a_i, b_i, and c_i.

Equation (4-20) may be viewed as the conditional distribution of the pattern $\mathbf{u}$ of item responses for a given individual with ability θ and for known item parameters $\mathbf{a}, \mathbf{b},$ and $\mathbf{c}$. In this case the u_i ($i = 1, 2, \ldots , n$) are random variables and $\theta, \mathbf{a}, \mathbf{b},$ and $\mathbf{c}$ are considered fixed.

If the u_i for an individual have already been determined from his answer sheet, they are no longer chance variables but known constants. In this case, assuming the item parameters to be known from pretesting, it is useful to think of (4-20) as a function of the mathematical variable θ, which represents the (un-known) ability level of the examinee. Considered in this way, (4-20) is the

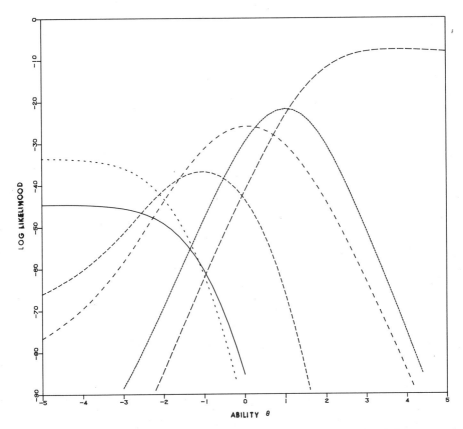

FIG. 4.9.1. Logarithm of likelihood functions for estimating the ability of six selected examinees from the SCAT II 2B Mathematics test.

likelihood function for θ. The *maximum likelihood estimate* $\hat{\theta}$ (see Section 4.13) of the examinee's ability is the value of θ that maximizes the likelihood (4-20) of his actually observed responses u_i ($i = 1, 2, \ldots, n$).

Figure 4.9.1 shows the logarithm of six logistic likelihood functions computed independently by (4-20) for six selected examinees taking a 100-item high school mathematics aptitude test. The maxima of these six curves are found at ability levels $\theta = -5.6, -4.6, -1.0, .1, 1.0$, and 3.7. These six values are the maximum likelihood ability estimates $\hat{\theta}$ for the six examinees.

4.10. JOINT DISTRIBUTION OF ALL ITEM SCORES ON ALL ANSWER SHEETS

If N examinees can be treated as a random sample from a very large population of examinees, then the distributions of **u** for different examinees are statistically independent. Thus the joint distribution of the N different $\mathbf{u}$ for all examinees is the product of the separate distributions. This joint distribution is then

$$L(\mathbf{U} \mid \boldsymbol{\theta}; \mathbf{a}, \mathbf{b}, \mathbf{c}) \equiv L(\mathbf{u}_1, \mathbf{u}_2, \ldots, \mathbf{u}_N \mid \boldsymbol{\theta}) = \prod_{a=1}^{N} \prod_{i=1}^{n} P_{ia}^{u_{ia}} \, Q_{ia}^{1-u_{ia}}, \quad (4\text{-}21)$$

where the subscript a distinguishes the contribution of examinee a ($a = 1$, $2, \ldots, N$) and where $P_{ia} \equiv P_i(\theta_a)$, $\mathbf{U}$ is the matrix $\|u_{ia}\|$, and $\boldsymbol{\theta}$ is the vector $\{\theta_1, \theta_2, \ldots, \theta_N\}'$.

When examinee responses have already been recorded on a pile of answer sheets, (4-21) may be viewed as the likelihood function of both the ability parameters $\theta_1, \theta_2, \ldots, \theta_N$ and the item parameters $a_1, b_1, c_1, a_2, b_2, c_2, \ldots, a_n, b_n, c_n$. The maximum likelihood estimates are the values $\hat{\theta}_a$ ($a = 1, 2, \ldots, N$) and $\hat{a}_i, \hat{b}_i, \hat{c}_i$ ($i = 1, 2, \ldots, n$) that together maximize (4-21). If the item parameters are known, then (4-21) is simply the likelihood function of all the θ_a.

Does it seem unlikely that we can successfully estimate $N + 3n$ parameters all at the same time from just one pile of answer sheets? Actually, we do almost the same thing in everyday practice. We obtain a score (ability estimate) for each examinee and also do an item analysis on the same pile of answer sheets, obtaining indices of item difficulty and item discriminating power. It is reasonable to do this if nN, the total number of observations, is large compared to both N and n. If n is 50 and N is 1000, we have about 43 observations for each parameter estimated.

4.11.   LOGISTIC LIKELIHOOD FUNCTION

The likelihood function (4-20) for θ for one examinee can also be written

$$L(\mathbf{u} \mid \Theta) = \prod_{i=1}^{n} \left(\frac{P_i}{Q_i} \right)^{u_i} \cdot \prod_{i=1}^{n} Q_i.$$

In general, this is not helpful; but in the case of the logistic function [Eq. (2-1)] when $c_i = 0$,

$$\frac{P_i}{Q_i} = \frac{\dfrac{1}{1 + e^{-DL_i}}}{1 - \dfrac{1}{1 + e^{-DL_i}}} = e^{DL_i}, \qquad (4\text{-}22)$$

where D is the constant $\equiv 1.7$ and

$$L_i \equiv a_i(\theta - b_i). \qquad (4\text{-}23)$$

Substituting (4-22) in the preceding likelihood function gives the logistic likelihood function

$$L(\mathbf{u}|\theta) = \exp\left(\sum_{i=1}^{n} u_i L_i\right) \prod_{i=1}^{n} Q_i$$

$$= \exp\left(-D\sum_{i=1}^{n} a_i b_i u_i\right) e^{D\theta s} \prod_{i=1}^{n} Q_i(\theta), \qquad (4\text{-}24)$$

where

$$s \equiv s(\mathbf{u}) \equiv \sum_{i=1}^{n} a_i u_i. \qquad (4\text{-}25)$$

In Appendix 4, it is shown that *if*

1. *the item response function is logistic,*
2. *there is no guessing* ($c_i = 0$ *for all* i),
3. *the item parameters are known.*

then the weighted item score

$$s \equiv \Sigma_i^n \ a_i u_i$$

is a sufficient statistic for estimating examinee ability θ.

4.12. SUFFICIENT STATISTICS

The key property of a sufficient statistic s is that the conditional distribution of the observations given s is independent of some parameter θ. This means that once s is given, the data contain no further information about θ. This justifies the usual statement that *the sufficient statistic* s *contains all the information in the data concerning the unknown parameter* θ.

Note that s in (4-25) is a kind of test score, although different from the usual number-right score x. Note also that s ranges from 0 to $\Sigma_i^n a_i$. Clearly, s is not a consistent estimator of θ, which ranges from $-\infty$ to $+\infty$.

Since

$$\mathcal{E}(u_i|\theta) = P_i(\theta) \qquad (4\text{-}26)$$

the expectation of s is

$$\mathcal{E}(s|\theta) = \sum_{i=1}^{n} a_i P_i(\theta). \qquad (4\text{-}27)$$

Note that (4-27) is a kind of true score, although different from the usual number-right score ξ. A consistent estimator $\hat{\theta}$ of θ is found by solving for $\hat{\theta}$ the equation.

$$\Sigma_i a_i P_i(\hat{\theta}) = s. \qquad (4\text{-}28)$$

It is shown in Section 4.14 that the $\hat{\theta}$ obtained from Eq. (4-28) is also the maximum likelihood estimator of θ under the logistic model with all $c_i = 0$.

If s is sufficient for θ, so is any monotonic function of s. It is generally agreed that when a sufficient statistic s exists for θ, any statistical inference for θ should be based on some function of s and not on any other statistic.

The three conditions stated at the end of the preceding section are the most general conditions for the existence of a sufficient statistic for θ. There is no sufficient statistic when the item response function is a normal ogive, even though the normal ogive and logistic functions are empirically almost indistinguishable. There is no sufficient statistic when there is guessing, that is, when $c_i \neq 0$. This means that there is no sufficient statistic in cases, frequently reported in the literature, where the Rasch model (see Wright, 1977) is (improperly) used when the items can be answered correctly by guessing.

4.13. MAXIMUM LIKELIHOOD ESTIMATES

When no sufficient statistic exists, the statistician uses other estimation methods, such as maximum likelihood. As already noted in Section 4.10, the maximum likelihood estimates $\hat{\theta}_a$ ($a = 1, 2, \ldots, N$) and $\hat{a}_i$, $\hat{b}_i$, and $\hat{c}_i$ ($i = 1, 2, \ldots, n$) are by definition the parameter values that maximize (4-21) when the matrix of observed item responses $\mathbf{U} \equiv \|u_{ia}\|$ is known. In practice, the maximum likelihood estimates are found by taking derivatives of the logarithm of the likelihood function, setting the derivatives equal to zero, and then solving the resulting *likelihood equations*.

The natural logarithm of (4-21), to be denoted by l, is

$$l \equiv \ln L(\mathbf{U}|\boldsymbol{\Theta};\mathbf{a},\mathbf{b},\mathbf{c}) = \sum_{a=1}^{N} \sum_{i=1}^{n} [u_{ia} \ln P_{ia} + (1 - u_{ia}) \ln Q_{ia}]. \quad (4\text{-}29)$$

If χ represents θ_a, a_j, b_j, or c_j, the derivative of the log likelihood with respect to χ is

$$\frac{\partial l}{\partial \chi} = \sum_{a=1}^{N} \sum_{i=1}^{n} \left[u_{ia} \frac{P'_{ia}}{P_{ia}} - (1 - u_{ia}) \frac{P'_{ia}}{Q_{ia}} \right]$$

$$= \sum_{a=1}^{N} \sum_{i=1}^{n} (u_{ia} - P_{ia}) \frac{P'_{ia}}{P_{ia} Q_{ia}}, \quad (4\text{-}30)$$

where $P'_{ia} \equiv \partial P_{ia}/\partial \chi$. An explicit expression for P'_{ia} can be written as soon as the mathematical form of P_{ia} is specified, as by Eq. (2-1) or (2-2). The result for the three-parameter logistic model is given by Eq. (4-40). Some practical procedures for solving the likelihood equations (4-29) are discussed in Chapter 12.

When $\mathbf{a}, \mathbf{b}, \mathbf{c}$ are known from pretesting, the likelihood equation for estimating the ability of each examinee is obtained by setting (4-30) equal to zero:

$$\sum_{i=1}^{n} (u_{ia} - P_{ia}) \frac{P'_{ia}}{P_{ia} Q_{ia}} = 0. \qquad (4\text{-}31)$$

This is a nonlinear equation in just one unknown, θ_a. The maximum likelihood estimate $\hat{\theta}_a$ of the ability of examinee a is a root of this equation. The roots of (4-31) can be found by iterative numerical procedures, once the mathematical form for P_{ia} is specified.

If the number of items is small, (4-31) may have more than one root (Samejima, 1973). This may cause difficulty if the number of test items n is 2 or 3, as in Samejima's examples. Multiple roots have not been found to occur in practical work with $n \geqslant 20$.

If the number of items is large enough, the long test being formed by combining parallel subtests, the uniqueness of the root $\hat{\theta}$ of the likelihood equation (4-31) is guaranteed by a theorem of Foutz (1977). The unique root is a *consistent estimator;* that is, it converges to the true parameter value as the number of parallel subtests becomes large.

4.14. MAXIMUM LIKELIHOOD ESTIMATION FOR LOGISTIC ITEMS WITH $c_i = 0$

If P_{ia} is logistic [Eq. (2-1)] and each $c_i = 0$, it is found that

$$\frac{\partial P_{ia}}{\partial \theta_a} = D a_i P_{ia} Q_{ia}. \qquad (4\text{-}32)$$

Substituting this for P'_{ia} in (4-31) and rearranging gives the likelihood equation

$$\sum_{i=1}^{n} a_i P_{ia}(\theta_a) = \sum_{i=1}^{n} a_i u_{ia}. \qquad (4\text{-}33)$$

This again in a nonlinear equation in a single unknown, θ_a.

Note that its root $\hat{\theta}_a$, the maximum likelihood estimator, is a function of the sufficient statistic (4-25). Thus (4-33) is the same as (4-28). It is a general property that a maximum likelihood estimator will be a function of sufficient statistics whenever the relevant sufficient statistics exist.

4.15. MAXIMUM LIKELIHOOD ESTIMATION FOR EQUIVALENT ITEMS

Suppose all items have the same response function $P(\theta)$. We shall call this the case of *equivalent items*. This is not likely to occur in practice, but it is a limiting case that throws some light on practical situations.

In the case of equivalent items, the likelihood equation (4-31) for estimating θ becomes $(P'/PQ) \Sigma_i (u_i - P) = 0$ or

$$P(\theta) = \frac{1}{n} \sum_{i=1}^{n} u_i \equiv z, \tag{4-34}$$

where $z \equiv x/n$ is the proportion of items answered correctly. The maximum likelihood estimator $\hat{\theta}$ is found by solving (4-34) for θ:

$$\hat{\theta} = P^{-1}(z), \tag{4-35}$$

where $P^{-1}(\ )$ is the inverse function to $P(\ )$, whatever the item response function may be.

Note that when all items are equivalent, a sufficient statistic for estimating ability θ is $s = \Sigma_i a u_i = a \Sigma_i u_i = ax$. Thus, in this special case, both the number-right score x and the proportion-correct score z are sufficient statistics for estimating ability.

Exercise 4.15.1

Suppose that $P(\theta)$ is given by Eq. (2-1) and all items have $a_i = a$, $b_i = b$, and $c_i = c$, where a, b, and c are known. Show that the maximum likelihood estimator $\hat{\theta}$ of ability is given by

$$\hat{\theta} = \frac{1}{Da} \ln \frac{z - c}{1 - z} + b. \tag{4-36}$$

(Here and throughout this book, "ln" denotes a natural logarithm.) If $c = 0$, $\hat{\theta}$ is a linear function of the logarithm of the odds ratio (probability of success)/(probability of failure).

4.16. FORMULAS FOR FUNCTIONS OF THE THREE-PARAMETER LOGISTIC FUNCTION

A few useful formulas involving the three-parameter logistic function [Eq. (2-1)] are recorded here for convenient reference. These formulas do not apply to the three-parameter normal ogive [Eq. (2-2)].

$$P_i = c_i + \frac{1 - c_i}{1 + e^{-DL_i}} = \frac{c_i + e^{DL_i}}{1 + e^{DL_i}}, \tag{4-37}$$

where $D \equiv 1.7$ and $L_i \equiv a_i(\theta - b_i)$.

$$Q_i \equiv 1 - P_i = \frac{1 - c_i}{1 + e^{DL_i}}. \tag{4-38}$$

$$\frac{P_i}{Q_i} = \frac{c_i + e^{DL_i}}{1 - c_i}. \tag{4-39}$$

$$P_i' \equiv \frac{dP_i}{d\theta} = \frac{Da_i}{1 - c_i} Q_i (P_i - c_i) = \frac{Da_i (1 - c_i)}{e^{DL_i} + 2 + e^{-DL_i}}. \tag{4-40}$$

$$\frac{P_i'}{Q_i} = \frac{Da_i}{1 + e^{-DL_i}}. \tag{4-41}$$

$$w_i (\theta) \equiv \frac{P_i'}{P_i Q_i} = \frac{Da_i}{1 - c_i} \frac{P_i - c_i}{P_i} = \frac{Da_i}{1 + c_i e^{-DL_i}}. \tag{4-42}$$

$$I\{\theta, u_i\} \equiv \frac{P_i'^2}{P_i Q_i} = \frac{D^2 a_i^2 (1 - c_i)}{(c_i + e^{DL_i}) (1 + e^{-DL_i})^2}. \tag{4-43}$$

$$\frac{d^2 P_i}{d\theta^2} = \frac{D^2 a_i^2}{(1 - c_i)^2} Q_i (P_i - c_i)(Q_i - P_i + c_i). \tag{4-44}$$

$$\frac{P_i - c_i}{P_i} = \frac{1 - c_i}{1 + c_i e^{-DL_i}}. \tag{4-45}$$

4.17.   EXERCISES

4-1   Compute $P(\theta)$ under the normal ogive model [Eq. (2-2)] for $a = 1/1.7$, $b = 0$, $c = .2$, and $\theta = -3, -2, -1, 0, 1, 2, 3$. Compare with the results given for item 2 in Table 4.17.1 under the logistic model. Plot the item response function $P(\theta)$ for each item in test 1, using the values given in Table 4.17.1.

TABLE 4.17.1
Item Response Function $P(\theta)$ and Related Functions for Test 1,
Composed of $n = 3$ Items with Parameters $a_1 = a_2 = a_3 = 1/1.7$,
$b_1 = -1$, $b_2 = 0$, $b_3 = +1$, $c_1 = c_2 = c_3 = .2$

θ							
Item No.*			$P(\theta)$	$P(\theta)Q(\theta)$	$P'(\theta)$	P'^2/PQ	P'/PQ
1	2	3					
3	4	5	.985611	.014182	.014130	.014078	.996350
2	3	4	.962059	.036501	.036142	.035785	.990141
1	2	3	.904638	.086268	.083994	.081780	.973646
0	1	2	.784847	.168862	.157290	.146511	.931466
-1	0	1	.6	.24	.2	.166667	.833333
-2	-1	0	.415153	.242801	.157290	.101895	.647814
-3	-2	-1	.295362	.208123	.083994	.033898	.403582
-4	-3	-2	.237941	.181325	.036142	.007204	.199318
-5	-4	-3	.214389	.168426	.014130	.001185	.083894

*For item i, enter the table with the θ values shown in column i ($i = 1, 2, 3$).

4-2   Compute from Eq. (4-1) for examinees at $\theta = 0$ the frequency distribution $\phi(x|\theta)$ of the number-right score on a test composed of $n = 3$ equivalent items, given that $P_i(0) = .6$ for each item. Compute the mean score from the $\phi(x|\theta)$, also from (4-2). Compute the standard deviation (4-3) of number-right scores. Compute the mean of the proportion-correct score $z \equiv x/n$.

4-3   Compute from (4-1) the frequency distribution of number-right score x on test 1 when $\theta = 0$, given that $P_1(0) = .7848$, $P_2(0) = .6$, $P_3(0) = .4152$. Compute $\mu_{x|\theta}$, $\mu_{z|\theta}$, and $\sigma_{x|\theta}$. Compare with the results of Exercise 4-2.

4-4   Note that $\sigma_{x|\theta}$ is the standard error of measurement, (4-8). Check the value found in Exercise 4-3, using Eq. (4-4).

4-5   Compute from Table 4.3.1 the standard deviation of the conditional distribution $\phi(x|\theta)$ of number-right scores when $\theta = -3, 0, +2.25$. (Because of rounding errors, the columns do not add to exactly 100; compute the standard deviation of the distribution as tabled.)

4-6   What is the range of number-right true scores ξ on test 1 (see Table 4.17.1)?

4-7   In Table 4.3.1, find very approximately a (equal-tailed) 94% confidence interval for θ when $x = 26$.

4-8   Given that $P_1(0) = .7848$, $P_2(0) = .6$, $P_3(0) = .4152$, as in Exercise 4-3, compute from (4-20) the likelihood when $\theta = 0$ of every possible pattern of responses to this three-item test.

4-9   Given that $u_1 = 0$, $u_2 = 0$, and $u_3 = 1$, compute for $\theta = -3, -2, -1, 0, 1, 2, 3$ and plot the likelihood function (4-24) for a three-item test composed of equivalent items with $a = 1/1.7$, $b = 0$, and $c = 0$ for each item. The necessary values of $P(\theta)$ are given in Table 4.17.2.

4-10   For Exercise 4-9, show that the right side of (4-33) exceeds the left side when $\theta_a = -1$ but that the left side exceeds the right side when $\theta_a = 0$; consequently the maximum likelihood estimator $\hat{\theta}_a$ satisfying (4-33) lies between -1 and 0.

4-11   Find from (4-36) the maximum likelihood estimate $\hat{\theta}$ for the situation in Exercises 4-9 and 4-10.

TABLE 4.17.2
Logistic Item Response Function $P(\theta)$ when $a = 1/1.7$, $b = 0$, $c = 0$

θ	-3	-2	-1	0	1	2	3
$P(\theta)$	.047426	.119203	.268941	.5	.731059	.880797	.952574
PQ	.045177	.104994	.196612	.25	.196612	.104994	.045177
P'	.045177	.104994	.196612	.25	.196612	.104994	.045177

APPENDIX

Proof that Σau Is a Sufficient Statistic for θ

Using a line of proof provided by Birnbaum (1968, Chapter 18), we can see that s is a sufficient statistic for estimating ability. By a familiar general formula relating conditional, marginal, and joint distributions,

$$\text{Prob}(A \text{ and } B) = \text{Prob}(A) \cdot \text{Prob } (B|A). \tag{4-46}$$

If θ is fixed, this becomes

$$\text{Prob}(A \text{ and } B|\theta) = \text{Prob}(A|\theta) \cdot \text{Prob}(B|A, \theta). \tag{4-47}$$

Substitute s_o for A and $\mathbf{u}_o$ for B in (4-47) where the subscript indicates corresponding but otherwise arbitrary values of $s \equiv s(\mathbf{u})$ and $\mathbf{u}$. Rearrange to obtain

$$\text{Prob}(\mathbf{u}_o|s_o, \theta) = \frac{\text{Prob}(s_o \text{ and } \mathbf{u}_o|\theta)}{\text{Prob}(s_o|\theta)}.$$

Now $s \equiv s(\mathbf{u})$ depends entirely on $\mathbf{u}$, so $\text{Prob}(s \text{ and } \mathbf{u}|\theta) \equiv \text{Prob}(\mathbf{u}|\theta)$ and

$$\text{Prob}(\mathbf{u}_o|s_o, \theta) = \frac{\text{Prob}(\mathbf{u}_o|\theta)}{\text{Prob}(s_o|\theta)}.$$

From this and (4-25),

$$\text{Prob}(\mathbf{u}_o|s_o, \theta) = \frac{\text{Prob}(\mathbf{u}_o|\theta)}{\displaystyle\sum_{\mathbf{u}|s_o} \text{Prob}(\mathbf{u}|\theta)},$$

where the summation is over all vectors $\mathbf{u}$ for which $\Sigma_i u_i u_i - s_o$. By (4-24),

$$\text{Prob}(\mathbf{u}_o|s_o, \theta) = \frac{\exp(-D\Sigma_i a_i b_i u_{oi})e^{D\theta s_o}\Pi_i Q_i(\theta)}{\displaystyle\sum_{\mathbf{u}|s_o} \exp(-D\Sigma_i a_i b_i u_i)e^{D\theta s_o}\Pi_i Q_i(\theta)}$$

$$= \frac{\exp(-D\Sigma_i a_i b_i u_{oi})}{\displaystyle\sum_{\mathbf{u}|s_o} \exp(-D\Sigma_i a_i b_i u_i)}.$$

The point of this result is not the formula obtained but the fact that it does not depend on θ. In view of the definition of a sufficient statistic (see Section 4.12), we therefore have the following: *If*

1. *the item response function is logistic,*
2. *there is no guessing ($c_i = 0$ for all i),*
3. *the item parameters are known,*

then the weighted item score

$$s \equiv \Sigma_i^n \, a_i u_i$$

is a sufficient statistic for estimating examinee ability θ.

REFERENCES

Birnbaum, A. Test scores, sufficient statistics, and the information structures of tests. In F. M. Lord & M. R. Novick, *Statistical theories of mental test scores*. Reading, Mass.: Addison-Wesley, 1968.

Foutz, R. V. On the unique consistent solution to the likelihood equations. *Journal of the American Statistical Association*, 1977, *72*, 147–148.

Kendall, M. G., & Stuart, A. *The advanced theory of statistics* (Vol. 1, 3rd ed.). New York: Hafner, 1969.

Lord, F. M., & Novick, M. R. *Statistical theories of mental test scores*. Reading, Mass.: Addison-Wesley, 1968.

Samejima, F. A comment on Birnbaum's three-parameter logistic model in the latent trait theory. *Psychometrika*, 1973, *38*, 221–233.

Wright, B. D. Solving measurement problems with the Rasch model. *Journal of Educational Measurement*, 1977, *14*, 97–116.

5
Information Functions and Optimal Scoring Weights

5.1. THE INFORMATION FUNCTION FOR A TEST SCORE

The information function $I\{\theta, y\}$ *for any score* y *is by definition inversely proportional to the square of the length of the asymptotic confidence interval for estimating ability* θ *from score* y (Birnbaum, 1968, Section 17.7). In this chapter, an asymptotic result means a result that holds when the number n of items (not the number N of people) becomes very large. In classical test theory, it is usual to consider that a test is lengthened by adding items "like those in the test," that is, by adding test forms that are strictly parallel (see Section 1.4) to the original test. This guarantees that an examinee's proportion-correct true score ("zayta") $\zeta \equiv \xi/n$ is not changed by lengthening the test. We shall use *lengthening* in this sense here and throughout this book.

Denote by $z \equiv x/n$ the observed proportion-correct score (proportion of n items answered correctly). The regression of z on ability θ is by Eq. (4-2) and (4-9)

$$\mu_{z|\theta} = \frac{1}{n}\sum_{i=1}^{n} P_i(\theta) = \zeta. \tag{5-1}$$

This regression is not changed by lengthening the test. The variance of z for fixed θ is seen from Eq. (4-3) and (4-4) to be

$$\sigma_{z|\theta}^2 = \frac{1}{n^2}\sum_{i=1}^{n} P_i Q_i = \frac{1}{n}(\overline{PQ} - \sigma_{P|\theta}^2). \tag{5-2}$$

This variance approaches zero as n becomes large.

The distribution of z for fixed θ is generated by Eq. (4-1). As n becomes large, and $\sigma_{z\,|\theta} \to 0$, the conditional distribution of z shrinks toward a single point, its mean.

Now consider Fig. 4.8.1, replacing the number-right scale for x on the vertical axis by $z \equiv x/n$, which ranges from $z = 0$ to $z = 1$. The regression $\mu_{z|\theta}$ of z on θ may be visualized as an ogive-shaped curve lying midway between the two step functions, which approximate the 2½ and the 97½ percentiles of the distributions of z given θ. As n becomes large, this regression does not change, but $\sigma^2_{z\,|\theta}$ shrinks toward zero, so that the step functions crowd in toward the regression curve. At the same time, the number of steps increases so that the step functions increasingly approximate smooth curves. When the conditional distribution of z given θ has become approximately normal, the distance from the regression curve to the 2½ percentile, also to the 97½ percentile, will be about 1.96 standard deviations or $(1.96/n)\sqrt{\Sigma_i^n P_i Q_i}$.

We can visualize the mathematics of the situation by imagining examining Fig. 4.8.1 under a microscope while n becomes large. If, inappropriately, the microscope magnifies n times, the bounds of the confidence region will still appear as step functions. This is true because this view of the figure is equivalent to examining $\mu_{nz\,|\theta} = \mu_{x\,|\theta}$, the mean number-right score for fixed θ. The number of steps will increase directly with n; no regularities will appear. The bounds of the confidence region will appear to move away from the regression line, since $\sigma_{z|\theta}$ in (5-2) decreases as $\sqrt{n}$, while the magnification increases as n.

We shall avoid this by looking at $\sqrt{n}(z - \zeta)$ rather than at z. As n becomes large, the conditional variance of $\sqrt{n}(z - \zeta)$ remains finite:

$$\sigma^2[\sqrt{n}(z - \zeta)|\theta] = \bar{P}\bar{Q} - \sigma^2_p ,$$

and the conditional distribution of $\sqrt{n}(z - \zeta)$ approaches normality. Thus the appropriate microscope magnifies only $\sqrt{n}$ times. With this magnification, the bounds of the confidence region will approach smooth curves that appear to remain at a fixed distance (proportional to $\bar{P}\bar{Q} - \sigma^2_p$) from the regression line as both n and the magnification are increased simultaneously. At sufficient magnification, the portions of curves in any small region will appear to be straight lines, as in Fig. 5.1.1. The bounds of the confidence region and the regression line will appear parallel because $\sigma_{z\,|\theta}$ does not change appreciably over a small range of θ.

The asymptotic confidence interval corresponding to z_0 is $(\underline{\theta}, \bar{\theta})$. The length of the confidence interval, the distance $\overline{AB}$, describes the effectiveness of the test as a measure of ability. In the triangle ABC,

$$\tan \alpha = \frac{\overline{CB}}{\overline{AB}} = \frac{2(1.96\sigma_{z|\theta})}{\overline{AB}}$$

or

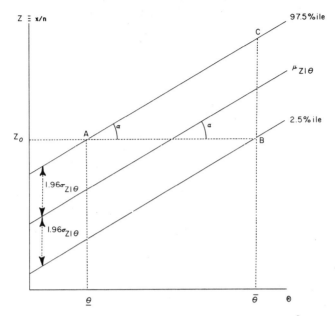

FIG. 5.1.1.   Construction of a 95% asymptotic confidence interval $(\underline{\theta}, \bar{\theta})$ for ability θ.

$$\overline{AB} = \frac{3.92\sigma_{z|\theta}}{\tan \alpha} \; .$$

Since $\tan \alpha$ is the slope of the regression line $\mu_{z|\theta}$, the information function, as defined at the beginning of this chapter, for score z is proportional to

$$\frac{1}{\overline{AB}^2} \equiv \frac{\left(\dfrac{d}{d\theta}\,\mu_{z|\theta}\right)^2}{(3.92)^2 \; \mathrm{Var}\,(z|\theta)} \; .$$

Figure 5.1.1 was derived for estimating ability from the proportion-correct score z. For unidimensional tests, the same line of reasoning applies quite generally to almost all kinds of test scores in practical use. Thus Birnbaum (1968) defines the information function for *any* score y to be

$$I\{\theta,\,y\} \equiv \frac{\left(\dfrac{d}{d\theta}\,\mu_{y|\theta}\right)^2}{\mathrm{Var}\,(y|\theta)} \; . \tag{5-3}$$

The information function for score y *is by definition the square of the ratio of the slope of the regression of* y *on* θ *to the standard error of measurement of* y *for fixed* θ.

Now true score η, corresponding to observed score y, is fixed whenever θ is fixed. (If this were not true, the test items would be systematically measuring some dimension other than θ, contrary to the requirement of unidimensionality.) Thus, as in Eq. (4-7), Var $(y|\theta)$ is identical to the familiar squared standard error of measurement $\sigma^2_{y\,|\eta}$.

The information provided by score y for estimating θ varies at different θ levels. The variation comes from two distinguishable sources:

1. *The smaller the standard error of measurement $\sigma_{y\,|\eta}$, the more information y provides about θ.*

2. *The steeper the slope of the regression $\mu_{y\,|\theta}$ (the more sharply y varies with θ), the more information y provides about θ.*

If two tests have the same true-score scale, their effectiveness as measuring instruments can properly be summarized by their standard errors of measurement at various true-score levels. If, however, the tests measure the same trait but their true-score scales are nonlinearly related, the situation is different. This will ordinarily be the case whenever the tests are not parallel forms (see Chapter 13). In this case, it is not enough to compare standard errors of measurement; we must also take the relation of their true-score scales into account. This is the reason why the score information function depends not only on the standard error of measurement but also on the slope of the regression of score on ability.

Example 5.1

The use of (5-3) can be illustrated by deriving the information function for the proportion correct score z. From (5-1),

$$\frac{d\mu_{z|\theta}}{d\theta} = \left(\frac{1}{n}\right) \Sigma_i P'_i(\theta),$$

where $P'_i(\theta)$ is the derivative of $P_i(\theta)$ with respect to θ. From (5-3) and (5-2) we can now write the information function for z:

$$I\{\theta,\ z\} = \frac{\left[\displaystyle\sum_{i=1}^{n} P'_i(\theta)\right]^2}{\displaystyle\sum_{i=1}^{n} P_i(\theta)Q_i(\theta)}.$$

This result is the same as the information function for number-right score, which is derived from a more general result in the sequel and presented as Eq. (5-13).

5.2. ALTERNATIVE DERIVATION OF THE SCORE INFORMATION FUNCTION

A nonasymptotic derivation of (5-3) was given by Lord (1952, Eq. 57) before the term *score information function* was coined and also in a different context, by

Mandel and Stiehler (1954). Suppose that we are using test score y in an effort to discriminate individuals at θ' from individuals at θ''. Figure 5.2.1 illustrates the two frequency distributions $\phi(y|\theta)$ at θ' and θ'' and shows the mean $\mu_{y|\theta}$ of each distribution.

A natural statistic to use to measure the effectiveness of y for this purpose is the ratio

$$\frac{\mu_{y|\theta''} - \mu_{y|\theta'}}{\sigma^*_{y|\theta}} ,$$

where the denominator is some sort of average of $\sigma_{y|\theta'}$ and $\sigma_{y|\theta''}$. The displayed ratio is proportional to the difference between means divided by its standard error, sometimes called a *critical ratio*.

If θ' and θ'' are close together, $\mu_{y|\theta}$ will be an approximately linear function of θ in the interval (θ', θ''). Thus the numerator of our ratio will be proportional to the distance $\theta'' - \theta'$. The coefficient of proportionality is the slope of the regression, given by the derivative $d\mu_{y|\theta}/d\theta$. Over short distances, it will make no difference whether this slope is taken at θ'' or at θ'. Also, $\sigma_{y|\theta''}$ will be close to $\sigma_{y|\theta}$, so their average will differ little from $\sigma_{y|\theta'}$. Thus our ratio can be written

$$\frac{(\theta'' - \theta')(d\mu_{y|\theta}/d\theta)_{\theta=\theta'}}{\sigma_{y|\theta'}} .$$

The information function (5-3) when $\theta = \theta'$ is directly proportional to the square of the ratio just derived. The coefficient of proportionality is $(\theta'' - \theta')^2$, a quantity of no relevance for assessing the discriminating power of test score y at ability level $\theta = \theta'$.

If asymptotic values of $\mu_{y|\theta}$ and Var $(y|\theta)$ are used in (5-3), we find an asymptotic information function explicable in terms of the length of the asymptotic confidence interval. If exact values of $\mu_{y|\theta}$ and Var $(y|\theta)$ are used, the

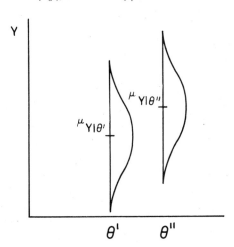

FIG. 5.2.1.   Using score y to discriminate two ability levels.

resulting information function may be justified by the nonasymptotic derivation of the present section. The language used need not always distinguish asymptotic and nonasymptotic information functions, provided no serious confusion arises.

5.3.   THE TEST INFORMATION FUNCTION

The maximum likelihood estimator $\hat{\theta}$ is a kind of test score. Thus, we can use (5-3) to find the information function of the maximum likelihood estimator. To do this, we need (asymptotic) formulas for the regression $\mu_{\hat{\theta}|\theta}$ and for the variance $\sigma^2_{\hat{\theta}|\theta}$.

There is a general theorem, under regularity conditions, satisfied here whenever the item parameters are known from previous testing: A maximum likelihood estimator $\hat{\theta}$ of a parameter θ is asymptotically normally distributed with mean θ_0 (the unknown true parameter value) and variance

$$\mathrm{Var}(\hat{\theta}|\theta_0) = \frac{1}{\mathscr{E}\left[\left(\dfrac{d \ln L}{d\theta}\right)^2_{\theta_0}\right]}, \tag{5-4}$$

where L is the likelihood function.

When the item parameters are known, we have from Eq. (5-4) and (4-30) that

$$\frac{1}{\mathrm{Var}\ (\hat{\theta}|\theta_0)} = \mathscr{E}\left\{\left[\sum_{i=1}^{n} (u_i - P_i)P_i'/P_iQ_i\right]^2 \Big|\theta_0\right\}$$

$$= \mathscr{E}\left\{\left[\sum_{i=1}^{n} (u_i - P_i)P_i'/P_iQ_i\right]\right.$$

$$\left. \cdot \left[\sum_{j=1}^{n} (u_j - P_j)P_j'/P_jQ_j\right]\Big|\theta_0\right\}$$

$$= \sum_{i=1}^{n}\sum_{j=1}^{n} \frac{P_{io}'P_{jo}'}{P_{io}P_{jo}\,Q_{io}Q_{jo}}\,\mathscr{E}[(u_i - P_i)(u_j - P_j)|\theta_0].$$

Since $\mathscr{E}(u_i|\theta_0) = P_{i0}$, the expectation under the summation sign is a covariance. Because of local independence, u_i is distributed independently of u_j for fixed θ. Consequently the covariance is zero except when $i = j$, in which case it is a variance. Thus

$$\frac{1}{\mathrm{Var}\ (\hat{\theta}|\theta_0)} = \sum_{i=1}^{n} \frac{P_i'^2}{P_i^2 Q_i^2}\,\mathrm{Var}\ (u_{io}|\theta_0) = \sum_{i=1}^{n} \frac{P_{io}'^2}{P_{io}^2 Q_{io}^2}\,P_{io}Q_{io}.$$

Dropping the subscript o, the formula for the asymptotic sampling variance of the maximum likelihood estimator is thus

$$\text{Var } (\hat{\theta}|\theta) = \frac{1}{\displaystyle\sum_{i=1}^{n} \frac{P_i'^2}{P_i Q_i}}. \tag{5-5}$$

Now, as already stated, $\hat{\theta}$ is a consistent estimator; so asymptotically $\mu_{\hat{\theta}|\theta} \rightarrow \theta$. Thus asymptotically the numerator of the information function (5-3) for score $\hat{\theta}$ is $(d\mu_{\hat{\theta}|\theta}/d\theta)^2 = 1$. Thus the (asymptotic) information function (5-3) of the maximum likelihood estimator of ability is the reciprocal of the asymptotic variance (5-5):

$$I\{\theta\} \equiv I\{\theta,\hat{\theta}\} = \sum_{i=1}^{n} \frac{P_i'^2}{P_i Q_i} . \tag{5-6}$$

Let us note an obvious theorem in passing:

Theorem 5.3.1. *The information function for an unbiased (consistent) estimator of ability is the reciprocal of the (asymptotic) sampling variance of the estimator.*

Equation (5-6) is of such importance that it is given a special name and symbol. It is called the *test information function* and is denoted simply by $I\{\theta\}$. Information functions for ordinary published tests are usually roughly bell-shaped. Such a test information function is shown in Fig. 5.5.1.

The importance of the test information function comes partly from the fact that it provides an (attainable) upper limit to the information that can be obtained from the test, no matter what method of scoring is used:

Theorem 5.3.2. *The test information function $I\{\theta\}$ given by (5-6) is an upper bound to the information that can be obtained by any method of scoring the test.*

Proof: Suppose t is an unbiased estimator of some function θ. Denote this function of θ by $\tau(\theta)$. According to the Cramér–Rao inequality (Kendall & Stuart, 1973, Section 17.23),

$$\text{Var } (t|\theta) \geq \frac{[\tau'(\theta)]^2}{\mathscr{E}\left[\left(\dfrac{d \ln L}{d\theta}\right)^2\right]} , \tag{5-7}$$

where $\tau'(\theta)$ is the derivative of $\tau(\theta)$. Since $\mathscr{E}(t|\theta) \equiv \tau(\theta)$, we have from (5-3), (5-4), and (5-7) asymptotically

$$I\{\theta, t\} = \frac{[\tau'(\theta)]^2}{\text{Var } (t|\theta)} \leq \mathscr{E}\left[\left(\frac{d \ln L}{d\theta}\right)^2\right] = \frac{1}{\text{Var } (\hat{\theta}|\theta)} = I\{\theta\}. \tag{5-8}$$

This result holds under rather general regularity conditions on the item response function $P_i(\theta)$.

5.4.   THE ITEM INFORMATION FUNCTION

A very important feature of (5-6) is that *the test information consists entirely of independent and additive contributions from the items. The contribution of an item does not depend on what other items are included in the test.* The contribution of a single item is $P_i'^2/P_iQ_i$. This contribution is called *the item information function:*

$$I\{\theta, u_i\} = \frac{P_i'^2}{P_iQ_i} \, . \tag{5-9}$$

Item information functions for five familiar items are shown in Figure 2.5.1 along with the $I\{\theta\}$ for the five-item test.

In classical test theory, by contrast, the validity coefficient ρ_{xC} for number-right test score (correlation between score and criterion C) is given by Eq. (1-25) in terms of item intercorrelations ρ_{ij} and item-criterion correlations ρ_{iC}. There is no way to identify the contribution of a single item to test validity; the contribution of the item depends in an intricate way on the choice of items included in the test. The same may be said of an item's contribution to coefficient alpha, as shown by Eq. (1-24), and to other test reliability coefficients.

For emphasis and clarity, let us elaborate here Birnbaum's (1968) suggested procedure for test construction, previewed in Chapter 2. The procedure operates on a pool of items that have been calibrated by pretesting, so that we have the item information curve for each item.[1]

1. Decide on the shape desired for the test information function. Remember that this information function is inversely proportional to the squared length of the asymptotic confidence interval for estimating ability from test score. What accuracy of ability estimation is required of the test at each ability level? The desired curve is the *target information curve.*

2. Select items with item information curves that will fill the hard-to-fill areas under the target information curve.

3. Cumulatively add up the item information curves, obtaining at all times the information curve for the part-test composed of items already selected.

4. Continue (back-tracking if necessary) until the area under target information curve is filled up to a satisfactory approximation.

The item information curve for the three-parameter logistic model in Eq. (2-1) can be written down from (5-9) in many forms, such as

---

[1]These rules are reproduced with special permission from F. M. Lord, Practical applications of item characteristic curve theory. *Journal of Educational Measurement,* Summer 1977, *14,* No. 2, 117–138. Copyright 1977, National Council on Measurement in Education, Inc., East Lansing, Mich.

$$I\{\theta, \ u_i\} = D^2 a_i^2 \frac{Q_i}{P_i} \left(\frac{P_i - c_i}{1 - c_i}\right)^2,$$

$$I\{\theta, \ u_i\} = \frac{D^2 a_i^2 (1 - c_i)}{(c_i + e^{DL_i})(1 + e^{-DL_i})^2},$$

where $L_i \equiv a_i(\theta - b_i)$.

5.5. INFORMATION FUNCTION FOR A WEIGHTED SUM OF ITEM SCORES

Suppose the test score is the weighted composite $y \equiv \Sigma_i w_i u_i$, where the w_i are any set of weights. Since each u_i is a (locally) independent binomial variable, we have

$$\mu_{\Sigma w u | \theta} = \Sigma_i w_i P_i, \tag{5-10}$$

$$\sigma^2_{\Sigma w u | \theta} = \Sigma_i w_i^2 P_i Q_i. \tag{5-11}$$

By (5-3), the information function for the weighted composite is

$$I\{\theta, \ \Sigma_i w_i u_i\} = \frac{(\Sigma_i w_i P_i')^2}{\Sigma_i w_i^2 P_i Q_i}. \tag{5-12}$$

If the weights are all 1, y is the usual number-right score x. Thus the information function for number-right score x is

$$I\{\theta, \ x\} = \frac{(\Sigma_i P_i')^2}{\Sigma_i P_i Q_i}. \tag{5-13}$$

Note that (5-12) and (5-13) cannot be expressed as simple sums of independent additive contributions from individual items, as in (5-6).

Figure 5.5.1 shows the estimated information function $I\{\theta, \ x\}$ for the number-right score on a high school-level verbal test (SCAT II, Form 2A) composed of 50 four-choice word-relations items. For comparison, the test information function $I\{\theta\}$ is shown and also two other information functions to be discussed later. The test characteristic curve is given also.

We have seen that the squared slope of the test characteristic curve is the numerator of the information function for number-right score. The inflection point of the test characteristic curve in the figure is to the left of the maximum information, showing the effect of the denominator (squared standard error of measurement).

The relation shown between the number-right curve and the upper bound $I\{\theta\}$ is fairly typical of plots seen by the writer. This relation is of interest since it limits the extent to which we can hope to improve the accuracy of measurement by improving the method of scoring the test.

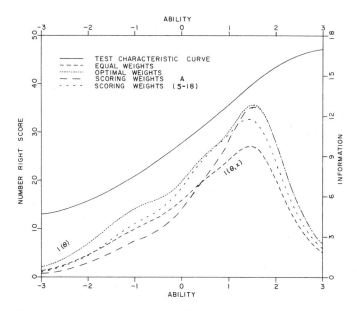

FIG. 5.5.1.   Test characteristic curve (solid line) and various information curves (dashed lines) for SCAT II 2A Verbal test. Item-scoring weights for the information curves are specified in the legend.

5.6.   OPTIMAL SCORING WEIGHTS

Suppose we allow the item-scoring weight w_i to be a function of θ. In particular, consider using as item-scoring weight the function $w_i(\theta) \equiv P_i'/P_iQ_i$. Substituting this weight into (5-12) gives the result

$$I\left\{ \theta, \Sigma_i \frac{P_i'u_i}{P_iQ_i} \right\} = \frac{(\Sigma_i P_i'^2/P_iQ_i)^2}{\Sigma_i P_iQ_i(P_i'/P_iQ_i)^2} = \Sigma_i \frac{P_i'^2}{P_iQ_i} . \qquad (5\text{-}14)$$

We have the surprising result that the information function for the weighted composite $\Sigma_i (P_i'/P_iQ_i)u_i$ is the same as the test information function, which is the maximum information attainable by any scoring method. Thus

$$w_i(\theta) \equiv \frac{P_i'(\theta)}{P_i(\theta)Q_i(\theta)} \qquad (5\text{-}15)$$

is the optimal scoring weight for item i.

   In practice, we do not know θ for any individual; hence we cannot know $w_i(\theta)$. We can approximate θ and thus $w_i(\theta)$, however.

   If the item response function is three-parameter logistic [Eq. (2-1)], it is easily verified that

$$P_i' = \frac{Da_i Q_i (P_i - c_i)}{1 - c_i} \tag{5-16}$$

From (5-15) and (5-16), the optimal item-scoring weights are

$$w_i(\theta) = \frac{Da_i (P_i - c_i)}{P_i (1 - c_i)} = \frac{Da_i}{1 + c_i e^{-DL_i}} \tag{5-17}$$

where $L_i \equiv a_i(\theta - b_i)$. Note that when $c_i = 0$, the optimal weight is $1.7a_i$ or since we may divide all the weights by 1.7, simply a_i.

At high ability levels $P_{ia}(\theta) \to 1$, consequently $w_i(\theta) \to Da_i$. Thus, we see that at high ability levels optimal scoring weights under the logistic model are proportional to item discriminating power a_i.

The optimal weights $w_i(\theta)$ under the logistic model are shown in Fig. 2.5.2 for five familiar items. Note the following facts about optimal item weights for the logistic model, visible from the curves in the figure.[2]

1. As ability increases, the curve representing optimal item weight as a function of ability sooner or later becomes virtually horizontal. Thus, for sufficiently high ability levels, the optimal item weights are virtually independent of ability level. The optimum weight at this upper asymptote is proportional to the item parameter a_i. This occurs because there is no guessing at high ability levels.

2. As ability decreases from a very high level, the optimal weight curves for the difficult items begin to decline. The reason is that at lower ability levels random guessing destroys the value of these items.

3. As ability decreases further, the optimal weights for these difficult items become virtually zero. Such items will not be wanted if the test is used only to discriminate among examinees at low ability levels.

In summary, under the logistic model, the optimal weight to be assigned to an item for discriminating at high ability levels depends on the general discriminating power of the item. The optimal weight to be used for discriminating at lower ability levels depends not only on the general discriminating power of the item but also very much on the amount of random guessing occurring on the item at these ability levels. Thus, all moderately discriminating items are of use for discriminating at high ability levels, whereas only the easy items are of appreciable use for discriminating at low ability levels.

Item-scoring weights that are optimal for a particular examinee can never be determined exactly, since we do not know the examinee's ability θ exactly.[3] A

---

[2]The remainder of this paragraph is taken with permission from F. M. Lord, An analysis of the Verbal Scholastic Aptitude Test using Birnbaum's three-parameter logistic model. *Educational and Psychological Measurement*, 1968, *28*, 989–1020.

[3]The remainder of this section is adapted and reprinted with special permission from F. M. Lord, Practical applications of item characteristic curve theory. *Journal of Educational Measurement*, Summer 1977, *14*, No. 2, 117–138. Copyright 1977, National Council on Measurement in Education, Inc., East Lansing, Mich.

crude procedure for obtaining item-scoring weights is to substitute the conventional item difficulty p_i (proportion of correct answers in the total group of examinees) for $P_i(\theta)$ in (5-17). This crude procedure would use the resulting weight for scoring item i on all answer sheets regardless of examinee ability level. Since $D = 1.7$ is a constant, we can drop it and use the weight

$$w_i = \frac{a_i}{1 - c_i} \frac{p_i - c_i}{p_i}. \qquad (5\text{-}18)$$

This same item-scoring weight, except for the a_i, was recommended on other grounds by Chernoff (see Lord & Novick, 1968, p. 310).

The effect of using the crude scoring weights is illustrated for the SCAT II-2A verbal test in Fig. 5.5.1. For this test, the crude weights are almost everywhere better than no weights at all.

A better but more complicated procedure for determining scoring weights for a conventional test might be somewhat as follows.

1. Score the test in the usual way.
2. Divide the examinees into three or more subgroups according to the usual scores.
3. Separately for each subgroup, use (5-18) to find a roughly optimal scoring weight for each item.
4. Rescore all answer sheets using the item-scoring weights from step 3 (different weights in each subgroup).
5. Equate the three score scales obtained from the three sets of scoring weights. Conventional equating methods (Angoff, 1971) may be used for this.
6. Use the equating to place everyone on the same score scale.

The foregoing procedure should improve measurement effectiveness, since each answer sheet is scored with weights roughly appropriate for the examinee's ability level. Too much should not be expected, however. If only a third of the items in a test are useful for measuring examinees at a certain ability level, no amount of statistical manipulation will make the test a really good one for such examinees.

5.7. OPTIMAL SCORING WEIGHTS NOT DEPENDENT ON θ

Is there an item response function $P(\theta)$ such that the optimal weights $w(\theta)$ actually do not depend on θ? If so, then

$$w(\theta) \equiv \frac{P'(\theta)}{P(\theta)Q(\theta)} = A,$$

where A is some constant. This leads to the differential equation

$$\frac{dP}{P(1 - P)} = A \, d\theta.$$

Integrating, we have uniquely

$$-\ln \frac{1 - P}{P} = A\theta + B,$$

where B is a constant of integration. Solving for P, we find

$$P \equiv P(\theta) = \frac{1}{1 + e^{-A\theta - B}} = \frac{1}{1 + e^{-Da(\theta - b)}},$$

where $A \equiv Da$ and $B \equiv -Dab$.

In summary, *when the item response function is a two-parameter logistic function, the optimal scoring weight* $w_i(\theta)$ *does not depend on* θ. *The optimal weight is* $w_i = a_i$, *the item discrimination index. The optimally weighted composite of item scores is* s $\equiv \Sigma_i a_i u_i$, *the sufficient statistic of Section 4.12. The two-parameter logistic function, which does not permit guessing, is the most general item response function for which the optimal item scoring weights do not depend on* θ.

Figure 5.5.1 shows the information curve obtained when the weights $w_i = a_i$ are used for the SCAT II-2A verbal test. The score $\Sigma a_i u_i$ is optimally efficient at high ability levels but is less efficient than number-right score at low ability levels. This is the result to be expected on a multiple-choice test, since $w_i = a_i$ is optimal only when there is no guessing.

5.8. MAXIMUM LIKELIHOOD ESTIMATE OF ABILITY

From Eq. (4-31) and (5-15), if the item parameters are known from pretesting, the maximum likelihood estimate of ability is obtained by solving, for $\hat{\theta}$, the equation

$$\sum_{i=1}^{n} \frac{P_i'(\hat{\theta})}{Q_i(\hat{\theta})} = \sum_{i=1}^{n} w_i(\hat{\theta}) u_i. \qquad (5\text{-}19)$$

Thus we see that the maximum likelihood estimator $\hat{\theta}$ is itself a function of the optimally weighted composite of item scores $\Sigma_i w_i(\theta) u_i$ with $\hat{\theta}$ substituted for θ. This is true regardless of the form of the item response function $P_i(\theta)$.

5.9. EXERCISES

5-1 For test 1, compute from Table 4.17.1 the mean number-right score x at $\theta = -3, -2, -1, 0, 1, 2, 3$ using Eq. (4-2). Plot the regression of x on θ. This is the test characteristic function.

5-2   As in Exercise 5-1, compute the standard deviation [Eq. (4-3)] of number-right score for integer values of θ. Plot on the same graph as the regression $\mu_{x\,|\theta}$.

5-3   From Table 4.17.1, plot on a single graph the item information function for each of the three items in test 1.

5-4   Compute from Table 4.17.1 the test information function (5-6) of test 1. Plot on the same graph as $\mu_{x\,|\theta}$ and $\sigma_{x\,|\theta}$. Also plot on the same graph as the item information functions.

5-5 to 5-8   Using Table 4.17.2, repeat Exercises 5-1 to 5-4 for a three-item test with $a = 1/1.7$, $b = 0$, $c = 0$ for all items. Compare with the results of test 1.

5-9   Compute from (5-5) the variance of $\hat{\theta}$ at integral values of θ for test 1.

5-10   From Table 4.17.1, compute the score information function (5-13) for the number-right score x. Plot this and the test information function (5-6) from Exercise 5-4 on the same graph.

5-11   For each item in test 1, plot the optimal scoring weights (5-15) as a function of θ.

5-12   For test 1, compute the optimally weighted composite score $\Sigma_i w_i(\theta)u_i$ for examinees at ability level $\theta = 0$ responding $u_1 = 1$, $u_2 = 0$, $u_3 = 0$. Repeat for $u_1 = 0$, $u_2 = 1$, $u_3 = 0$; also repeat for $u_1 = 0$, $u_2 = 0$, $u_3 = 1$. Can you explain why the scores for the three patterns should be in the rank order you have found?

5-13   Compute the optimal item-scoring weight (5-15) at each θ level for the items in Table 4.17.2. Explain.

APPENDIX

Information Functions for Transformed Scores

What is the effect on the score information function (5-3) of transforming the score scale? Let $Y \equiv Y(y)$ denote a monotonic transformation of the score y, and let $\eta \equiv \mathcal{E}(y|\theta)$ be the true score corresponding to y.

For present purposes, score y will be assumed to have the property that $\eta \equiv \mathcal{E}(y|\theta)$ does not depend on test length n. For most conventional scoring methods, this is usually a trivial requirement. For example, if x is the number of right answers, $\xi \equiv \mathcal{E}x = \Sigma^n P_i(\theta)$ is not independent of test length. Instead of using x, however, we simply use z, the proportion of right answers. The proportion-correct true score $\zeta \equiv \mathcal{E}z = [\Sigma^n P_i(\theta)]/n$ does not vary if n is increased by adding test forms parallel to the original test (see Section 5.1).

Now y is an unbiased estimate of η, and $\mathcal{E}(y - \eta)^2$ is the sampling variance of the estimator y. It is usual to find that such sampling variances are *of order* $1/n$; this means that for sufficiently large n the sampling variance can be written as

$(1/n)$ times a constant term (a term that does not vary with n) and also that $\mathscr{E}(y - \eta)^3$, the third sampling moment of y, is of order $n^{-3/2}$ (is a constant divided by $n^{3/2}$). We assume this in all that follows.

Expanding $Y(y)$ by Taylor's formula, we have

$$Y(y) - Y(\eta) = Y'(\eta)(y - \eta) + \tfrac{1}{2}Y''(\eta)(y - \eta)^2 + \delta Y'''(\eta)(y - \eta)^3, \tag{5-20}$$

where $0 < \delta < 1$ and $Y'(\eta)$, $Y''(\eta)$, $Y'''(\eta)$ are derivatives of $Y(\eta)$ with respect to η. Rearranging (5-20) and taking expectations, we find that the expectation of Y is

$$\mathscr{E}(Y|\theta) = Y(\eta) + \text{terms of order } \frac{1}{n}. \tag{5-21}$$

Squaring (5-20) and taking expectations, we find a formula for the sampling variance of Y:

$$\text{Var}(Y|\theta) \equiv \mathscr{E}\{[Y(y) - Y(\eta)]^2|\theta\} = [Y'(\eta)]^2 \text{ Var }(y|\theta) + \text{terms of order } n^{-3/2}. \tag{5-22}$$

From (5-21),

$$\frac{d}{d\theta}\mathscr{E}(Y|\theta) = Y'(\eta)\frac{d\eta}{d\theta} + \text{terms of order} \frac{1}{n}.$$

From this and (5-22) and (5-3), we obtain the information function for the transformed score $Y(y)$:

$$I\{\theta, Y(y)\} = \frac{(d\eta/d\theta)^2}{\text{Var}(y|\theta)} + \text{neglected terms.}$$

Since Var $(y|\theta)$ is a constant times $1/n$ and the numerator is independent of n, the fraction on the right is of order n (a constant times n). The largest neglected terms are easily seen to be constant with respect to n. For large n, the largest neglected terms are therefore small compared to term retained. The term retained is seen to be the information function of the untransformed score y. Asymptotically,

$$I\{\theta, Y(y)\} = I\{\theta, y\}. \tag{5-23}$$

In summary, if (1) y is a score chosen so that the corresponding true score does not vary with n, (2) $Y(y)$ is a monotonic transformation of y not involving n, (3) Var $(y|\theta)$ is of order $1/n$ and $\mathscr{E}[(y - \eta)^3|\theta]$ is of order $n^{-3/2}$, then *the score transformation* $Y(y)$ *does not change the asymptotic score information function*. The first restriction in this summary is readily removed for most sensible methods of scoring. The number-right true score ξ, for example, varies with n, whereas the proportion-correct true score $\zeta \equiv \xi/n$ does not; yet both ξ and ζ have the same information: $I\{\theta, \xi\} = I\{\theta, \zeta\}$.

The invariance (5-23) of $I\{\theta, Y(y)\}$ is important; however, it is not surprising in view of the definition of information. A monotonic transformation of score y should not change the confidence interval for θ.

REFERENCES

Angoff, W. H. Scales, norms, and equivalent scores. In R. L. Thorndike (Ed.), *Educational measurement* (2nd ed.). Washington, D.C.: American Council on Education, 1971.

Birnbaum, A. Some latent trait models. In F. M. Lord & M. R. Novick, *Statistical theories of mental test scores*. Reading, Mass.: Addison-Wesley, 1968.

Kendall, M. G., & Stuart, A. *The advanced theory of statistics* (Vol. 2, 3rd ed.). New York: Hafner, 1973.

Lord, F. M. A theory of test scores. *Psychometric Monograph No. 7*. Psychometric Society, 1952.

Lord, F. M., & Novick, M. R. *Statistical theories of mental test scores*. Reading, Mass.: Addison-Wesley, 1968.

Mandel, J., & Stiehler, R. D. Sensitivity—A criterion for the comparison of methods of test. *Journal of Research of the National Bureau of Standards*, 1954, *53*, 155–159.

II APPLICATIONS OF ITEM RESPONSE THEORY

6

The Relative Efficiency of Two Tests

6.1. RELATIVE EFFICIENCY

The *relative efficiency* of test score y with respect to test score x is the ratio of their information functions:

$$\text{RE } \{y, x\} \equiv \frac{I\{\theta, y\}}{I\{\theta, x\}} . \tag{6-1}$$

Scores x and y may be scores on two different tests of the same ability θ, or x and y may result from scoring the same test in two different ways. Relative efficiency is defined only when the θ in $I\{\theta, y\}$ is the same θ as in $I\{\theta, x\}$. Although the notation does not make it explicit, it should be clear that the relative efficiency of two test scores varies according to ability level.

The dashed curve in Fig. 6.7.1 shows estimated relative efficiency of a "regular" test compared to a "peaked" test. Both are 45-item verbal tests composed of five-choice items. The regular test (y) consists of the even-numbered items in a 90-item College Board SAT. The peaked test (x) consists of 45 items from the same test with difficulty parameters nearest the average b_i (the average over all 90 items).

There is considerable overlap in items between the two 45-item tests, but this does not impair the comparison. As the figure shows, from the third percentile up through the thirtieth, the regular test with its wide spread of item difficulty is less than half as efficient as the peaked test. In other words, the regular test would have to be lengthened to more than 90 items in order to be as efficient as the 45-item peaked test within this range.

6.2.   TRANSFORMATIONS OF THE ABILITY SCALE

The ability scale θ is the scale on which all item response functions have the particular mathematical form $P_i(\theta)$. This is a specified form chosen by the psychometrician, such as Eq. (2-1) or (2-2). Except for the theoretical case where all items are equivalent, there is no transformation of the ability scale that will convert a set of normal ogive response functions to logistic, or vice versa.

Once we have found the scale θ on which all item response curves are (say) logistic, it is often thought that this scale has unique virtues. This conclusion is incorrect, however, as the following illustration shows.

Consider the transformations

$$\theta^* \equiv \theta^*(\theta) \equiv Ke^{k\theta}, \qquad b_i^* \equiv Ke^{kb_i}, \qquad a_i^* \equiv \frac{Da_i}{k}, \qquad (6\text{-}2)$$

where K and k are any positive constants. Under the logistic model

$$P_i \equiv c_i + \frac{1 - c_i}{1 + e^{-Da_i\theta}e^{Da_ib_i}}$$

$$\equiv c_i + \frac{1 - c_i}{1 + (b_i^*/\theta^*)^{a_i^*}} \qquad (6\text{-}3)$$

Also

$$Q_i = (1 - c_i)\frac{(b_i^*/\theta^*)^{a_i^*}}{1 + (b_i^*/\theta^*)^{a_i^*}} \ .$$

Thus

$$\frac{P_i - c_i}{Q_i} = \left(\frac{\theta^*}{b_i^*}\right)^{a_i^*}. \qquad (6\text{-}4)$$

This last equation relates probability of success on an item to the ratio of examinee ability θ^* to item difficulty b_i^*. The relation is so simple and direct as to suggest that the θ^* scale may be better for measuring ability than is the θ scale.

By assumption, all items have logistic response curves on the θ scale; however, it is equally true that all items have response curves given by (6-3) on the θ^* scale. Thus there is no obvious reason to prefer θ to θ^*.

6.3. EFFECT OF ABILITY TRANSFORMATION ON THE INFORMATION FUNCTION

If there is no unique virtue in the θ scale for ability, we should consider how a monotonic transformation of this scale affects our theoretical machinery. There is nothing about our definition or derivation of the information function [Eq. (5-3)] that requires us to use the θ scale rather than the θ^* scale. If θ^* is any monotonic transformation of θ, the information function for making inferences about θ^* from y is defined by Eq. (5-3) to be

$$I\{\theta^*, y\} \equiv \frac{(d\mu_{y|\theta*}/d\theta^*)^2}{\text{Var }(y|\theta^*)} \ . \tag{6-5}$$

Before proceeding, we need to clarify a notational paradox. Note that, for every θ_o,

$$\text{Var }(y|\theta=\theta_o) \equiv \text{Var }(y|\theta^*=\theta^*(\theta_o)).$$

The left-hand side is usually abbreviated as Var $(y|\theta_o)$, the right-hand side as Var $(y|\theta^*_o)$. The abbreviated equation Var $(y|\theta_o) = $ Var $(y|\theta^*_o)$ appears self-contradictory. This is the fault of the abbreviated notation and does not impair the validity of the unabbreviated result. Similarly (in abbreviated notation),

$$\mu_{y|\theta_o} \equiv \mu_{y|\theta*(\theta_o)} \equiv \mu_{y|\theta^*_o}.$$

By the chain rule for differentiation, $d/d\theta^* \equiv (d\theta/d\theta^*)(d/d\theta)$. Substituting the last three equations into (6-5) and dropping the subscript o, we have the important result

$$\begin{aligned} I\{\theta^*, y\} &= \frac{(d\mu_{y|\theta*}/d\theta)^2}{\text{Var }(y|\theta^*)} \left(\frac{d\theta}{d\theta^*}\right)^2 \\ &= \frac{(d\mu_{y|\theta}/d\theta)^2}{\text{Var }(y|\theta)} \left(\frac{d\theta}{d\theta^*}\right)^2 \\ &= \frac{I\{\theta, y\}}{\left(\frac{d\theta^*}{d\theta}\right)^2} \ . \end{aligned} \tag{6-6}$$

This result states: *When we transform θ monotonically to $\theta^*(\theta)$, the information function is divided by the square of the derivative of the transformation.*

This is as it should be. The confidence interval $(\underline{\theta}, \bar{\theta})$ in Fig. 5.1.1 transforms into the confidence interval $(\underline{\theta}^*, \bar{\theta}^*)$. Asymptotically, the length of the latter interval will be $d\theta^*/d\theta$ times the length of the former interval. Thus the information function $I\{\theta^*, x\}$ will equal $I\{\theta, x\}$ divided by $(d\theta^*/d\theta)^2$.

When $d\theta^*/d\theta$ varies along the ability scale, the shape of the information

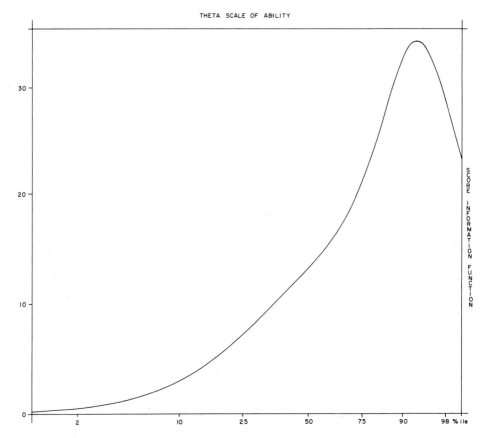

FIG. 6.3.1.   Score information function for measuring ability θ, SAT Mathematics test. Taken with permission from F. M. Lord, The 'ability' scale in item characteristic curve theory. *Psychometrika*, 1975, *40*, 205–217.

function may be drastically altered by the transformation. Worse yet, the ability level at which a test provides maximum information may be totally different when ability is measured by θ^* rather than by θ. Or $I\{\theta, x\}$ may have one maximum, whereas $I\{\theta^*, x\}$ has two separate maxima. Actually, *any single-valued continuous information function on θ may be transformed to any other such information function by a suitably chosen monotonic transformation $\theta^*(\theta)$.*

Figure 6.3.1 shows the information function $I\{\theta, x\}$ for number-right score on a 60-item College Board mathematics aptitude test. The baseline, representing ability, is marked off in terms of estimated percentile rank on ability for the group tested rather than in terms of θ values. Figure 6.3.2 shows a rather mild transformation $\theta^*(\theta) \equiv \omega(\theta)$. Figure 6.3.3 shows the resulting information func-

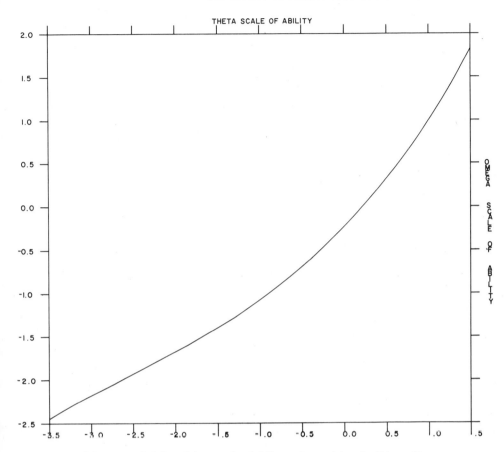

FIG. 6.3.2.   Relation of the ω scale of ability to the usual θ scale. Taken with permission from F. M. Lord, The 'ability' scale in item characteristic curve theory. *Psychometrika,* 1975, *40,* 205–217.

tion $I\{\omega, x\}$ on the ω scale for the same number-right score. The information functions for the same score x on the two different ability scales bear little resemblance to each other.

Clearly information is not a pure number; the units in terms of which information is measured depend on the units used to measure ability. This must be true, since information is defined by the length of a confidence interval, and this length is expressed in terms of the units used to measure ability. If we are uncertain what units to use to quantify ability, then to the same extent we do not know how to quantify information.

We cannot draw any useful conclusions from the shape of a single information function unless we assert that the ability scale we are using is unique except for a

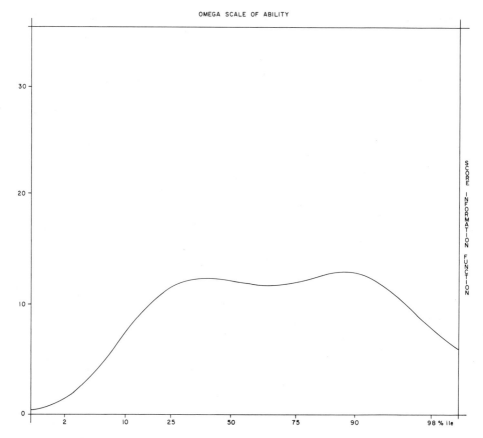

FIG. 6.3.3. Score information function for measuring ability ω, SAT Mathematics test. Taken with permission from F. M. Lord, The 'ability' scale in item characteristic curve theory. *Psychometrika,* 1975, *40,* 205-217.

linear transformation. Most important *we cannot know at what ability level the test or test score discriminates best, unless we have an ability scale that is not subject to challenge.*

Even though a single information curve may not be readily interpretable, comparisons between two or more information curves are not impaired by doubt about the ability scale. This important fact is easily proved in Section 6.4.

6.4. EFFECT OF ABILITY TRANSFORMATION ON RELATIVE EFFICIENCY

Suppose we transform the ability scale monotonically to $\theta^*(\theta)$ and then compute the relative efficiency of two scores, x and y (which may be scores on one test or on two different tests), for measuring $\theta*$. Replacing θ by $\theta*$ in (6-1) and using (6-6), we find

$$\text{RE } \{y, x\} = \frac{I\{\theta*, y\}}{I\{\theta*, x\}} = \frac{I\{\theta, y\}}{I\{\theta, x\}} \frac{(d\theta*/d\theta)^2}{(d\theta*/d\theta)^2} = \frac{I\{\theta, y\}}{I\{\theta, x\}}.$$

Comparing this with (6-1), we see that *relative efficiency is invariant under any monotonic transformation of the ability scale*. It is for this reason that the symbol θ does not appear in the notation RE $\{y, x\}$.

For the reasons outlined in Section 6.3, the practical application of item response theory in this book are not based on inference from an isolated information function. We shall compare information curves, or equivalently we shall rely on a study of relative efficiency. Such comparisons are not affected by the choice of scale for measuring ability.

6.5. INFORMATION FUNCTION OF OBSERVED SCORE ON TRUE SCORE

It was noted in Section 4.2 that number-right true score ξ is a monotonic increasing transformation of ability θ. What is the information function of number-right score x for making inferences about true score ξ?

If we substitute ξ for $\theta*$ and x for y in (6-5), we find

$$I\{\xi, x\} = \frac{(d\mu_{x|\xi}/d\xi)^2}{\sigma^2_{x|\xi}}. \tag{6-7}$$

Now the true score ξ is defined as the expectation of x. It follows that $\mu_{x|\xi} \equiv \xi$. If we substitute this into the numerator of (6-7), the desired information function is found to be

$$I\{\xi, x\} \equiv \frac{1}{\sigma^2_{x|\xi}}. \tag{6-8}$$

When using observed score x *to make inferences about the corresponding true score* ξ, *the appropriate information function* $I\{\xi,$ x$\}$ *is the reciprocal of the squared standard error of measurement of score* x *at* ξ. This result will hold for any score x, not just for number-right score, as long as $\xi \equiv \mu_{x|\xi}$ is a monotonic function of θ.

Figure 6.5.1 shows $I\{\xi,$ x$\}$ for the same test represented in Fig. 6.3.1 and 6.3.3. The reader should compare these three information functions, noting once again that information functions do not give a unique answer to the question: "At what ability level does the test measure best?"

The reader may have been startled to find from Fig. 6.5.1 that $I\{\xi,$ x$\}$ is greatest at high and at low ability levels and least at moderate ability levels. Actually, similar results would be found for most tests. Examinees at very high

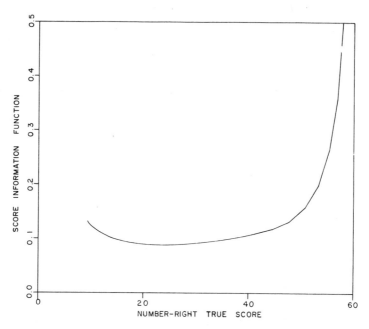

FIG. 6.5.1.   Score information function for measuring the true score ξ on SAT mathematics test.

ability levels are virtually certain to obtain a perfect score on the test. Thus for them the standard error of measurement $\sigma_{x\,|\xi}$ is nearly zero, their true score ξ is very close to n, the length of the confidence interval for estimating ξ from x is nearly zero, and consequently $I\{\xi, x\} \equiv 1/\sigma_{x\,|\xi}^2$ is very large. Clearly true score ξ can be estimated very accurately for such examinees: It is close to n. Their ability θ cannot be estimated accurately; however: We know that their θ is high without knowing how high. This situation is mirrored by the fact that $I\{\xi, x\}$ is very large for such examinees, whereas $I\{\theta, x\}$ is near zero. The reader should understand these conclusions if he is to make proper use of information functions (or of standard errors of measurement).

6.6.   RELATION BETWEEN RELATIVE EFFICIENCY AND TRUE-SCORE DISTRIBUTION

Suppose now that we have another test measuring the same ability θ as test x. Denote the observed score on the new test by y and the corresponding true score by η. As in (6-8), the information function for y on η will be

$$I\{\eta, y\} = \frac{1}{\sigma_{y\,|\eta}^2}. \tag{6-9}$$

For present purposes, it is not necessary that either x or y be a number-right score. Suppose merely that ξ is some monotonic increasing function of ability θ and that η also is. Then η is necessarily a monotonic increasing function of ξ; we write $\eta \equiv \eta(\xi)$. Also ξ is a monotonic increasing function of η. If x and y are number-right scores, $\eta(\xi)$ is found (numerically) by eliminating θ from the test characteristic curves $\xi = \Sigma_i P_i(\theta)$ and $\eta = \Sigma_j P_j(\theta)$. Figure 13.5.1 shows how the value of $\eta(\xi_o)$ may be determined graphically for any given ξ_o from $\xi = \Sigma_i P_i(\theta)$ and $\eta = \Sigma_j P_j(\theta)$.

Now, we can substitute ξ for θ^* and η for θ in (6-6) and then use (6-9) to write the information function of y on ξ:

$$I\{\xi, y\} = \frac{I\{\eta, y\}}{\left(\dfrac{d\xi}{d\eta}\right)^2} = \frac{\left(\dfrac{d\eta}{d\xi}\right)^2}{\sigma^2_{y|\eta}}.$$ (6-10)

The efficiency of y relative to x is the ratio of (6-10) to (6-8), or

$$RE\{y, x\} = \frac{\sigma^2_{x|\xi}}{\sigma^2_{y|\eta}}\left(\frac{d\eta}{d\xi}\right)^2.$$ (6-11)

Similarly,

$$RE\{x, y\} = \frac{\sigma^2_{y|\eta}}{\sigma^2_{x|\xi}}\left(\frac{d\xi}{d\eta}\right)^2.$$ (6-12)

Equations (6-11) and (6-12) are valid regardless of the scale used to measure ability (see Section 6.4). In particular, (6-11) and (6-12) do *not* assume that ability is to be measured on the true-score scale ξ.

Denote by $p(\xi)$ the frequency distribution (density) of true score ξ in some population of examinees. The distribution $q(\eta)$ of $\eta \equiv \eta(\xi)$ in this same population is then found from

$$q(\eta)\, d\eta \equiv p(\xi)\, d\xi.$$ (6-13)

Rearranging, we have

$$\frac{d\eta}{d\xi} \equiv \frac{p(\xi)}{q(\eta)}.$$

Substituting this into (6-11), we find

$$RE\{y, x\} = \frac{\sigma^2_{x|\xi}}{\sigma^2_{y|\eta(\xi)}}\frac{p^2(\xi)}{q^2[\eta(\xi)]}.$$ (6-14)

To our surprise, this formula shows that the relative efficiency of two tests can be expressed directly in terms of true-score frequency distributions and standard errors of measurement. The formulas agree with the vague intuitive notion that a test is more discriminating at true-score levels where the scores are spread out and less discriminating at true-score levels where the scores pile up.

6.7.   AN APPROXIMATION FOR RELATIVE EFFICIENCY

If estimated item parameters are available, estimated relative efficiency can be directly and simply computed from (6-1) and from the formula for the appropriate information function, such as Eq. (5-6), (5-12), or (5-13). If estimated item parameters are not conveniently available, it may be possible to estimate the necessary quantities on the right side of (6-14), thus approximating relative efficiency without requiring the item parameters a_i, b_i, and c_i. A method for estimating true-score distributions $p(\zeta)$ and $q(\eta)$ is the subject of Chapter 16. The following application is presented here rather than in Chapter 16 because it leads to the much simpler approximation described in Section 6.8. An approximation for the standard error of measurement is given by (Lord, 1965; Eq. 9, 34):

$$\sigma_{x|\xi} = \frac{(n_x - 2k_x)\xi(n_x - \xi)}{n_x^2}, \tag{6-15}$$

$$k_x \equiv \frac{\tfrac{1}{2}n_x^2(n_x - 1)s_p^2}{[\bar{x}(n_x - \bar{x}) - s_x^2 - n_x s_p^2]}, \tag{6-16}$$

where $\bar{x}$ and s_x^2 are the sample mean and variance (over people) of the number-right scores, s_p^2 is the sample variance (over items) of the p_i, and p_i is the sample proportion of correct answers to item i; $\sigma_{y|\eta}$ is obtained similarly, from the same group or from an equivalent group of examinees.

When item parameters a_i, b_i, and c_i have not been estimated, the relation $\eta(\xi)$ between η and ξ may be obtained as follows. Integrating (6-13), we have, for any value ξ_0,

$$\int_{-\infty}^{\eta(\xi_0)} q(\eta)\, d\eta \equiv \int_{-\infty}^{\xi_0} p(\xi)\, d\xi . \tag{6-17}$$

In more familiar terms, this equation says that $\eta_0 \equiv \eta(\xi_0)$ has the same percentile rank in $q(\eta)$ as ξ_0 does in $p(\xi)$. Thus for any value of ξ, $\eta \equiv \eta(\xi)$ is to be obtained by standard equipercentile equating. The distributions $q(\eta)$ and $p(\xi)$ must be for the same group or for statistically equivalent groups of examinees. Given estimates of $q(\eta)$ and $p(\xi)$, the integration and equating are done by numerical methods by the computer (see Section 17.3).

A computer program (Stocking, Wingersky, Lees, Lennon, & Lord, 1973), is available to compute (6-14). The program uses estimates $p(\xi)$ and $q(\eta)$ obtained by the methods of Chapter 16. It then uses (6-17) to find equivalent values of ξ and η. Finally, using approximation (6-15), it computes relative efficiencies by (6-14).

In Fig. 6.7.1, the solid curve is the approximate relative efficiency from (6-14). The dotted curve is the ratio of information functions computed by (6-1)

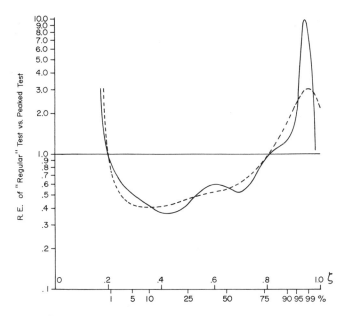

FIG. 6.7.1.   Approximation (solid line) to relative efficiency [Eq. (6-14)] compared with estimate (dashed line) from Eq. (6-1) and (5-13). (From F. M. Lord, The relative efficiency of two tests as a function of ability level. *Psychometrika*, 1974, *39*, 351–358.)

from estimated item response function parameters. The two tests under comparison are the regular test (y) and the peaked test (x), described in more detail in Section 6.1. Approximation (6-14) tends to oscillate about the estimated relative efficiency (6-1), but the approximation is adequate for the practical purpose of comparing the effectiveness of the tests over a range of ability levels. The agreement found here and in later sections of this chapter between relative efficiency calculated from item parameters and relative efficiency approximated from totally different sources is a reassuring illustration of the adequacy of item response theory and of the procedures used for estimation of item parameters.

As noted in Section 6.4, the relative efficiency of two tests remains the same under any monotonic transformation of the ability scale. Thus, the RE curve can be plotted against any convenient baseline. In Fig. 6.7.1, the baseline is scaled in terms of true score $\zeta \equiv \xi/n \equiv \Sigma_i P_i(\theta)/n$ for the peaked test [see Eq. (4-5)].

Is it a good rule of test construction to spread the items over a wide range of item difficulty, so as to have some items that are appropriate for each examinee? Or will a peaked test with all items of equal difficulty be better for everyone? In Fig. 6.7.1, the peaked test (really only partially peaked—it is hard to find 45 items that are identical in difficulty) is better than the regular (unpeaked) test for all examinees from the first through the seventy-fifth percentile. If the peaked test were more difficult, it might be better from perhaps the tenth percentile up through the nintieth.

6.8. DESK CALCULATOR APPROXIMATION FOR RELATIVE EFFICIENCY

Although the approximation of Section 6.7 avoids the need to estimate item response function parameters, the method (see Chapter 16) for estimating $p(\xi)$ and $q(\eta)$ is far from simple. Section 6.7 is included here because it leads to the suggestion that a simple approximation to relative efficiency can be obtained by substituting observed-score relative frequencies, f_x and f_y, say, for the true-score densities $p(\xi)$ and $q(\eta)$.

A simple approximation to $\sigma_{x|\xi}$ and $\sigma_{y|\eta}$ is also available. If the n_x items in test x are considered as a random sample from an infinite pool of items, then the sampling distribution of number-right score x for a particular examinee, over successive random samples of items, is the familiar binomial distribution

$$\binom{n_x}{x}\zeta^x(1 - \zeta)^{n_x-x},$$

where ζ is a parameter characterizing the individual. Since $\mathscr{E}(x|\zeta) = n_x\zeta \equiv \xi$ for the binomial, ζ or ξ is the individual's true score. [Although it may not seem so, the fact is that the binomial model just described holds just as well when the items are of widely varying difficulty as when they are all of the same difficulty. A simple discussion of this fact is given by Lord (1977).]

Under the binomial model just outlined, the sampling variance of an examinee's number-right score x over random samples of items is given by the familiar formula

$$\sigma^2_{x|\zeta} = n_x\zeta(1 - \zeta) \tag{6-18}$$

or, equivalently,

$$\sigma^2_{x|\xi} = \frac{\xi(n_x - \xi)}{n_x}. \tag{6-19}$$

A similar formula holds for y.

If we substitute these into (6-14) and replace ξ by x, η by y, we have

$$\text{RE}\,\{y, x\} \cong \frac{n_y x(n_x - x)}{n_x y(n_y - y)} \frac{f_x^2}{f_y^2} \tag{6-20}$$

This is the shortcut approximation recommended for calculating relative efficiency. Note that here x and y are number-right scores with the same percentile rank in some group of examinees (as determined by equipercentile equating); f_x and f_y are relative frequencies for the same group or for equivalent groups ($\Sigma f_x = \Sigma f_y = 1$). Note also that test x and test y must be measures of the same ability or trait.

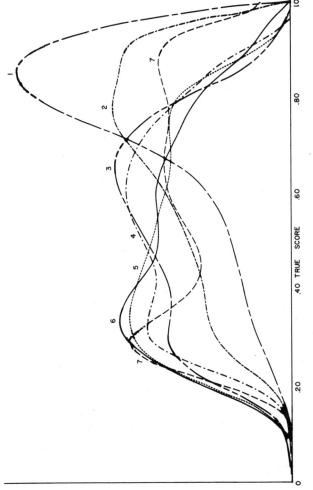

FIG. 6.8.1. Estimated true-score distribution for the sixth-grade data for STEP (1), MAT (2), CAT (3), ITBS (4), Stanford (5), CTBS (6), and SRA (7).

95

Equation (6-20) will work best with a large sample of examinees, perhaps several thousand. If the sample size is smaller, the equipercentile equating of x and y will be irregular because of local irregularities in f_x and f_y. This can be overcome by smoothing distributions f_x and f_y. Smaller samples can then be used, but at some cost in labor.

In order to investigate the adequacy of (6-20), the relative efficiencies of the vocabulary sections of seven nationally known reading tests were approximated by formula (6-20) and also by the computer program (Stocking et al., 1973) described in Section 6.7. For each test, a carefully selected representative national sample of 10,000 or more sixth graders from the Anchor Test Study (Loret, Seder, Bianchini, & Vale, 1974) supplies the frequency distribution of number-right vocabulary score needed for the two methods. The number of items per vocabulary section ranges from $n = 30$ through $n = 50$.

Figure 6.8.1 shows the true-score distributions for the seven vocabulary tests as estimated by the method of Chapter 16. These are the $p(\xi)$ and $q(\eta)$ used in (6-14) to obtain the smooth curves in Fig. 6.9.1-6.9.6. As already noted, a test in general tends to be less efficient where the true scores pile up and more efficient where the true scores are spread out.

6.9. RELATIVE EFFICIENCY OF SEVEN SIXTH-GRADE VOCABULARY TESTS[1]

Figures 6.9.1 to 6.9.6 show the efficiency curves for six of the tests relative to the Metropolitan Reading Tests (1970), Intermediate Level, Form F, Word Analysis subtest (MAT). The smooth curves are obtained from (6-14); the broken lines are obtained from (6-20), after grouping together adjacent pairs of raw scores in order to reduce zigzags due to sampling fluctuations.

Although (6-20) gives only approximate results, the approximation is seen to be quite adequate for many purposes. Rough calculations using (6-20) can be conveniently made under circumstances not permitting the use of an elaborate computer program.

Figure 6.9.1 shows the relative efficiency of STEP (Sequential Tests of Educational Progress) Series II (1969), Level 4, Form A, Reading subtest. STEP is more efficient than MAT for the bottom fifth or sixth of the pupils and less efficient for the rest of the students. Between the fortieth and eightieth percentiles, STEP would have to be tripled in length in order to be as effective as MAT. STEP ($n_y = 30$) is actually three-fifths as long as MAT ($n_x = 50$), as shown by

---

[1]This section is revised and printed with special permission from F. M. Lord, Quick estimates of the relative efficiency of two tests as a function of ability level. *Journal of Educational Measurement,* Winter 1974, *11,* No. 4, 247–254. Figures 6.9.1, 6.9.6, and Table 6.9.1 are taken from the same source. Copyright 1974, National Council on Measurement in Education, Inc., East Lansing, Mich.

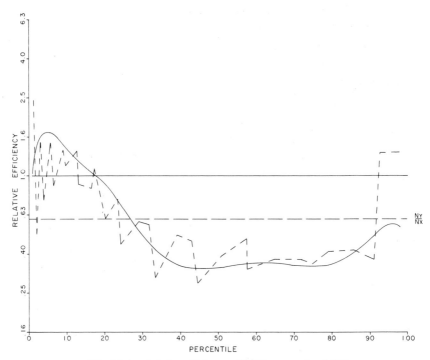

FIG. 6.9.1.   Relative efficiency of STEP compared to MAT.

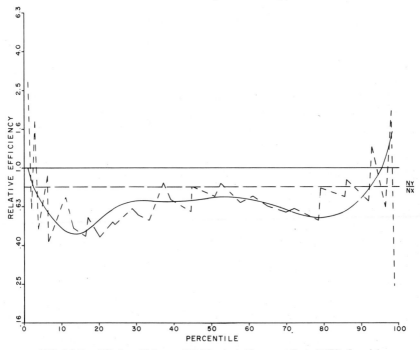

FIG. 6.9.2.   Relative efficiency of California Achievement Tests (1970), Level 4,
Form A, Reading Vocabulary compared to MAT.

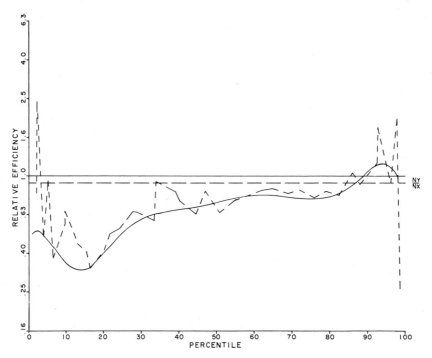

FIG. 6.9.3.   Relative efficiency of Iowa Test of Basic Skills (1970), Level 12, Form 5, Vocabulary compared to MAT.

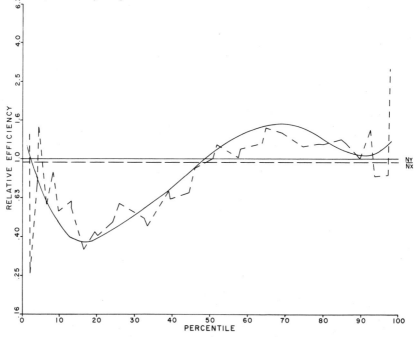

FIG. 6.9.4.   Relative efficiency of Stanford Reading Tests (1964), Intermediate II, Form W, Word Meaning compared to MAT.

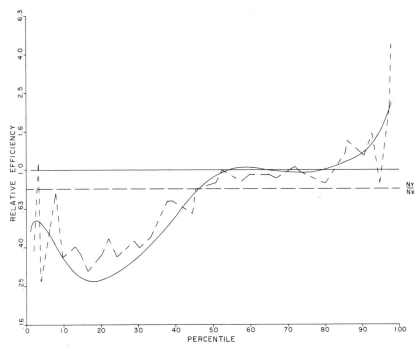

FIG. 6.9.5.   Relative efficiency of Comprehensive Tests of Basic Skills (1968), Level 3, Form Q, Reading Vocabulary compared to MAT.

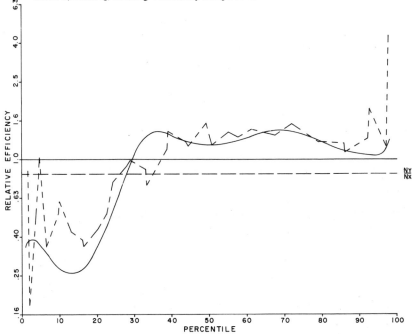

FIG. 6.9.6.   Relative efficiency of SRA Achievement Series (1971), Green Edition, Form E, Vocabulary compared to MAT.

99

the dashed line representing the ratio n_y/n_x. The dashed line represents the relative efficiency that would be expected if the two tests differed only in length.

The fact that STEP is more efficient for low-ability students and less efficient at higher ability levels is to be expected in view of the fact that this STEP (Level 4) is extremely easy for most sixth-grade pupils in the representative national sample. It has long been known that an easy test discriminates best at low ability levels and is less effective at higher levels than a more difficult test would be.

Similar conclusions can be drawn from the other figures. It is valuable to have such relative efficiency curves whenever a choice has to be made between tests measuring the same ability or trait.

Numerical Example

For illustrative purposes, Table 6.9.1 shows a method for computing RE $\{y, x\}$ for one set of data, with $N = 10,000$, $n_x = 50$, $n_y = 30$. The method illustrated is a little rough but seems adequate for the purpose.

The raw data for the table are the frequency distributions given by the un-italicized figures in columns f_x and f_y. The score ranges covered by the table are

TABLE 6.9.1
Illustrative Computations for Relative Efficiency*

Percentile Rank	Test X			Test Y			RE $\{y, x\}$
	x	f_x	F_x	y	f_y	F_y	
⋮	⋮	⋮	⋮				
	17.5		1141	⋮	⋮	⋮	⋮
	18	176		14	203		
12.70	18.23	(175.08)		14.5	204.5	1270	1.13
13.17	18.5	174	1317	14.73	(205.19)		1.12
	19	172		15	206		
14.76	19.42	(166.96)		15.5	228	1476	.85
14.89	19.5	166	1489	15.55	(230.20)		.83
	20	160		16	250		
16.49	20.5	171	1649	16.19	(258.74)		.71
17.26	20.92	(180.24)		16.5	273	1726	.71
	21	182					
18.31	21.5	186.5	1831	16.85	(289.10)		.69
	22	191		17	296		
20.22	22.5	196	2022**	17.50	(313)	2022**	.67
	23	201		18	330		
⋮	⋮	⋮	⋮	⋮	⋮	⋮	⋮

*Italicized figures are obtained by linear interpolation. The remaining figures indicate exact values obtained from the data.

**These two numbers are identical only by coincidence.

shown by the corresponding integers in the x and y columns. Computational steps are the following:

1. Enter the half-integer scores in the x and y columns as shown.
2. Obtain from the raw data the cumulative frequency distributions shown in columns F_x and F_y. (The frequency f_x is treated as spread evenly over the interval from $x - .5$ to $x + .5$.)
3. Compute from the F_x and F_y columns the percentile rank of each half-integer score (the proportion of cases lying below the half-integer score) and enter this in the first column.
4. Using linear interpolation, compute and record in the x or y column the score (percentile) for each percentile rank listed in column 1. In the table, these percentiles are in italics. (Note that, by definition, the score having a given percentile rank is called the *percentile*.)
5. For each half-integer score, record (in italics) in the adjacent f column the average of f for the next higher integer score and the f for the next lower integer score.
6. For each (italicized) score obtained in step 4, compute by linear interpolation and record in parentheses in the adjacent f column the f for the score.
7. For each row of the table that contains an entry in the first column, compute RE $\{y, x\}$ by (6-20).

6.10.   REDESIGNING A TEST

When a test is to be changed, we normally have response data for a typical group of examinees. Such data are not available when a new test is designed. This section deals chiefly with changing or *re*designing an existing test. Procedures for redesign are best explained by citing a concrete example.

Recently, it was decided to change slightly the characteristics of the College Entrance Examination Board's Scholastic Aptitude Test, Verbal Section. It was desired to make the test somewhat more appropriate at low ability levels without impairing its effectiveness at high ability levels. The possibility of simultaneously shortening the test was also considered.

A first step was to estimate the item parameters for all items in a typical current form of the Verbal test. A second step was to compute from the item parameters the information curves for variously modified hypothetical forms of the Verbal test. Each of these curves was compared to the information curve of the actual Verbal test. The ratio of the two curves is the relative efficiency of the modified test, which varies as a function of ability level.

Let us now consider some typical questions: How would the relative efficiency of the existing test be changed by

1. Shortening the test without changing its composition?
2. Adding five more items just like the five easiest items in the existing test?
3. Cutting out five items of medium difficulty?
4. Replacing five items of medium difficulty by five very easy items?
5. Replacing all reading items by a typical set of nonreading items?
6. Discarding the easiest half of the test items?
7. Scoring only the easiest half of the test items?
8. Replacing all items by items of medium difficulty?

These questions are taken up one by one in the correspondingly numbered paragraphs that follow, illustrating the results of various design changes on the SAT Verbal test. In Figure 6.10.1, the horizontal scale representing the ability measured by the test has for convenience been marked off to correspond to College Board true scaled scores.

   (The test-score information curves are computed for hypothetical examinees who omit no items. The SAT is normally scored with a "correction for guessing," but when there are no omitted items, the corrected score is perfectly correlated with number-right score. For this reason, the relative efficiencies dis-

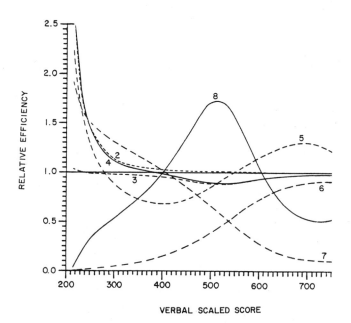

FIG. 6.10.1.   Relative efficiency of various modified SAT Verbal tests. (From F. M. Lord, Practical applications of item characteristic curve theory. *Journal of Educational Measurement*. Summer 1977, *14*, No. 2, 117–138. Copyright 1977, National Council on Measurement in Education, Inc., East Lansing, Mich.)

cussed below are equally appropriate for corrected scores and for number-right scores. See Section 15.11 for a detailed discussion of work with formula scores.)

1. Reducing the test from n_1 to n_2 items without changing its composition produces a new test with efficiency RE $= n_2/n_1$ relative to the original test. If such an RE were shown in Figure 6.10.1, it would appear as a horizontal straight line.

2. The effect of adding five very easy items to the SAT Verbal test is shown by curve 2. The efficiency of the lengthened verbal test, relative to the usual SAT Verbal, is increased at all ability levels, as might be expected. The change in efficiency at any particular level indicates the (relative) extent to which the five easy items are useful for measurement at that level. These items are of little use above the ability level represented by a (true) score of 400, because above this level most people answer these items correctly.

3. The effect of simply cutting out five items of medium difficulty from the SAT Verbal test is shown by curve 3. The efficiency of the shortened verbal test, relative to the usual full-length verbal test, is decreased at all ability levels above a (true) score of 245. It may seem strange that omitting five items actually increases relative efficiency below 245. The reason will be pointed out in the discussion of question 7.

4. Replacing five medium difficulty items by five very easy items simply adds together the changes made in paragraphs 2 and 3 above. If asymptotically optimal (maximum likelihood) scoring were used, the relative efficiency of (SAT Verbal + easy items − medium items) would be exactly equal to (RE of SAT Verbal + RE of easy items − RE of medium items). Since number-right scoring is used, the foregoing relationship holds only as a useful approximation. Curve 4 in Figure 6.10.1 shows the combined effects of the changes of curves 2 and 3.

5. Curve 5 shows the result of first omitting all reading items and then bringing the SAT Verbal test back to its original length without further changes in composition. This curve is given purely to illustrate a kind of question that can be answered. The particular result obtained cannot be generalized to other tests. It also ignores the fact that reading items require more testing time than other verbal item types. This last fact could be taken into account, if desired.

6. The effect of discarding the easiest half of the test items is shown by curve 6. The test loses most of its effectiveness except at high ability levels, where there is a loss of about 10% in efficiency.

7. In contrast, discarding the most difficult half of the test items greatly improves measurement efficiency for low-ability examinees. A similar but smaller effect was observed in answer to question 3. The reason is that random guessing by low-level examinees on the harder items adds so much "noise" to the measuring process that it would be better simply not to score these items for low-ability examinees. The half test actually measures better than the full-length test at low ability levels.

8. Replacing all items by items of medium difficulty produces a "peaked" SAT that is much more efficient than the actual SAT for the average examinee, who scores near 500. The peaked test is more efficient than the actual SAT for examinees from 400 to 610, less efficient for examinees at more extreme ability levels. (Curve 8 is obtained by changing all b_i to an average value, all other SAT item response parameters being unchanged.)

The foregoing illustrates how typical questions involved in redesigning a test can be answered by predicting the relative efficiency of a suitably modified test. A more general redesign problem may be stated: How can we change the present test to produce a new test with a specified relative efficiency curve? It would be possible to devise mathematical methods for answering this general question. For the present, however, it may be more convenient to answer it by trial and error: by devising a variety of redesigned tests, computing their RE curves, then choosing the best of these, and modifying the tests further until the desired RE curve is achieved.

6.11.   EXERCISES

6-1   Using Table 4.17.1, compute the test information function for a three-item test with $a = 1/1.7$, $b = 0$, $c = .2$ for all items. Plot it.

6-2   Using Table 4.17.2, plot on the same graph the test information function for a three-item test with $a = 1/1.7$, $b = 0$, $c = 0$ (see Exercise 5-8).

6-3   Compute and plot the efficiency of the test in Exercise 6-1 relative to test 1 (see Exercise 5-4).

6-4   Compute and plot the efficiency of the test in Exercise 6-2 relative to test 1 (see Exercise 5-4).

6-5   For each item in test 1, plot $P(\theta)$ from Table 4.17.1 against $\theta^* \equiv e^\theta$. These are the item response functions when θ^* is used as the measure of ability. Compare with Exercise 4-1.

6-6   Using Table 4.17.1, compute and plot against θ^* the item information function $I\{\theta^*, u_i\}$ for each item in test 1. Compare with Exercise 5-3.

6-7   Using Table 4.17.1, plot the information function (6-8) of number-right observed score x on number-right true score ξ for test 1. Necessary values were calculated in Exercise 5-2.

6-8   Using Table 4.17.1, compute for test 1 at $\theta = -3, -2, -1, 0, 1, 2, 3$ the $\sigma^2_{x|\xi}$ of (6-19), and compare with the $\sigma^2_{x|\xi}$ of Eq. (4-3). The necessary values of $\xi \equiv \xi(\theta)$ are calculated in Exercise 5-1. Explain the discrepancy between the two sets of results.

6-9   Suppose test 1 is modified by replacing item 2 by an item exactly like item 1. Compute the information function for the modified test and plot its relative efficiency with respect to test 1 (see Exercise 5-4).

REFERENCES

Lord, F. M. A strong true-score theory, with applications. *Psychometrika*, 1965, *30*, 239–270.

Lord, F. M. Practical applications of item characteristic curve theory. *Journal of Educational Measurement*, 1977, *14*, 117–138.

Loret, P. G., Seder, A., Bianchini, J. C., & Vale, C. A. *Anchor Test Study—Equivalence and norms tables for selected reading achievement tests (grades 4, 5, 6)*. Washington, D.C.: U.S. Government Printing Office, 1974.

Stocking, M., Wingersky, M. S., Lees, D. M., Lennon, V., & Lord, F. M. *A program for estimating the relative efficiency of tests at various ability levels, for equating true scores, and for predicting bivariate distributions of observed scores*. Research Memorandum 73-24. Princeton, N.J.: Educational Testing Service, 1973.

7

Optimal Number of Choices Per Item[1]

7.1. INTRODUCTION

Typical multiple-choice tests have four or five alternative choices per item. What is the optimal number?

If additional choices did not increase total testing time or add to the cost of the test, it would seem from general considerations that the more choices, the better. The same conclusion can be reached by examination of the formula (4-43) for the logistic item information function: Information is maximized when $c \to 0$. An empirical study by Vale and Weiss (1977) reaches the same conclusion.

In practice, increasing the number of choices will usually increase the testing time. Each approach treated in this chapter makes the assumption that total testing time for a set of n items is proportional to the number A of choices per item. This means that nA, the total number of alternatives in the entire test, is assumed fixed.

It seems likely that many or most item types do not satisfy this condition, but doubtless some item types will be found for which the condition can be shown to hold approximately. The relation of n to A for fixed testing time should be determined experimentally for each given item type; the theoretical approaches given here should then be modified in obvious ways to determine the optimal

[1]This chapter is adapted by special permission from F. M. Lord, Optimal number of choices per item—a comparison of four approaches. *Journal of Educational Measurement,* Spring 1977, *14,* No. 1. Copyright 1977. National Council on Measurement in Education, Inc., East Lansing, Mich. Research reported was supported by grant GB-41999 from the National Science Foundation.

value of A for each item type. A useful procedure for doing this is described in Grier (1976).

In this chapter, some published empirical results, two published theoretical approaches, and also an unpublished classical test theory approach are compared with some new results obtained from item response theory. From some points of view, the contrasts between the different approaches are as interesting and instructive as the actual answers given to the question asked.

7.2. PREVIOUS EMPIRICAL FINDINGS

Ruch and Charles (1928), Ruch, DeGraff, and Gordon (1926, pp. 54–88), Ruch and Stoddard (1925, 1927), and Toops (1921), among others, reported data on the relative time required to answer items with various numbers of alternatives. Their empirical evidence regarding the optimal number of alternatives for maximum test reliability is somewhat contradictory. Ruch and Stoddard (1927) and Ruch and Charles (1928) concluded that because more of such items can be administered in a given length of time, two- and three-choice items give as good or better results than do four- and five-choice items.

More recently, Williams and Ebel (1957, p. 64) report that

> For tests of equal working time . . . three-choice vocabulary test items gave a test of equal reliability, and two-choice items a test of higher reliability, in comparison with standard four-choice items. However, neither of the differences was significant at the 10% level of confidence.

About 230 students were tested with each test.

Williams and Ebel eliminated choices by dropping those shown by item analysis to be least discriminating. This is a desirable practical procedure that should yield better results than simply eliminating distractors at random, as assumed by the theoretical approaches discussed below.

7.3. A MATHEMATICAL APPROACH

Tversky (1964) proposed that the optimal number of choices is the value of A that maximizes the "discrimination function" A^n. He chose this function because A^n is the total number of possible distinct response patterns on n A-choice items and also for other related reasons.

Tversky easily showed that when $nA = K$ is fixed, A^n is maximized by $A = e = 2.718$. For integer values of A, A^n is maximized by $A = 3$. Tversky concludes that when $nA = K$, three choices per item is optimal.

7.4. GRIER'S APPROACH

Grier (1975) investigated the same problem. He also found that three-choice items are best when the total number of alternatives is fixed. Two-choice items are next best.

Grier reached these conclusions by maximizing an approximation to the Kuder–Richardson Formula-21 reliability coefficient. This approximation, given as Eq. (7-2), is derived by Ebel (1969) on the assumption that the mean number-right score $\bar{x}$ is halfway between the maximum possible score n and the expected chance score n/A and also that the standard deviation of test scores s_x is one-sixth of the difference between the maximum possible score and the expected chance score:

$$
\begin{aligned}
\bar{x} &= \frac{1}{2}\left(n + \frac{n}{A} \right) , \\
s_x &= \frac{1}{6}\left(n - \frac{n}{A} \right) .
\end{aligned}
\tag{7-1}
$$

If (7-1) were true, the Kuder–Richardson Formula-21 reliability coefficient of the test would be

$$
r_{21} = \frac{n}{n-1}\left[1 - \frac{9(A+1)}{n(A-1)} \right] .
\tag{7-2}
$$

This formula (as Ebel points out) is not useful for small n. When $A = 3$, the value of r_{21} given by (7-2) is negative unless $n \geqslant 18$.

7.5. A CLASSICAL TEST THEORY APPROACH

A third approach is to use the knowledge-or-random-guessing assumption and work out the reliabilities for hypothetical tests composed of equivalent items. This is done below. The knowledge-or-random-guessing assumption is not ordinarily satisfied in practice, but it is not likely to lead to unreasonable conclusions for the present problem. In any case, the conclusions reached from this third approach agree to some extent with Tversky's and Grier's.

The intercorrelation between two equivalent items under the knowledge-or-random-guessing model is given by

$$
r' = \frac{r}{1 + 1/(A-1)p} ,
\tag{7-3}
$$

where r' is the product-moment intercorrelation between k-choice items when $k = A$. Here p and r denote, respectively, the difficulty (proportion of correct answers) and the product-moment intercorrelation of k-choice items when $k =$

∞. This formula is a generalization of Eq. (3-19) and may be derived by the same approach.

By the Spearman–Brown formula [Eq. (1-17)], the reliability r'_{tt} of number-right scores on a test composed of n equivalent A-choice items is found from (7-3) to be

$$r'_{tt} = \frac{nr'}{1 + (n - 1)r'} = \frac{nr}{(n - 1)r + 1 + 1/(A - 1)p} \tag{7-4}$$

Since $n = K/A$, Eq. (7-4) becomes

$$r'_{tt} = \frac{Kr}{Kr + (1 - r)A + A/(A - 1)p} . \tag{7-5}$$

We wish to know what value of A, the number of choices, will maximize the reliability r'_{tt}. The optimal value of A is the value that minimizes the denominator of (7-5). The derivative of the denominator with respect to A is $1 - r - 1/(A - 1)^2 p$. Setting this equal to zero and solving for A, the optimal value is found to be

$$A = 1 + \frac{1}{\sqrt{(1 - r)p}} . \tag{7-6}$$

It is easy to verify that this value of A provides a maximum rather than a minimum for r'_{tt}.

Some optimal values of A from (7-6) are shown in the following table:

	$p = .20$	$p = .50$	$p = .80$
$r = .10$	3.36	2.49	2.18
$r = .30$	3.67	2.69	2.34

For $p = .5$ these values agree rather well with those found by Grier (1975). Our optimal values, however, unlike Grier's, are independent of test length, as indeed they should be. For $p \neq .5$, the results are different from Grier's.

Some typical values of test reliability are shown in the following table for the case where $p = .5$:

	$A = 2$	$A = 3$	$A = 4$	$A = 5$
$K = 250, r = .20, r'_{tt} =$	.889	.902	.895	.885
$K = 150, r = .30, r'_{tt} =$	.893	.898	.892	.882

These values vary with A less than do those in Grier's Fig. 1.

7.6.   AN ITEM RESPONSE THEORY APPROACH

A different perspective appears when item response theory is applied to this problem. The 90-item Verbal section of the College Board Scholastic Aptitude Test, Form TSA13, was chosen for investigation. Logistic item parameters for this test had already been estimated in the course of another study. The median estimated c_i for the five-choice items in TSA13 is about .15. Four alternative hypothetical tests were built from TSA13 by replacing all the c_i parameters by .200, .250, .333, or .50 while leaving the a_i and b_i parameters unchanged.

The parameter c_i is the lower asymptote of the item response function. If very low-level examinees responded purely at random, these hypothetical c_i values would correspond, respectively, to five-, four-, three-, and two-choice items. The restriction $nA = K$ could then be written $n \propto c_i$. Accordingly, the number of items n in each test was specified to be proportional to its c_i value, as follows:

Test:	TSA13*	$c_i = .20$	$c_i = .25$	$c_i = .333$	$c_i = .50$
$n =$	90	120	150	200	300

*Median c_i is .15.

In actual practice, low-level examinees do less well than if they responded at random. Thus the current investigation really compares different values of c_i (subject to $n \propto c_i$) rather than comparing different values of A.

The efficiency of number-right scores on each of the other tests was computed relative to the test with $c_i = .333$. The resulting relative efficiencies are shown in Fig. 7.6.1 as functions of ability level. The ability scale along the baseline of the figure is calibrated to show true College Board scaled scores on TSA13.

At high ability levels, there is little random guessing and the relative efficiency of the five tests is determined by their length. Thus when ranked according to their efficiency at an ability level of 800, the tests, in order of merit, are $c_i = .50$, $c_i = .333$, $c_i = .25$, $c_i = .20$, and TSA13.

At low ability levels the effect of random guessing becomes of overwhelming importance. At an ability level of 215, the rank order of test efficiency is precisely the opposite of the order at 800. Thus, for any pair of tests, one test is better than the other over a certain range of ability but worse over the complementary range of ability.

The figure makes it obvious that it is not enough just to think about overall test reliability, as in earlier sections. *The effect of decreasing the number of choices per item while lengthening the test proportionately is to increase the efficiency of the test for high-level examinees and to decrease its efficiency for low-level examinees.* None of the empirical studies known to the writer has taken this effect into account when determining the optimal number of choices per item.

This effect may be offset by adjusting the difficulty level of the tests. The median value of b_i for TSA13, and hence for all the tests, was $b_i = .5$ approxi-

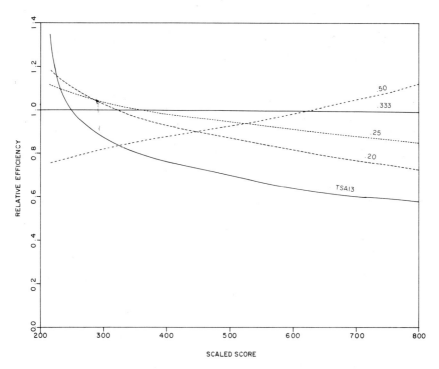

FIG. 7.6.1.   Relative efficiency of five SAT Verbal tests that differ only in test length and in the value of c_i.

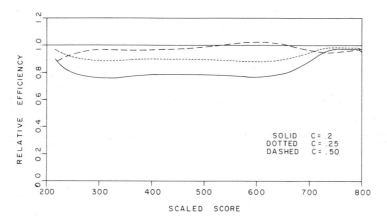

FIG. 7.6.2.   Efficiency of three SAT Verbal tests relative to the $c_i = .333$ test after the $c_i = .5$ test has been made easier and the $c_i = .2$ and $c_i = .25$ tests have been made harder.

mately. The dashed curve in Fig. 7.6.2 shows the relative efficiency of the $c_i = .50$ test when all its items are made slightly easier (all the item difficulty parameters b_i decreased by 0.1). The dotted curve shows the relative efficiency of the $c_i = .25$ test when all its items are made slightly harder (all b_i increased by 0.1). The solid curve shows a harder $c_i = .20$ test (all b_i increased 0.2). The efficiencies are shown relative to the test with $c_i = .333$. The test with $c_i = .333$ is clearly superior to the others.

Comparisons using item response theory assume that c_i can be changed without affecting the item discrimination power a_i. This would be true if examinees either knew the answer or guessed at random. When an examinee has partial information about an item, the value of a_i is likely to change with the number of alternatives. This effect could operate against reducing the number of alternatives per item. The extent of this effect cannot be confidently predicted here.

7.7. MAXIMIZING INFORMATION AT A CUTTING SCORE

If a test is to be used only to accept or to reject examinees, all items in the test ideally should be maximally informative at the cutting score. Now, the maximum possible information M_i obtainable from a logistic item with parameters a_i and c_i is given by Eq. (10-6). If all items have $a_i = a$ and $c_i = c$ and if the number of items that can be administered in the available testing time is proportional to c, what value of c will maximize the test information $I\{\theta\} = nM_i \propto cM_i$ at the cutting score? Numerical investigation of cM_i using Eq. (10-6) shows that the optimal value of c is $c = .4374$.

REFERENCES

Ebel, R. L. Expected reliability as a function of choices per item. *Educational and Psychological Measurement,* 1969, *29,* 565–570.

Grier, J. B. The number of alternatives for optimum test reliability. *Journal of Educational Measurement,* 1975, *12,* 109–112.

Grier, J. B. The optimal number of alternatives at a choice point with travel time considered. *Journal of Mathematical Psychology,* 1976, *14,* 91–97.

Ruch, G. M., & Charles, J. W. A comparison of five types of objective tests in elementary psychology. *Journal of Applied Psychology,* 1928, *12,* 398–404.

Ruch, G. M., DeGraff, M. H., & Gordon, W. E. *Objective examination methods in the social studies.* New York: Scott, Foresman and Co., 1926.

Ruch, G. M., & Stoddard, G. D. Comparative reliabilities of five types of objective examinations. *Journal of Educational Psychology,* 1925, *16,* 89–103.

Ruch, G. M., & Stoddard, G. D. *Tests and measurement in high school instruction.* Chicago: World Book, 1927.

Toops, H. A. Trade tests in education. *Teachers College Contributions to Education* (No. 115). New York: Columbia University, 1921.

Tversky, A. On the optimal number of alternatives of a choice point. *Journal of Mathematical Psychology,* 1964, *1*, 386–391.

Vale, C. D., & Weiss, D. J. *A comparison of information functions of multiple-choice and free-response vocabulary items.* Research Report 77-2. Minneapolis: Psychometric Methods Program, Department of Psychology, University of Minnesota, 1977.

Williams, B. J., & Ebel, R. L. The effect of varying the number of alternatives per item on multiple-choice vocabulary test items. *The Fourteenth Yearbook.* National Council on Measurements Used in Education, 1957.

8
Flexilevel Tests[1]

8.1. INTRODUCTION

It is well known (see also Theorem 8.7.1) that for accurate measurement the difficulty level of a psychological test should be appropriate to the ability level of the examinee. With conventional tests, this goal is achievable for all examinees only if they are fairly homogeneous in ability. College entrance examinations, for example, could provide more reliable measurement at particular ability levels if they did not need to cover such a wide range of examinee talent (see Section 6.10). Furthermore, in many situations it is psychologically desirable that the test difficulty be matched to the examinee's ability: A test that is excessively difficult for a particular examinee may have a demoralizing or otherwise undesirable effect.

There has recently been increasing interest in "branched," "computer-assisted," "individualized," "programmed," "sequential," or *tailored* testing (Chapter 10). When carefully designed, such testing comes close to matching the difficulty of the items administered to the ability level of the examinee. The practical complications involved in achieving this result are great, however.

Some simplification can be obtained by simple two-stage testing—by use of a routing test followed by the administration of one of several alternative second-stage tests (Chapter 9). This reduces the number of items needed and eliminates

---

[1]Sections 8.1 through 8.4 and Fig. 8.2.1 are taken with special permission and with some revisions from F. M. Lord, The self-scoring flexilevel test. *Journal of Educational Measurement,* Fall 1971, *8,* No. 3, 147–151. Copyright 1971, National Council on Measurement in Education, Inc., East Lansing, Mich.

the need for a computer to administer them. To obtain comparable scores from different second-stage tests, however, expensive equating procedures based on special large-scale administrations are required.

8.2.   FLEXILEVEL TESTS

To a degree, the same result, the matching of item difficulty with ability level, can be achieved with fewer complications. This can be done by modifying the directions, the test booklet, and the answer sheet of an ordinary conventional test. The modified test is called a *flexilevel test*.

Consider a conventional multiple-choice test in which the items are arranged in order of difficulty. The general idea of a flexilevel test is simply that the examinee starts with the middle item in the test and proceeds, taking an easier item each time he gets an item wrong and a harder item each time he gets an item right. He stops when he has answered half the items in the test.

Let us consider a concrete example, starting with a conventional test of $N = 75$ items. (In this chapter, the symbol N is used with this special meaning; in other chapters, N denotes the number of examinees.) For purposes of discussion, we assume that the items are arranged in order of difficulty; however, it is seen later that any rough approximation to this is adequate. The middle item of the conventional test (formerly item 38) is the first item in the flexilevel test. It is printed in the center at the top of the first page of the flexilevel test. The page below this, and subsequent pages, are divided in half vertically (see Fig. 8.2.1).

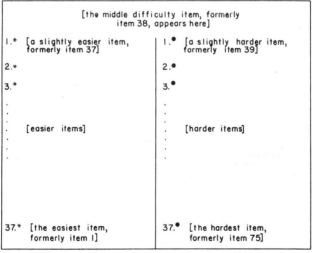

*numbers printed in red   •numbers printed in blue

FIG. 8.2.1.   Layout of printed flexilevel test booklet.

Items formerly numbered 39, 40, 41, . . . , 75 appear in that order in the right-hand columns, the hardest item (formerly item 75) at the bottom of the last page. In place of the old numbers, these items are numbered in blue as items 1, 2, 3, . . . , 37, respectively. Items formerly number 37, 36, 35, . . . , 1 appear in that order in the left-hand columns, the easiest item (formerly item 1) at the bottom of the last page. In place of the old numbers, these items are numbered in red as items 1, 2, 3, . . . , 37, respectively (the easiest item is now at the end and is numbered 37). The layout is indicated in Fig. 8.2.1.

The answer sheet used for a flexilevel test must inform the examinee whether each answer is right or wrong. When the examinee chooses a wrong answer, a red spot appears where he has marked or punched the answer sheet. When he chooses a right answer, a blue spot appears. Answer sheets similar to this are commercially available in a variety of designs.

In answering the test, the examinee must follow one rule. When his answer to an item is correct, he should turn next to the lowest numbered "blue" item not previously answered. When his answer is incorrect, he should work next on the lowest numbered "red" item not previously answered.

Each examinee is to answer just $\frac{1}{2}(N + 1) = 38$ items. One way to make it apparent to him when he has finished the test would be to print the answer sheet in two columns, using the same format as in Fig. 8.2.1 but with the second column inverted. Thus, the examinee works down from the top in the first column of the answer sheet and up from the bottom in the second column. The examinee can be told to stop (he has completed the test) when he has responded to one item in each *row* of the answer sheet.

It is now clear that the high-ability examinee who does well on the first items he answers will automatically be administered a harder set of items than the low-ability examinee who does poorly on the first items. Within limits, the flexilevel test automatically adjusts the difficulty of the items to the examinee's ability level.

8.3.   SCORING

Let us first agree that when examinees answer the same items, we will be satisfied to consider examinees with the same number-right score equal. A surprising feature of the flexilevel test is that even though different examinees take different sets of items, complicated and expensive scoring or equating procedures to put all examinees on the same score scale are not needed. The obvious validity of the scoring (by contrast with tailored testing) will keep examinees from feeling that they are the victims of occult scoring methods. Finally, the test is self-scoring—the examinee can determine his score without counting the number of correct answers.

The score on a flexilevel test will be the number of questions answered correctly, except that examinees who miss the last question they attempt receive a one-half point "bonus." Justification that this scoring provides comparable scores, as well as procedures for arriving at an examinee's score without counting the number of correct answers, is given in the following section.

8.4. PROPERTIES OF FLEXILEVEL TESTS

A flexilevel test has the following properties, which the reader should verify for himself. For convenience of exposition, we at first assume, as before, that the items in the conventional test are arranged in order of difficulty. Later on we see that any rough approximation will be adequate.

1. *If the items were ordered by difficulty, the items answered by a single examinee would always be a block of consecutive items.*

For simplicity, assume throughout that the examinee has completed the required $\frac{1}{2}(N + 1) = 38$ items (the complications arising when examinees do not have enough time are not dealt with here). Also, assume that the examinee has been instructed to indicate on the answer sheet the item he would have to answer next if the test were continued. (In an exceptional case, this might be a dummy "item 38," which need not actually appear in the test booklet, since no one will ever reach it.) An examinee who indicates that he would next try a blue item will be called a blue examinee; one who indicates a red item will be called a red examinee.

2. *For a blue examinee, the number of right answers is equal to the serial number of the item that would be answered next if the test were continued.*
3. *For a red examinee, the number of wrong answers is equal to the serial number of the item that would be answered next if the test were continued. The number of right answers is obtained by subtracting this serial number from $\frac{1}{2}(N + 1)$.* (A different serial numbering of the red items could give the number of right answers directly but might confuse the examinee while he is taking the test.)
4. *All blue examinees who have a given number-right score have answered the same block of items.*
5. *All red examinees who have a given number-right score have answered the same block of items.*

It can now be seen that all blue examinees can properly be compared with each other in terms of their number-right scores, even though examinees with different scores have not taken the same test. Consider two blue examinees, *A* and *B*, whose number-right scores differ by 1. The items answered by the two examinees are identical except that *A* had one item that was harder than any of

B's and B had one item that was easier than any of A's. The higher scoring examinee, A, is clearly the better of the two because he took the harder test.

The same reasoning shows that all red examinees can properly be compared with each other in terms of their number-right scores:

   6. *Examinees of the same color are properly compared by their number-right scores.*

In the foregoing discussion, the item taken by A and not by B was far apart on the difficulty scale from the item taken by B and not by A. Thus A still would be considered better than B even if the difficulty levels of individual items had been roughly estimated rather than accurately determined. It will be seen that still simpler considerations make exact determination of difficulty levels unnecessary for the remaining comparisons among examinees, discussed below. Thus:

   7. *Exact ranking of items on difficulty level is not necessary for proper comparison among examinees.*

It remains to be shown how blue examinees can be compared with red examinees. Consider a red examinee with a number-right score of x. If his very last response had been correct instead of wrong, he would have been a blue examinee with a score of $x + 1$. Clearly, his actual performance was worse than this; so we conclude that

   8. *A blue examinee with a number-right score of* $x + 1$ *has outperformed all red examinees with scores of* x.

Finally, we can compare a blue examinee and a red examinee, both having the same number-right score. Suppose we hypothetically administer to each examinee the item that he would normally take if the testing were continued. If both examinees answer this item correctly, they both become blue examinees with identical number-right scores. We have agreed that such examinees can be considered equal. In order hypothetically to reach this equality, however, the blue examinee had to answer a hard item correctly, whereas the red examinee had only to answer an easy item correctly. Clearly, without the hypothetical extra item, the standing of the blue examinee is inferior to the standing of the red examinee:

   9. *A red examinee has outperformed all blue examinees having the same number-right score.*

In view of this last conclusion, let us modify the scoring by adding one-half score point to the number-right score of each red examinee. Thus, once we agree to use number-right score for examinees answering the same block of items, we can say that

10. *On a flexilevel test, examinee performance is effectively quantified by number-right score, except that (roughly) one-half score point should be added to the score of each red examinee.*

If desired, all scores can be doubled to avoid fractional scores.

It is clear from the foregoing that to a considerable extent the flexilevel test matches the difficulty level of the items administered to the ability level of the examinee. This result is not achieved without some complication of the test administration. The complications are minor, however, compared with those arising in other forms of tailored testing.

8.5.   THEORETICAL EVALUATION OF NOVEL TESTING PROCEDURES

Item response theory is essential both for good design and for evaluation of novel testing procedures, such as flexilevel testing. If its basic assumptions hold, item response theory allows us to state precisely the relation between the parameters of the test design and the properties of the test scores produced.

Although the properties of test scores depend on the design parameters, the dependence is in general not a simple one. Item response theory will be most easily applicable if we make some simplifying assumptions. Even then, it is hard to state unequivocal rules for optimal test design. In the present state of the art, the following procedure is typical.

1. Evaluate various specific test designs.
2. Compare the results, seeking empirical rules.
3. Take the better designs and vary them systematically.
4. Repeat steps 1–4, evaluating and then modifying the better designs.
5. Stop when further effort leads to little or no improvement.
6. Try to draw general conclusions from a study of the results.

In this way, 100 or 200 different designs for some novel testing procedure can be tried out on the computer in a short time using simulated examinees.

Nothing like this could be done if 100 actual tests had to be built and administered to statistically adequate samples of real examinees. When we have learned as much as we can from simulated examinees, then we can design an adequate test, build it, administer it in a real testing situation, and evaluate the results. The real test administration is indispensable. Limits on testing time, attitudes of examinees, failure to follow directions, or other violations of the assumptions of the model may in practice invalidate all theoretical predictions.

The preliminary theoretical work and computer simulation are also important. Without them, the test actually built is likely to be a very inadequate one.

8.6. CONDITIONAL FREQUENCY DISTRIBUTION OF FLEXILEVEL TEST SCORES[2]

We can evaluate any given flexilevel test once we can determine $\phi(y|\theta)$, the conditional frequency distribution of test scores y for examinees at ability level θ. Given some mathematical form for the function $P_i \equiv P_i(\theta) \equiv P(\theta; a_i, b_i, c_i)$, the value of $\phi(y|\theta)$ can be determined numerically for any specified value of θ by the recursive method outlined below. In the case of flexilevel tests, the testing and scoring procedures are so fully specified that the item parameters are the only parameters involved. It is assumed that the item parameters have already been determined by pretesting.[3]

Assume the N test items to be arranged in order of difficulty, as measured by the parameter b_i. We choose N to be an odd number. For present purposes (not for actual test administration), identify the items by the index i, taking on the values $-n + 1, -n + 2, \ldots, -1, 0, 1, \ldots, n - 2, n - 1$, respectively, when the items are arranged in order of difficulty. Thus $n \equiv (N + 1)/2$ is the number of items answered by each examinee, and b_0 is the median item difficulty.

Consider, for example, the sequence of right (R) and wrong (W) answers $R\,W\,W\,R\,W\,R\,R\,R\,W\,R$. Following the rules given for a flexilevel test, we see that the corresponding sequence of items answered is

$$i = 0, +1, -1, -2, +2, -3, +3, +4, +5, -4, (+6).$$

Let I_v be the random variable denoting the vth item administered ($v = 1, 2, \ldots, n + 1$); thus I_v takes the integer values $i = -n + 1, -n + 2, \ldots, n - 1$. The general rule for flexilevel tests is that when $I_v \geq 0$, either

$$I_{v+1} = I_v + 1 \quad \text{or} \quad I_{v+1} = I_v - v,$$

and when $I_v \leq 0$, either

$$I_{v+1} = I_v - 1 \quad \text{or} \quad I_{v+1} = I_v + v.$$

For example, if the fourth item administered is indexed by $I_4 = -2$, the next item to be administered must be either $I_5 = -2 - 1 = -3$ or $I_5 = -2 + 4 = +2$, depending on whether item 4 is answered incorrectly or correctly.

Let $P_v(i'|i, \theta)$ denote the probability that item i' will be the next item ad-

---

[2]Sections 8.6 through 8.9 are revised and taken with permission from F. M. Lord, The theoretical study of the measurement effectiveness of flexilevel tests. *Educational and Psychological Measurement*, 1971, *31*, 805–813.

[3]The reader concerned only with practical conclusions may skip to Section 8.7.

ministered when the vth item administered was item i ($v = 1, 2, \ldots, n$). A simple restatement of the preceding rule gives us if $i \geq 0$,

$$P_v(i'|i, \theta) = \begin{cases} P_i(\theta) & \text{if } i' = i + 1, \\ Q_i(\theta) & \text{if } i' = i - v, \\ 0 & \text{otherwise.} \end{cases}$$

If $i \leq 0$,

$$P_v(i'|i, \theta) = \begin{cases} P_i(\theta) & \text{if } i' = i + v, \\ Q_i(\theta) & \text{if } i' = i - 1, \\ 0 & \text{otherwise.} \end{cases}$$

(8.1)

For examinees at ability level θ, let $p_v(i|\theta)$ denote the probability that item i is the vth item administered ($v = 1, 2, \ldots, n + 1$). For fixed v, the joint distribution of i and i' is the product of the marginal distribution $p_v(i|\theta)$ and the conditional distribution $P_v(i'|i, \theta)$. Summing this product over i, we obtain the overall probability that item i' will be administered on the $(v + 1)$th trial:

$$p_{v+1}(i|\theta) = \sum_{i=-n+1}^{n-1} p_v(i|\theta) P_v(i'|i, \theta).$$

(8-2)

The rightmost probability, P_v, is known from (8-1). The other probability on the right, p_v, can be found by the procedure described below.

The first item administered ($v = 1$) is always item $I_1 = 0$, so

$$p_1(i|\theta) = \begin{cases} 1 & \text{if } i = 0, \\ 0 & \text{otherwise.} \end{cases}$$

Starting with this fact and with a knowledge of all the $P_i(\theta)$ (item response functions) for a specified value of θ, the values of $p_2(i'|\theta)$ for each i' can be obtained from (8-2). Drop the prime from the final result. Repetition of the same procedure now gives us $p_3(i|\theta)$, the overall probability that item i ($i = -n + 1$, $-n + 2, \ldots, n - 1$) will be the third item administered. Successive repetitions of the same procedure now gives us $p_4(i|\theta)$, $p_5(i|\theta)$, $\ldots$, $p_{n+1}(i|\theta)$.

Now we can make use of an already verified feature of flexilevel tests. Again let i' represent the $(v + 1)$th item to be administered. *If* i' > 0, *then the number-right score* x *on the* v *items already administered was* x $= $ i'; *if* i' < 0, *then* x $= $ v $+ $ i'. Thus the frequency distribution of the number-right score x for examinees at ability level θ is given by $p_{n+1}(x|\theta)$ for those examinees who answered correctly the nth (last) item administered and by $p_{n+1}(x - n|\theta)$ for those who answered incorrectly. This frequency distribution can be computed recursively from (8-1) and (8-2).

As already noted, the actual score assigned on a flexilevel test is $y = x$ if the last item is answered correctly and $y = x + \frac{1}{2}$ if it is answered incorrectly. Consequently the conditional distribution of test scores is

$$\phi(y|\theta) = \begin{cases} p_{n+1}(y|\theta) & \text{if } y \text{ is an integer,} \\ p_{n+1}(y - n - \frac{1}{2}|\theta) & \text{if } y \text{ is a half integer.} \end{cases} \tag{8-3}$$

For any specified test design, this conditional frequency distribution $\phi(y|\theta)$ can be computed from (8-1) and (8-2) for $y = \frac{1}{2}, 1, 1\frac{1}{2}, \ldots, n$ for various values of θ.

Such a distribution constitutes the totality of possible information relevant to evaluating the effectiveness of y as a measure of ability θ. Having computed $\phi(y|\theta)$, we compute its mean $\mu_{y|\theta}$ and its variance $\sigma^2_{y|\theta}$. The necessary derivative $d\mu_{y|\theta}/d\theta$ is readily approximated by numerical methods:

$$\frac{d\mu_{y|\theta}}{d\theta} \cong \frac{\mu_{y|\theta+\Delta} - \mu_{y|\theta}}{\Delta}$$

approximately, when Δ is a small increment in θ. From these we compute the information function [Eq. (5-3)] for test score y.

8.7.   ILLUSTRATIVE FLEXILEVEL TESTS, NO GUESSING

The numerical results reported here are obtained on the assumption that P_i is a three-parameter normal ogive [Eq. (2-2)]. The results would presumably be about the same if P_i had been assumed logistic rather than normal ogive.

To keep matters simple, we consider tests in which all items have the same discriminating power a and also the same guessing parameter c. Results are presented here separately for $c = 0$ (no guessing) and $c = .2$. The results are general for any value of $a > 0$, since a can be absorbed into the unit of measurement chosen for the ability scale (see the baseline scale shown in the figures). Each examinee answers exactly $n = 60$ items. For simplicity, we consider tests in which the item difficulties form an arithmetic sequence, so that $b_{i+1} - b_i = d$, say, for $i = -n + 1, -n + 2, \ldots, n - 1$.

Figure 8.7.1 compares the effectiveness of four 60-item ($n = 60$, $N = 119$) flexilevel tests and three bench mark tests by means of score information curves. The "standard test" is a conventional 60-item test composed entirely of items of difficulty $b = 0$, scored by counting the number of right answers. There is no guessing, so $c = 0$. The values of a and c are the same for bench mark and flexilevel tests. The average value of b_i, averaged over items, is zero for all seven tests.

The figure shows that the standard test is best for discriminating among examinees at ability levels near $\theta = 0$. If good discrimination is important at $\theta = \pm 2/2a$ or $\theta = \pm 3/2a$, then a flexilevel test such as the one with $d = .033/2a$ or $d = .050/2a$ is better. The larger d is, the poorer the measurement at $\theta = 0$ but the better the measurement at extreme values of θ.

Suppose the best possible measurement is required at $\theta = \pm 2$, with $a = .5$. It might be thought that an effective conventional 60-item test for this limited purpose would consist of 30 items at $b = +2$ and 30 items at $b = -2$. The curve for this last test is shown in Fig. 8.7.1. It can be shown numerically that with $a = .5$ no conventional test with items at more than one difficulty level, scored

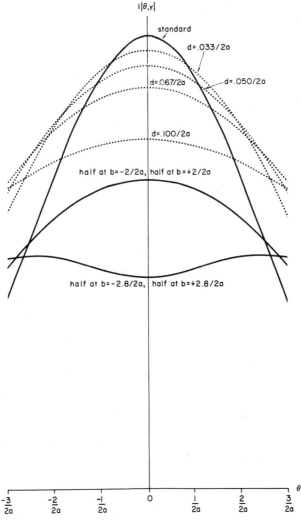

FIG. 8.7.1.   Score information functions for four 60-item flexilevel tests with $b_0 = 0$ (dotted curves) and three bench mark tests, $c = 0$. (From F. M. Lord, The theoretical study of the measurement effectiveness of flexilevel tests. *Educational and Psychological Measurement*, 1971, *31*, 805–813.)

number-right, can simultaneously measure as well both at $\theta = +2$ and at $\theta = -2$ as does the standard test (which has all items peaked at $b = 0$).

The situation is different if the best possible measurement is required at $\theta = \pm 3$, with $a = .5$. Using dichotomously scored items, the best 60-item conventional test for this purpose consists of 30 items at $b = -2.8$ and 30 items at $b = +2.8$, approximately. The curve for this test is shown in Fig. 8.7.1.

We know from Chapter 5 that $I\{\theta, y\}$ for a standard test is proportional to n, the test length. We thus see that when $a = .75$ (a common average value) the 60-item flexilevel test with $d = .033/2a = .022$ gives about as effective measurement as a

58-item standard test at $\theta = 0$,

64-item standard test at $\theta = \pm 1$,

86-item standard test at $\theta = \pm 2$.

At $\theta = \pm 2$, the 60-item flexilevel test with $d = .1/2a = .067$ is as effective as a 96-item standard test.

Comparisons between flexilevel tests and a "standard" peaked test are best understood in the light of the following.

Theorem 8.7.1. *When the a_i are equal and the c_i are equal for all items, no n-item test no matter how scored can provide more information at a given ability level θ_o than does number-right score on an n-item peaked test of suitable difficulty.*

Proof. Given $a_i = a$ and $c_i = c$, the test information function $\Sigma_i I\{\theta, u_i\}$ at fixed ability level θ_o depends only on the b_i ($i = 1, 2, \ldots, n$). Its maximum value is therefore $\Sigma_i \text{Max}_{b_i} I\{\theta, u_i\}$. The same value of b_i will maximize each item information function $I\{\theta, u_i\}$. Therefore, maximum information is produced by a peaked test (all items of equal difficulty). Number-right provides optimal scoring on such a test (Section 4.15).

8.8. ILLUSTRATIVE FLEXILEVEL TESTS, WITH GUESSING

Figure 8.8.1 compares the effectiveness of three 60-item flexilevel tests with each other and with five bench mark tests. All items have $c = .2$ and all have the same discriminating power a. Numerical labels on the curves are for $a = .75$. The standard test is a conventional 60-item test with all items at difficulty level $b = .5/2a$, scored by counting the number of right answers.

If all the item difficulties in any test were changed by some constant amount Δb, the effect would be simply to translate the corresponding curve by an amount Δb along the θ-axis. The difficulty level of each bench mark test and the starting

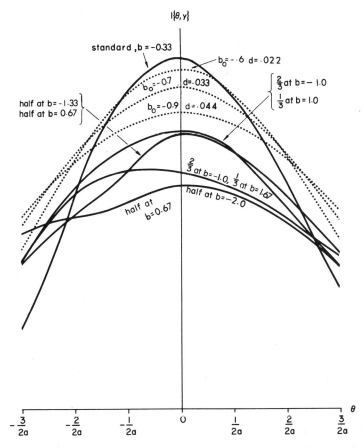

FIG. 8.8.1.   Information functions for three 60-item flexilevel tests (dotted curves) and five bench mark tests, $c = .2$. (Numerical labels on curves are for $a = .75$.) (From F. M. Lord, The theoretical study of the measurement effectiveness of flexilevel tests. *Educational and Psychological Measurement*, 1971, *31*, 805–813.

item difficulty level b_0 of each flexilevel test in Fig. 8.8.1 has been chosen so as to give maximum information somewhere in the neighborhood of $\theta = 0$.

The standard test is again found to be best for discriminating among examinees at ability levels near $\theta = 0$. At $\theta = \pm 2$ the flexilevel tests are better than any of the other conventional (bench mark) tests, although the situation is less clear than before because of the asymmetry of the curves.

When $a = .75$, the 60-item flexilevel test with $b_0 = -.6$ and $d = .022$ gives about as effective measurement as a

58-item standard test at $\theta = 0$,

60-item standard test at $\theta = \pm.67$,

83-item standard test at $\theta = +2$,

114-item standard test at $\theta = -2$.

At $\theta = -2$, the 60-item flexilevel test with $b_0 = .9$ and $d = .044$ is as effective as a 137-item standard test.

8.9.　CONCLUSION

Near the middle of the ability range for which the test is designed, a flexilevel test is less effective than is a comparable peaked conventional test. In the outlying half of the ability range, the flexilevel test provides more accurate measurement in typical aptitude and achievement testing situations than a peaked conventional test composed of comparable items. The advantage of flexilevel tests over conventional tests at low ability levels is significantly greater when there is guessing than when there is not.

Since most examinees lie in the center of the distribution where the peaked conventional test is superior, a flexilevel test may not have a higher reliability coefficient for the total group than the peaked conventional test. The flexilevel test is designed for situations where it is important to measure well at both high and low ability levels. As shown by the unpeaked bench mark tests in the figures, unpeaked conventional tests cannot do as well in any part of the range as a suitably designed flexilevel test. The most likely application of flexilevel tests is in situations where it would otherwise be necessary to unpeak a conventional test in an attempt to obtain adequate measurement at the extremes of the ability range. Such situations are found in nationwide college admissions testing and elsewhere.

Empirical studies need to answer such questions as the following:

1. To what extent are different types of examinees confused by flexilevel testing?
2. To what extent does flexilevel testing lose efficiency because of an increase in testing time per item?
3. How adequately can we score the examinee who does not have time to finish the test?
4. How can we score the examinee who does not follow directions?
5. What other serious inconveniences and complications are there in flexilevel testing?
6. Is the examinee's attitude and performance improved when a flexilevel test "tailors" the test difficulty level to match his ability level?

Empirical investigations should study tests designed in accordance with the theory used here. Otherwise, it is likely that a poor choice of d and especially b_0 will result in an ineffective measuring instrument.

Several empirical studies of varied merit have already been carried out, with various results. The reader is referred to Betz and Weiss (1975), where several of these are discussed, to Harris and Pennell (1977), and to Seguin (1976).

8.10. EXERCISES

Suppose the items in a flexilevel test are indexed by $i = -n + 1, -n + 2, \ldots,$ $0, \ldots, n - 1$. Suppose for all items $a = 1/1.7$, $c = .2$, and $b_i = i$. The examinee starts by taking item 0. Assume the examinee's true ability is $\theta = 0$.

8-1 Using Table 4.17.1, obtain the probability that the second item the examinee takes is item 1, and also the probability that the second item he takes is item -1.

8-2 Without using the formulas developed in this chapter, compute the probability that the third item the examinee takes is item j ($j = -2, -1, 1, 2$).

8-3 If $n = 2$ for this flexilevel test, write the relative frequency distribution $\phi(y|\theta)$ of the final scores for an examinee at $\theta = 0$.

8-4 Repeat Exercises 8-1, 8-2, 8-3 for an examinee at $\theta = -1$. Compare $\phi(y|-1)$ and $\phi(y|\theta)$ graphically.

REFERENCES

Betz, N. E., & Weiss, D. J. *Empirical and simulation studies of flexilevel ability testing*. Research Report 75-3. Minneapolis: Psychometric Methods Program, Department of Psychology, University of Minnesota, 1975.

Harris, D. A., & Pennell, R. J. *Simulated and empirical studies of flexilevel testing in Air Force technical training courses*. Report No. AFHRL-TR-77-51. Brooks Air Force Base, Texas: Human Resources Laboratory, 1977.

Seguin, S. P. *An exploratory study of the efficiency of the flexilevel testing procedure*. Unpublished doctoral dissertation, University of Toronto, 1976.

9 Two-Stage Procedures[1] and Multilevel Tests

9.1. INTRODUCTION

A two-stage testing procedure consists of a *routing* test followed by one of several alternative second-stage tests. All tests are of conventional type. The choice of the second-stage test administered is determined by the examinee's score on the routing test.

The main advantage of such a procedure lies in matching the difficulty level of the second test to the ability level of the examinee. Since conventional tests are usually at a difficulty level suitable for typical examinees in the group tested, two-stage testing procedures are likely to be advantageous chiefly at the extremes of the ability range.

One will usually want to have some way of scoring the routing test quickly, so that testing can proceed at a single session. Various paper-and-pencil procedures that do not involve electronic machinery are possible. For example, the answer sheet for the routing test can automatically produce a duplicated copy. The original copy is collected at once and later scored as the official record of the examinee's performance. The duplicate copy is retained by the examinee, who scores it according to directions given by the examiner. The score assigned by the examinee determines the second-stage test administered to him forthwith.

Two-stage testing is discussed by Cronbach and Gleser (1965, Chapter 6), using a decision theory approach. They deal primarily with a situation where examinees are to be selected or rejected. Their approach is chiefly *sequential* in

---

[1] Sections 9.1–9.8 are revised and printed with permission from F. M. Lord, A theoretical study of two-stage testing. *Psychometrika*, 1971, *36*, 227–242.

the special sense that the second-stage test is administered only to borderline examinees. The advantages of this procedure come from economy in testing time.

In contrast, the present chapter is concerned with situations where the immediate purpose of the testing is measurement, not classification. Here, the total number of test items administered to a single examinee is fixed. Any advantage of two-stage testing appears as improved measurement.

This chapter attempts to find, under specified restrictions, some good designs for two-stage testing. A "good" procedure provides reasonably accurate measurement for all examinees including those who would obtain near-perfect or near-zero (or near-chance-level) scores on a conventional test.

The particulars at our disposal in designing a two-stage testing procedure include the following:

1. The total number of items given to a single examinee (n).
2. The number of alternative second-stage tests available for use.
3. The number of alternative responses per item.
4. The number of items in the routing test (n_1).
5. The difficulty level of the routing test.
6. The method of scoring the routing test.
7. The cutting points for deciding which second-stage test an examinee will take.
8. The difficulty levels of the second-stage tests.
9. The method of scoring the entire two-stage procedure.

It does not seem feasible to locate truly optimal designs. We proceed by investigating several designs, modifying the best of these in various ways, choosing the best of the modifications, and continuing in this fashion as long as any modifications can be found that noticeably improves results.

Two different two-stage procedures will be considered in this chapter. Sections 9.2–9.8 deal with the first two-stage procedure. Sections 9.9–9.13 deal with the second.

9.2.   FIRST TWO-STAGE PROCEDURE—ASSUMPTIONS

The mathematical model to be used assumes that $P_i(\theta)$, the probability of a correct response to item i, is a three-parameter normal ogive [Eq. (2-2)]. We rewrite this as

$$P_i \equiv P_i(\theta) = c_i + (1 - c_i)\Phi[a_i(\theta - b_i)], \qquad (9\text{-}1)$$

where $\Phi(t)$ denotes the area of the standard normal curve lying below t.

For the sake of simplicity, we assume that the available items differ only in difficulty, b_i. They all have equal discrimination parameters a and equal guessing parameters c. Also, we consider here only the case where the routing test and each of the second-stage tests are *peaked;* that is, each subtest is composed of items all of equal difficulty. These assumptions mean that within a subtest all items are statistically equivalent, with item response function $P \equiv P(\theta)$. (Sections 9.9–9.13 describe an approach that avoids these restrictive assumptions.)

9.3.   SCORING

For a test composed of statistically equivalent items, number-right score x is a sufficient statistic for estimating an examinee's ability θ, regardless of the form of the item characteristic curve (Section 4.15). Thus at first sight it might seem that there is no problem in scoring a two-stage testing procedure when all subtests are peaked. It is clear, however, that different estimates of θ should be used for examinees who obtain the same number-right score on different second-stage tests having different difficulty levels.

What is needed is to find a function of the sufficient statistic x that is an unbiased estimator or at least a consistent estimator of θ. The maximum likelihood estimator, to be denoted by $\hat{\theta}$, satisfies these requirements and will be used here. (The reader who is mainly interested in the conclusions reached may skip to Section 9.5.)

For an m-item peaked subtest, the likelihood equation (4-31) becomes

$$\frac{\partial \ln L}{\partial \theta} = \frac{P'}{PQ}(x - mP) = 0,$$

where P' is the derivative of P with respect to θ. Solving, we obtain the equation

$$P(\hat{\theta}) = \frac{x}{m}. \tag{9-2}$$

Substituting (9-2) into (9-1) and solving for Φ, we have

$$\Phi[a(\hat{\theta} - b)] = \frac{x/m - c}{1 - c},$$

where a, b, and c describe each item of the peaked subtest. The maximum likelihood estimator [compare Eq. (4-36)] is found by solving for $\hat{\theta}$:

$$\hat{\theta} = \frac{1}{a}\Phi^{-1}\left(\frac{x/m - c}{1 - c}\right) + b, \tag{9-3}$$

where Φ^{-1} is the inverse of the function Φ (Φ^{-1} is the relative deviate corresponding to a given normal curve area).

Equation (9-3) gives a sufficient statistic that is also a consistent estimator of θ and has minimum variance in large samples. The separate use of (9-3) for the routing test and for the second-stage test yields two such estimates, $\hat{\theta}_1$ and $\hat{\theta}_2$, for any given examinee. These are jointly sufficient statistics for θ. They must be combined into a single estimate. In the situation at hand, it would be inefficient to discard $\hat{\theta}_1$ and use only $\hat{\theta}_2$. Unfortunately, there is no uniquely best way to combine the two jointly sufficient statistics.

For present purposes, $\hat{\theta}_1$ and $\hat{\theta}_2$ will be averaged after weighting them inversely according to their (estimated) large-sample variances. It is well known that this weighting produces a consistent estimator with approximately minimum large-sample variance (see Graybill and Deal, 1959). Thus, an examinee's score $\bar{\theta}$ on the two-stage test will be proportional to

$$\frac{\hat{\theta}_1}{\hat{V}(\hat{\theta}_1)} + \frac{\hat{\theta}_2}{\hat{V}(\hat{\theta}_2)} \, ,$$

where $\hat{V}$ is an estimate of large-sample variance, to be denoted by Var. We multiply this by $\hat{V}(\hat{\theta}_1)\hat{V}(\hat{\theta}_2)/[\hat{V}(\hat{\theta}_1) + \hat{V}(\hat{\theta}_2)]$ to obtain the examinee's overall score, defined as

$$\bar{\theta} = \frac{\hat{\theta}_1 \hat{V}(\hat{\theta}_2) + \hat{\theta}_2 \hat{V}(\hat{\theta}_1)}{\hat{V}(\hat{\theta}_1) + \hat{V}(\hat{\theta}_2)} \, . \tag{9-4}$$

The multiplying factor is chosen so that $\bar{\theta}$ is asymptotically unbiased:

$$\mathscr{E}\bar{\theta} \cong \frac{\theta \ \text{Var} \ \hat{\theta}_2 + \theta \ \text{Var} \ \hat{\theta}_1}{\text{Var} \ \hat{\theta}_1 + \text{Var} \ \hat{\theta}_2} = \theta.$$

From Eq. (5-5), for equivalent items,

$$\text{Var} \ \hat{\theta} = \frac{PQ}{mP'^2} \, . \tag{9-5}$$

From (9-1),

$$P' = (1 - c)a\phi[a(\theta - b_i)], \tag{9-6}$$

where $\phi(t)$ is the normal curve ordinate at the relative deviate t. Thus, $\hat{V}(\hat{\theta}_1)$ or $\hat{V}(\hat{\theta}_2)$ can be obtained by substituting $\hat{\theta}_1$ or $\hat{\theta}_2$, respectively, for θ in the right-hand sides of (9-5) and (9-6).

When $x = m$ (a perfect score) or $x = cm$ (a ''pseudo-chance score''), the $\hat{\theta}$ defined by (9-3) would be infinite. A crude procedure will be used to avoid this. Whenever $x = m$, x will be replaced by $x = m - \frac{1}{2}$. All scores no greater than cm will be replaced by $(l + cm)/2$ where l is the smallest integer above cm.

9.4. CONDITIONAL DISTRIBUTION OF TEST SCORE $\bar{\theta}$

If there are n_1 items in the routing test and $n_2 = n - n_1$ items in the second-stage test, there are at most $(n_1 + 1)(n_2 + 1)$ different possible numerical values for $\bar{\theta}$. Let $\bar{\theta}_{xy}$ denote the value of $\bar{\theta}$ when the number-right score on the routing test is x

and on the second-stage test is y. By Eq. (4-1), the frequency distribution of x for fixed θ is the binomial

$$\binom{n_1}{x} P^x Q^{n_1 - x},$$

where P is given by (9-1) with $a_i = a$, $c_i = c$, and b_i equal to the difficulty level (b, say) of the routing test. The distribution of y is the binomial

$$\binom{n_2}{y} P_y^y Q_y^{n_2 - y},$$

where P_y is similarly given by (9-1) with b_i equal to the difficulty level of the second-stage test, this being a numerical function of x, here denoted by $b(x)$, assigned in advance by the psychometrician.

These two binomials are independent when θ is fixed. Given numerical values for n_1, n_2, a, b, c and for $b(x)$ ($x = 0, 1, \ldots , n_1$), the exact frequency distribution p_{xy} of the examinee's score $\hat{\theta}$ for an examinee at any given ability level θ can be computed from the product of the two binomials:

$$p_{xy} \equiv \text{Prob}(\hat{\theta} = \hat{\theta}_{xy} | \theta) = \binom{n_1}{x} P^x Q^{n_1 - x} \binom{n_2}{y} P_y^y Q_y^{n_2 - y}. \qquad (9\text{-}7)$$

This frequency distribution contains all possible information relevant for choosing among the specified two-stage testing procedures.

In actual practice, it is necessary to summarize somehow the plethora of numbers computed from (9-7). This is done by using the information function for $\hat{\theta}$ given by Eq. (5-3). For given θ, the denominator of the information function is the variance of $\hat{\theta}$ given θ, computed in straightforward fashion from the known conditional frequencies (9-7). We have similarly for the numerator

$$\mathcal{E}(\hat{\theta} | \theta) = \sum_{x=0}^{n_1} \sum_{y=0}^{n_2} p_{xy} \, \hat{\theta}_{xy}.$$

Since $\hat{\theta}_{xy}$ is not a function of θ,

$$\frac{\partial}{\partial \theta} \mathcal{E}(\hat{\theta} | \theta) = \sum_{x=0}^{n_1} \sum_{y=0}^{n_2} \hat{\theta}_{xy} \frac{\partial p_{xy}}{\partial \theta}.$$

A formula for $\partial p_{xy} / \partial \theta$ is easily written from (9-7) and (9-1), from which the numerical value of the numerator of Eq. (5-3) is calculated for given θ. In this way, $I\{\theta, \hat{\theta}\}$ is evaluated numerically for all ability levels of interest.

9.5.   ILLUSTRATIVE 60-ITEM TWO-STAGE TESTS, NO GUESSING

Figure 9.5.1 shows the information functions for five different testing procedures. For $c = 0$ (no guessing), only information curves symmetrical about $\theta =$

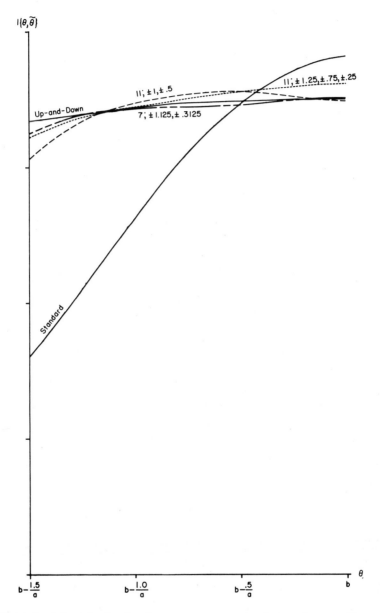

$I(\theta, \tilde{\theta})$

Up-and-Down

$11; \pm 1, \pm .5$

$7; \pm 1.125, \pm .3125$

$11; \pm 1.25, \pm .75, \pm .25$

Standard

$b-\dfrac{1.5}{a}$ $b-\dfrac{1.0}{a}$ $b-\dfrac{.5}{a}$ b θ

FIG. 9.5.1.   Information functions for some two-stage testing designs when $n = 60$, $c = 0$.

b were investigated. For this reason, only the left portion of each curve is shown in Fig. 9.5.1.

The two solid curves are benchmarks, with which the two-stage procedures are to be compared. The "standard" curve shows the information function for the number-right score on a 60-item peaked conventional test whose items all have the same difficulty level, *b*, and the same discriminating power, *a*. The "up-and-down" benchmark curve is the "best" of those obtained by the *up-and-down* method of tailored testing (see Chapter 10; the benchmark curve of Fig. 9.5.1 here is taken with permission from Fig. 7.6 of Lord, 1970).

If an examiner wants accurate measurement for typical examinees in the group tested and is less concerned about examinees at the extremes of the ability range, he should use a peaked conventional test. If a two-stage procedure is to be really valuable, it will usually be because it provides good measurement for extreme as well as for typical examinees. For this reason, an attempt was made to find two-stage procedures with information curves similar to (or better than) the "up-and-down" curve shown in the figure. For Sections 9.5 and 9.6 nearly 200 different two-stage designs were simulated for this search. Obviously, empirical investigations of 200 designs would have been out of the question.

Surprisingly, Fig. 9.5.1 shows that when there is no guessing, it is possible for a 60-item two-stage procedure to approximate the measurement efficiency of a good 60-item up-and-down tailored testing procedure throughout the ability range from $\theta = b - 1.5/a$ to $\theta = b + 1.5/a$. The effectiveness of the two-stage procedures shown falls off rather sharply outside this ability range, but this range is adequate or more than adequate for most testing purposes.

The label "11; ± 1, ± .5" indicates that the routing test contains $n_1 = 11$ items (at difficulty *b*) and that there are four alternative 49-item second-stage tests with difficulty levels $b \pm 1/a$ and $b \pm .5/a$. The cutting points on this routing test are equally spaced in terms of number-right scores, x_1: If $x_1 = 0-2$, the examinee is routed to the easiest second-stage test; if $x_1 = 3-5$, to the next easiest; and so on.

The label "7; ± 1.125, ±.3125" is similarly interpreted, the examinees being routed according to the score groupings $x_1 = 0-1$, $x_1 = 2-3$, $x_1 = 4-5$, and $x_1 = 6-7$. The label "11; ±1.25, ±.75, ±.25" similarly indicates a procedure with six alternative second-stage procedures, assigned according to the groupings $x_1 = 0-1$, $x_1 = 2-3, \ldots, x_1 = 10-11$.

A 60-item up-and-down procedure in principle requires 1830 items before testing can start; in practice, 600 items might be adequate without seriously impairing measurement. Two of the two-stage procedures shown in Fig. 9.5.1 require only slightly more than 200 items.

The two-stage procedures shown in Figure 9.5.1 are the "best" out of approximately sixty 60-item procedures studied with $c = 0$. None of the two-stage procedures that at first seemed promising according to armchair estimates turned out well. From this experience, it seems that casually designed two-stage tests are likely to provide fully effective measurement only over a relatively narrow range of ability, or possibly not at all.

9.6.   DISCUSSION OF RESULTS FOR 60-ITEM TESTS WITH NO GUESSING

Table 9.6.1 shows the information at four different ability levels obtainable from some of the better procedures. The following generalizations are plausible and should hold in most situations.

Length of Routing Test.   If the routing test is too long, not enough items are left for the second-stage test, so that measurement may be effective near $\theta = b$ but not at other ability levels. The test is not adaptive. If the routing test is too short, then examinees are poorly allocated to the second-stage tests. In this case, if the second-stage tests all have difficulty levels near b, then effective measurement may be achieved near $\theta = b$ but not at other ability levels; if the second-stage tests differ considerably in difficulty level, then the misallocation of examinees may lead to relatively poor measurement at all ability levels. The results shown in Fig. 9.5.1 and Table 9.6.1 suggest that $n_1 = 3$ is too small and $n_1 = 11$

TABLE 9.6.1
Information for Various 60-Item Testing Procedures with $c = 0$

Procedure*			Information** *at*			
			$\theta = b - 1.5/a$	$b - 1/a$	$b - 0.5/a$	b
Up-and-down (benchmark)			33.5	34.3	34.9	35.1
7;	±1.125,	±.3125	32.5	34.4	34.5	35.1
7;	±1,	±.25	31.1	34.2	35.1	35.8
7;	±1,	±.25*	27.0	31.4	35.8	37.0
7;	±1.25,	±.25	33.2	33.7	33.7	35.1
7;	± .75,	±.25	28.0	33.7	35.9	36.5
11;	±1,	±.25	30.4	34.1	35.5	36.8
11;	±1,	±.5	30.6	34.8	35.6	34.9
11;	±1.25,.	±.375	32.6	34.0	34.6	35.5
3;	± .75,	±.25	27.6	32.9	34.9	35.2
3;	± .75,	±.5	28.0	33.8	34.0	33.4
7;	± .75		28.6	34.4	34.5	31.4
7;	± .5		24.4	32.9	36.0	34.9
3;	± .5		24.5	32.5	34.5	34.4

*All cutting points are equally spaced, except for the starred procedure, which has score groups $x_1 = 0$, $x_1 = 1\text{-}3$, $x_1 = 4\text{-}6$, $x_1 = 7$.

**All information values are to be multiplied by a^2.

is too large for the range $b \pm 1.5/a$ in the situation considered, assuming that no more than four second-stage tests are used.

Number of Second Stage Tests.   There cannot usefully be more than $n_1 + 1$ second-stage tests. The number of such tests will also often be limited by considerations of economy. If there are only two second-stage tests, good measurement may be obtained in the subranges of ability best covered by these tests but not elsewhere (see "7; $\pm$ .75" in Table 9.6.1). On the other hand, a short routing test cannot make sufficiently accurate allocations to justify a large number of second-stage tests. In the present study, the number of second-stage tests was kept as low as possible; however, at least four second-stage tests were required to achieve effective measurement over the ability range considered.

Difficulty of Second-Stage Tests.   If the difficulty levels of the second-stage tests are all too close to b, there will be poor measurement at extreme ability levels (see "7; $\pm$.75, $\pm$.25" in Table 9.6.1). If the difficulty levels are too extreme, there will be poor measurement near $\theta = b$.

Cutting Points on Routing Test.   It is clearly important that the difficulty levels of the second-stage tests should match the ability levels of the examinees allocated to them, as determined by the cutting points used on the routing test. It is difficult to find an optimal match by the trial-and-error methods used here. Although many computer runs were made using unequally spaced cutting points, like those indicated in the footnote to Table 9.6.1, equally spaced cutting points turned out better. This matter deserves more careful study.

9.7.   ILLUSTRATIVE 15-ITEM TWO-STAGE TESTS WITH NO GUESSING

Some 40-odd different procedures were tried out for the case where a total of $n = 15$ items with $c = 0$ are to be administered to each examinee. The "best" of these—those with information curves near the up-and-down bench mark—are shown in Fig. 9.7.1. The bench mark here is again one of the "best" up-and-down procedures [see Stocking (1969), Fig. 2].

Table 9.7.1 shows results for various other two-stage procedures not quite so "good" as those in Fig. 9.7.1. In general, these others either did not measure well enough at extreme ability levels or else did not measure well enough at $\theta = b$. The results for $n = 15$ seem to require no further comment, since the general principles are the same as for $n = 60$.

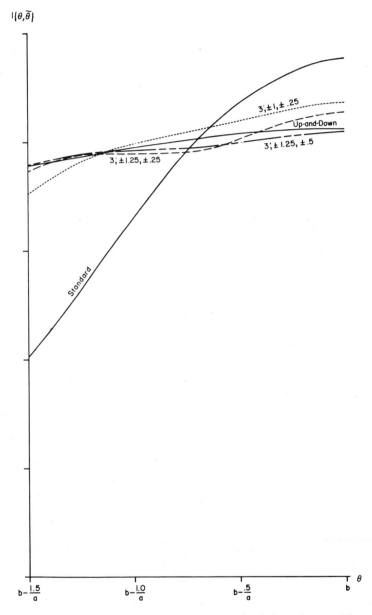

$I\{\theta,\tilde{\theta}\}$

3; ±1, ± .25

Up-and-Down

3; ± 1.25, ± .5

3; ± 1.25, ± .25

Standard

$b-\dfrac{1.5}{a}$ $b-\dfrac{1.0}{a}$ $b-\dfrac{.5}{a}$ b θ

FIG. 9.7.1.   Information functions for some two-stage testing designs when $n = 15$, $c = 0$.

137

TABLE 9.7.1
Information for Various 15-Item Testing Procedures with $c = 0$

Procedure*	Information** at			
	$\theta = b - 1.5/a$	$b - 1/a$	$b - 0.5/a$	b
Up-and-down (benchmark)	7.6	7.9	8.1	8.2
3; ±1.25, ± .5	7.6	7.8	8.0	8.2
3; ±1.25, ± .25	7.4	7.8	8.0	8.5
3; ±1, ± .25	7.0	8.0	8.4	8.7
7; ±1.25, ± .5	6.5	7.6	8.4	8.5
5; ±1.5, ±1, ±.5	7.2	7.7	8.0	8.1
4; ±1, 0*	7.1	8.0	8.0	8.0
2; ±1, 0	7.2	8.0	8.0	7.9
3; ± .25	4.8	7.1	8.7	9.1
7; ±1	6.2	7.8	8.0	7.5

*All cutting points are equally spaced, except for the starred procedure, which has score groups $x_1 = 0\text{-}1$, $x_1 = 2$, $x_1 = 3\text{-}4$.

**All information values are to be multiplied by a^2.

9.8.   ILLUSTRATIVE 60-ITEM TWO-STAGE TESTS WITH GUESSING

About 75 different 60-item two-stage procedures with $c = .20$ were tried out. The "best" of these are shown in Fig. 9.8.1 along with an appropriate bench mark procedure (see Lord, 1970, Fig. 7.8).

Apparently, when items can be answered correctly by guessing, two-stage testing procedures are not so effective for measuring at extreme ability levels as are the better up-and-down procedures. Unless some really "good" two-stage procedures were missed in the present investigation, it appears that a two-stage test might require 10 or more alternative second stages in order to measure well throughout the range shown in Fig. 9.8.1. Such tests were not studied here because the cost of producing so many second stages may be excessive. Possibly a three-stage procedure would be preferable.

When there is guessing, maximum information is likely to be obtained at an ability level higher than $\theta = b$, as is apparent from Fig. 9.8.1. This means that the examiner will probably wish to choose a value of b (the difficulty level of the routing test) somewhat below the mean ability level of the group to be tested. If a value of b were chosen near μ_θ, the mean ability level of the group, as might well be done if there were no guessing, then the two-stage procedures shown in Fig. 9.8.1 would provide good measurement for the top examinees (above $\theta = b +$

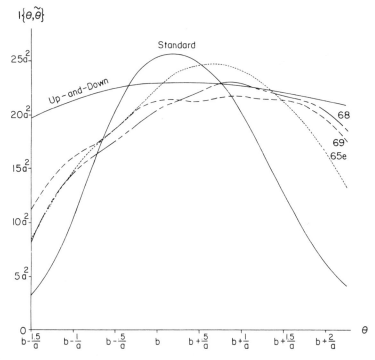

FIG. 9.8.1. Information functions for some two-stage testing designs when $n = 60$, $c = .2$.

$1/a$) but quite poor measurement for the bottom examinees (below $\theta = b - 1/a$). If an examiner wants good measurement over two or three standard deviations on each side of the mean ability level of the group, he should choose the value of b for the two-stage procedures in Fig. 9.8.1 so that μ_θ falls near $b + .75/a$. In this way, the ability levels of his examinees might be covered by the range from $\theta = b - .75/a$ to $\theta = b + 2.25/a$, for example.

The three two-stage tests shown in Fig. 9.8.1 are as follows. Test 68 has an 11-item routing test with six score groups $x_1 = 0–3, 4, 5–6, 7–8, 9–10, 11$, corresponding to six alternative second-stage tests at difficulty levels b_2 where $a(b_2 - b) = -1.35, -.65, -.325, +.25, +.75$, and $+1.5$. Test 69 has a 17-item routing test with $x_1 = 0–5, 6–7, 8–10, 11–13, 14–15, 16–17$ and $a(b_2 - b) = -1.5, -.75, -.25, +.35, +.9, +1.5$. Test 65e is an 11-item routing test with $x_1 = 0–2, 3–4, 5–6, 7–8, 9–10, 11$ and $a(b_2 - b) = -1.5, -.9, -.3, +.2, +.6, +1.0$.

A table of numerical values would be bulky and is not given here. Most of the conclusions apparent from such a table have already been stated.

9.9.   CONVERTING A CONVENTIONAL TEST TO A MULTILEVEL TEST

In many situations, the routing test can be a take-home test, answered and scored by the examinee at his leisure. This allows efficient use of the available supervised testing time. In this case, the examinee's score on the routing test cannot properly be used except for routing. If the examinee takes or scores the routing test improperly, the main effect is simply to lower the accuracy of his final (second-stage) score.

Our purpose in the rest of this chapter is to design and evaluate various hypothetical two-stage versions of the College Board Scholastic Aptitude Test, Mathematics section. College Board tests are ordinarily scored and reported in terms of College Board Scaled Scores. These scores presumably have a mean of 500 and a standard deviation of 100 for some imperfectly known historic group of examinees.

Instead of making detailed assumptions about the nature of the routing test, followed by complicated deductions about the resulting conditional distribution of routing test scores, we proceed here with some simple practical assumptions: (1) After suitable equating and scaling, the routing test yields scores on the College Board scale; (2) an examinee's routing test scaled score is (approximately) normally distributed about his true scaled score with a known standard deviation (standard error of measurement). This standard error will be taken to be 75 scaled score points, except where otherwise specified.

Since different examinees take different second-stage tests, it is necessary that all second-stage tests be equated to each other. It does not matter for present purposes whether the equating is done by conventional methods or by item characteristic curve methods (Chapter 13). We assume that after proper scaling and equating, each level of the second-stage test yields scaled scores on the College Board scale and that the expected value of each examinee's scaled score is the same regardless of the test administered to him. Although this goal of scaling and equating will never be perfectly achieved, the discrepancies should not invalidate the relative efficiency curves obtained here.

For economy of items, the second-stage tests should be overlapping. In simple cases, the basic design of the second-stage tests can be conveniently described by three quantities:

L number of second-stage tests,

n_2 number of items per second-stage test,

n total number of items.

Another quantity of interest is

m number of items common to two adjacent second-stage tests.

If, as we assume, the overlap is always the same, then

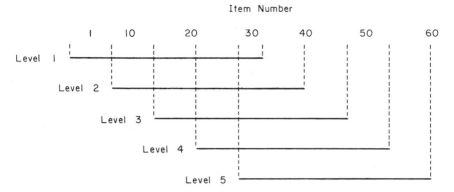

FIG. 9.9.1.   Allocation of 60 items, arranged in order of difficulty, to five over-lapping 32-item levels (second-stage tests).

$$m = \left(\frac{n_2 L - n}{L - 1} \right).$$

In practice, L, m, n_2, and n are necessarily integers. There is no cause for confusion, however, if for convenience this restriction is sometimes ignored in theoretical work.

In what follows, we frequently refer to a second-stage test as a *level*. Figure 9.9.1 illustrates a second-stage design with $L = 5$, $n_2 = 32$, $n = 60$, and $m = 25$.

If there are too many second-stage tests, the scaling and equating of these tests becomes burdensome. In any case, it will be found that there is relatively little gain from having more than a few second-stage tests.

9.10. THE RELATIVE EFFICIENCY OF A LEVEL

In order to determine the efficiency of a particular level, it is necessary to have quantitative information about the items in it. If this information is to be available before the level is constructed and administered, it is necessary that the level be described in terms of items whose parameters are known. This is most readily done by a specification, as in the following purely hypothetical example:

> Level 1 of the proposed SAT mathematics aptitude test will consist of (1) two sets of 5 items, each set having the same item parameters as the 5 easiest items in the published Form SSA 45; (2) 15 items having the same item parameters as the next 15 easiest items in Form SSA 45.

With such a specification, assuming the item parameters of Form SSA 45 to have been already estimated, it is straightforward to compute from the item parameters the efficiency of the proposed level 1, relative to Form SSA 45.

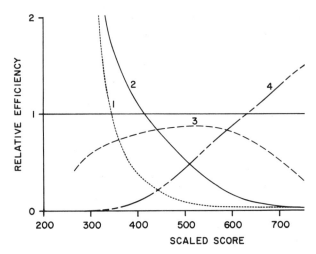

FIG. 9.10.1. Efficiency of each of the four levels of a poorly designed two-stage test, relative to Form SSA 45.

Figure 9.10.1 shows the relative efficiency curves obtained in this way for the four (second-stage) levels of a hypothetical two-stage mathematics aptitude test. This four-level test was the first trial design worked out by the writer after studying the item parameters obtained for the SAT mathematics aptitude test, Form SSA 45. It is presented here to emphasize that armchair designs of two-stage tests, even when based on more data than are usually available, are likely to be very inadequate.

The high relative efficiency of level 1 at scores below 300 was a desired part of the design. The similar high efficiency of level 2 below 300 is completely unnecessary, unplanned, and undesirable. Level 2 is too easy and too much like level 1.

The intention was that each level should reach above 100% relative efficiency for part of the score scale. Level 3 falls seriously short of this. As a result, the four-level test design would be inferior to the regular SAT for the majority of examinees. The shortcomings of level 3 could be remedied by restricting its range of item difficulty. Level 4 may be unnecessarily effective at the top of the score range and beyond. It should perhaps be easier.

9.11. DEPENDENCE OF THE TWO-STAGE TEST ON ITS LEVELS

The design inadequacies apparent in Fig. 9.10.1 can be rather easily covered up by increasing the number of levels and restricting the difficulty range of each level. After trying about a dozen different designs, the seven-level test shown in Fig. 9.11.1 was devised.

The solid curves in the figure are the relative efficiency curves for the seven levels (the lower portion of each curve is not shown). The dashed lines are relative efficiency curves for the entire seven-level two-stage test (formulas for obtaining the relative efficiency curve of the entire two-stage test from the curves of the individual levels are derived in the Appendix at the end of this chapter).

The lower dashed curve assumes the routing test score has a standard error of measurement of 90 scaled-score units. The upper curve assumes the very low value of 30. To achieve a standard error of 30, the routing test would have to be as long or longer than the present SAT—an impractical requirement included for its theoretical interest.

As mentioned earlier, subsequent results to be given here assume the standard error of measurement of the routing test to be 75 scaled-score points. This value is bracketed by the two values shown. A standard error of about 75 would be expected for a routing test consisting of 12 mathematics items.

The relationship between the efficiency curves for the individual levels and the efficiency curve of the entire two-stage test is direct and visually obvious from the figure. The effect of lowering the accuracy of the routing test is also clear and simple to visualize. The effect is less than might be expected.

Each level in Fig. 9.11.1 has only two-thirds as many items as the regular SAT mathematics aptitude test. Thus use of a two-stage test may enable us to increase the accuracy of measurement while reducing the official testing time for each examinee (ignoring the time required for the self-administered routing test, answered in advance of the regular testing).

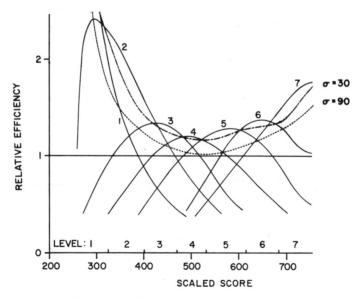

FIG. 9.11.1.   Relation between the relative efficiency of a two-stage test and the relative efficiency of the individual levels.

TABLE 9.12.1
Determination of Cutting Points for
Assigning Levels of the Two-Stage
Test in Fig. 9.11.1

Level	Scores at which RE = 1.00	Cutting Score
1	389	
		324
2	259* 465	
		400
3	335 519	
		469
4	419 577	
		531
5	485 671	
		616
6	561 759*	
		685
7	611	

*Values obtained by extrapolation.

9.12. CUTTING POINTS ON THE ROUTING TEST

In order to use a routing test for assigning examinees to levels, the score scale must be divided by cutting points that determine, for each scaled score on the routing test, the level to be assigned. There is no simple and uniquely optimal way to determine these cutting points.

A method that seems effective is illustrated in Table 9.12.1. for the multilevel test of Fig. 9.11.1. The cutting score between two adjacent levels in the table is taken to be the average of the two numbers connected by oblique lines. The cutting scores so obtained are indicated along the baseline of Fig. 9.11.1.

A convincing justification for this procedure is not immediately apparent. The procedure has been found to give good results as long as the levels are reasonably spaced and exceed a relative efficiency of 1.00 in a suitable score interval. Small changes in the cutting scores will have little effect on the RE curve of the two-stage test.

9.13. RESULTS FOR VARIOUS TWO-STAGE DESIGNS

Further experimentation with different designs shows that, with care, good results can be achieved with a two-stage test having only three or four (second-

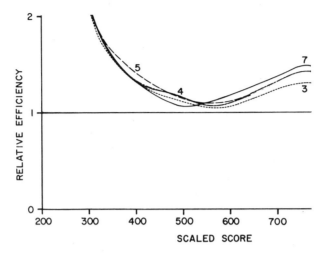

FIG. 9.13.1.   Relative efficiency of each of four hypothetical two-stage SAT Mathematics tests.

stage) levels. Relative efficiency curves for four different two-stage test designs are shown in Fig. 9.13.1. The curves were obtained in an effort to raise the lowest point of the curve without changing its general overall shape. It is probably not possible to make any great improvement from this point of view on the designs shown. This may account for the fact that the four curves shown differ little from each other. It would, of course, be easy to design two-stage tests with very differently shaped curves, if that were desired.

The identifying number on each curve in Figure 9.13.1 is its L value, the number of levels. The four designs shown are partially described in Table 9.13.1. A full description of each two-stage test would require listing all item parameters for each level and would not add much of value to the illustrative examples given.

TABLE 9.13.1
Description of Two-Stage Designs Shown in Fig. 9.13.1

Number of levels L	Total number of items n	Number of items per level n_2	Minimum RE
3	102	45	1.045
4	114	45	1.076
5	114	45	1.101
7	123	41	1.074

9.14. OTHER RESEARCH

Marco (1977) describes a "multilevel" test that resembles a two-stage test except that there is no routing test; instead, each examinee routes himself to levels that seem of appropriate difficulty to him. Item response theory cannot predict how a person will route himself. The present results may nevertheless be relevant if his errors in self-routing are similar to the errors made by some kind of routing test.

Empirical studies of two-stage testing are reported by Linn, Rock, and Cleary (1969) and by Larkin and Weiss (1975). Other studies are cited in these references. A simulation study of two-stage testing is reported by Betz and Weiss (1974).

Simulation studies in general confirm, or at least do not disagree with, conclusions reached here. Empirical studies frequently do not yield clear-cut results. This last might well be expected whenever total group reliability or validity coefficients are used to compare two-stage tests with conventional tests.

If the conventional test contains a wide spread of item difficulties, the two-stage test may be better at all ability levels, in which case it will have higher total-group reliability. If the conventional test is somewhat peaked at the appropriate difficulty level, however, it will be better than the two-stage test at moderate ability levels where most of the examinees are found; the two-stage test will be better at the extremes of the ability range. The two-stage test will in this case probably show lower total-group reliability than the conventional test, because most of the group is at the ability level where the conventional test is peaked.

Two-stage tests will be most valuable in situations where the group tested has a wider range of ability than can be measured effectively by a peaked conventional test.

9.15. EXERCISES

9-1   If $a = .8$, $b = 0$, $c = .2$, what is the maximum likelihood estimate (9-3) of ability when the examinee answers 25% of the items correctly on the routing test? 50%? 60%? 70%? 80%; 90%?

9-2   What is the square root of the estimated sampling variance of the maximum likelihood estimates found in Exercise 9-1, as estimated by substituting $\hat{\theta}$ for θ in (9-5) with $m = 9$? Comment on your results.

9-3   Suppose the three cutting scores on a seven-item routing test divide the score range as follows: 0–1, 2–3, 4–5, 6–7. If $a = .8$, $b = 0$, and $c = .2$, what proportion of examinees at $\theta = 0$ will take each of the four second-stage tests? At $\theta = +2$? At $\theta = -2$?

APPENDIX

Information Functions for the Two-Stage Tests of Sections 9.9–9.13

An individual's score on a two-stage test of the type discussed in Sections 9.9–9.13 is simply his score on the second stage. As already noted, it is assumed here that (after scaling and equating) this score, to be denoted by y, is expressed on the College Board scale. In this case, the true score for y, to be denoted by η, is the true (College Board) scaled score.

The scaled score y is a linear function of the number-right observed score. (When the observed score is a formula score involving a "correction for guessing," this statement will still be correct if we restrict consideration to examinees who answer all items, as discussed in detail in Chapter 15.) Since y is a linear function of number-right observed score, η is a linear function of number-right true score. Thus [Eq. (4-5)], η is a monotonic increasing function of ability θ.

Instead of using an information function on the θ scale of ability, it will be convenient here to use an information function on the η scale of ability (see Section 6.5). To compute the required information function $I\{\eta, y\}$, we need formulas for $\mu_{y|\eta}$ and for $\sigma_{y|\eta}$, where y is the (scaled) score on the level (second-stage test) assigned to the examinee.

We have assumed that the equating is carried out so that an examinee's score y has the same expected value regardless of the level administered to him. Let l denote the level administered ($l = 1, 2, \ldots, L$) and y_l, the score obtained on that level. By definition of true score, $\mu(y_l|\eta) = \eta$ for each examinee and each level. It follows that the expected score of an examinee across levels is $\mu_{y|\eta} = \eta$, also.

By a common identity from analysis of variance,

$$\sigma_{y|\eta}^2 = \sum_{l=1}^{L} p_{l|\eta} \operatorname{Var}(y_l|\eta) + \text{variance across levels of } \mu(y_l|\eta),$$

where $p_{l|\eta}$ is the probability that an examinee with true score η will be assigned to level l. Since $\mu(y_l|\eta)$ is constant, the last term is zero. Thus the denominator of $I\{\eta, y\}$ is

$$\sigma_{y|\eta}^2 = \sum_{l=1}^{L} p_{l|\eta} \operatorname{Var}(y_l|\eta).$$

The numerator of $I\{\eta, y\}$ is the square of $d\mu_{y|\eta}/d\eta = 1$. Thus the desired information function on η for the entire two-stage testing procedure is

$$I\{\eta, y\} = \frac{1}{\sum_{l=1}^{L} p_{l|\eta} \operatorname{Var}(y_{l|\eta})}. \tag{9-8}$$

The information function on η for a single second-stage test ("level") is clearly

$$I\{\eta, y_l\} = \frac{1}{\text{Var}\ (y_l|\eta)}. \tag{9-9}$$

Thus the information function on η for the entire two-stage testing procedure is the harmonic mean of the L information functions $I\{\eta, y_l\}$ for the L separate second-stage tests. In forming the harmonic mean, the L levels are weighted according to the probability $p_{l|\eta}$ of their occurrence.

In the particular problem at hand, it was assumed that the routing test score was normally distributed about η with known standard deviation. Once some set of cutting scores for the routing has been chosen as, for example, in Table 9.12.1, the probabilities $p_{l|\eta}$ are readily found from normal curve tables.

Let x_l denote number-right score on second-stage test l ($l = 1, 2, \ldots, L$). Since scaled-score y_l is a linear function of x_l, we write $y_l = A_l + B_l x_l$ and $\eta_l = A_l + B_l \xi_l$, where A_l and B_l are the constants used to place x_l on the College Board scale. The conditional variance of x_l when $\eta = \eta_o$ is

$$\text{Var}\ (x_l|\eta_o) = \text{Var}\ (x_l|\theta_o),$$

where, because of Eq. (4-5), θ_o is defined in terms of η_o by

$$\eta_o = A_l + B_l \xi_o = A_l + B_l \sum_i^{(l)} P_i (\theta_o), \tag{9-10}$$

the summation $\Sigma_i^{(l)}$ being over all items in test l. By Eq. (4-3),

$$\text{Var}\ (x_l|\theta_o) = \Sigma_i^{(l)}\ P_i(\theta_o)Q_i(\theta_o).$$

Thus, once the item response parameters have been determined, we can compute $I\{\eta, y_l\}$ from (9-9), (9-10), and

$$\text{Var}\ (y_l|\eta_o) = B_l^2\ \text{Var}\ (x_l|\eta_o) = B_l^2 \sum_i^{(l)} P_i (\theta_o)Q_i(\theta_o). \tag{9-11}$$

REFERENCES

Betz, N. E., & Weiss, D. J. *Simulation studies of two-stage ability testing*. Research Report 74-4. Minneapolis: Psychometric Methods Program, Department of Psychology, University of Minnesota, 1974.

Cronbach, L. J., & Gleser, G. C. *Psychological tests and personnel decisions* (2nd ed.). Urbana, Ill.: University of Illinois Press, 1965.

Graybill, F. A., & Deal, R. Combining unbiased estimators. *Biometrics*, 1959, *15*, 543–550.

Larkin, K. C., & Weiss, D. J. *An empirical comparison of two-stage and pyramidal adaptive ability testing*. Research Report 75-1. Minneapolis: Psychometric Methods Program, Department of Psychology, University of Minnesota, 1975.

Linn, R. L., Rock, D. A., & Cleary, T. A. The development and evaluation of several programmed testing methods. *Educational and Psychological Measurement,* 1969, *29,* 129–146.

Lord, F. M. Some test theory for tailored testing. In W. H. Holtzman (Ed.), *Computer assisted instruction, testing, and guidance.* New York: Harper and Row, 1970.

Marco, G. L. Item characteristic curve solutions to three intractable testing problems. *Journal of Educational Measurement,* 1977, *14,* 139–160.

Stocking, M. *Short tailored tests.* Research Bulletin 69-63 and Office of Naval Research Technical Report N00014-69-C-0017. Princeton, N.J.: Educational Testing Service, 1969.

10 Tailored Testing

10.1. INTRODUCTION[1]

It seems likely that in the not too distant future many mental tests will be administered and scored by computer. Computerized instruction will be common, and it will be convenient to use computers to administer achievement tests also.

The computer can test many examinees simultaneously with the same or with different tests. If desired, each examinee can be allowed to answer test questions at his own rate of speed. This situation opens up new possibilities. The computer can do more than simply administer a predetermined set of test items. Given a pool of precalibrated items to choose from, the computer can design a different test for each examinee.

An examinee is measured most effectively when the test items are neither too difficult nor too easy for him. Thus for any given psychological trait the computer's main task at each step of the test administration might be to estimate tentatively the examinee's level on the trait, on the basis of his responses to whatever items have already been administered. The computer could then choose the next item to be administered on the basis of this tentative estimate.

Such testing has been called adaptive testing, branched testing, individualized testing, programmed testing, sequential item testing, response-contingent testing, and computerized testing. Clearly, the procedure could be implemented

---

[1]This section is a revised version of the introductory section in F. M. Lord, Some test theory for tailored testing. In W. H. Holtzman (Ed.), *Computer assisted instruction, testing, and guidance.* New York: Harper and Row, 1970, pp. 139–183. Used by permission.

without a computer. Here, emphasizing the key feature, we shall speak of *tailored testing*. This term was suggested by William W. Turnbull in 1951.

It should be clear that there are important differences between testing for instructional purposes and testing for measurement purposes. The virtue of an instructional test lies ultimately in its effectiveness in changing the examinee. At the end we would like him to be able to answer every test item correctly. A measuring instrument, on the other hand, should not alter the trait being measured. Moreover (see Section 10.2), measurement is most effective when the examinee only knows the answers to about half of the test items. The discussion here is concerned exclusively with measurement problems and not at all with instructional testing.

10.2.   MAXIMIZING INFORMATION

Suppose we have a pool of calibrated items. Which single item from the pool will add the most to the test information function at a given ability level?

According to Eq. (5-6), each item contributes independently to the test information function $I\{\theta\}$. This contribution is given by

$$I\{\theta, u_i\} = \frac{P_i'^2}{P_i Q_i} , \tag{5-9}$$

the item information function. To answer the question asked, compute Eq. (5-9) for each item in the pool and then pick the item that gives the most information at the required ability level θ. It is useful here to discuss the maximum of the item information function in some detail, so as to provide background for tailored testing applications.

Under the logistic model [Eq. (2-1)] when there is no guessing, $P_i' = Da_i P_i Q_i$. The item information function [Eq. (5-9)] is thus

$$I\{\theta, u_i\} = D^2 a_i^2 P_i(\theta) Q_i(\theta). \tag{10-1}$$

Now, $P_i Q_i$ is a maximum when $P_i = .5$. It follows that *when there is no guessing, an item gives its maximum information for those examinees who have a 50% chance of answering correctly*. When $P_i(\theta) = .5$, we have $\theta = b_i$. Thus, when there is no guessing, an item gives its maximum information for examinees whose ability θ is equal to the item difficulty b_i. All statements in this paragraph may be shown to hold for the normal ogive model also.

The maximum information, to be denoted by M_i, for the logistic model with no guessing is seen from (10-1) to be

$$M_i = \frac{D^2 a_i^2}{4} = .722 a_i^2. \tag{10-2}$$

For the normal ogive model with no guessing,

$$M_i = \frac{2a_i^2}{\pi} = .637a_i^2. \tag{10-3}$$

Note that maximum information M_i is proportional to the square of the item discriminating power a_i. Thus an item at the proper difficulty level with $a_i = 1.0$ is worth as much as four items with $a_i = .5$.

On a certain item, suppose that examinees guess at random with probability p of success whenever they do not know the correct answer. (Item response theory does *not* use this assumption; it is used here only as a bench mark.) According to this supposition, the actual proportion of correct answers to the item at ability level θ will be $P_i(\theta) + pQ_i(\theta)$. Accordingly, a common rule of thumb for test design is that the average "item difficulty" (= proportion of correct answers in the group tested) should be .5 when there is no guessing and $\frac{1}{2}(1 + p)$ when there is random guessing with chance of success p. Let us check this rule using item information functions.

It is not difficult to show (Birnbaum, 1968, Eq. 20.4.21) for the three-parameter logistic model that an item gives maximal information at ability level $\theta = \theta_i$ where

$$\theta_i = b_i + \frac{1}{Da_i} \ln \frac{1 + \sqrt{1 + 8c_i}}{2}. \tag{10-4}$$

When $c_i = 0$, the item gives maximal information when $\theta = b_i$. When $c_i \neq 0$, $\theta_i > b_i$. The distance from the item difficulty level b_i to the optimal θ_i is inversely proportional to the item discriminating power a_i.

It is readily found from (10-4) that when ability and item difficulty b_i are optimally matched, the proportion of correct answers is

$$P_i(\theta_i) = \frac{1}{4}(1 + \sqrt{1 + 8c_i}). \tag{10-5}$$

If we substitute c_i for p in the old rule of thumb for test design and subtract the results from (10-5), the difference vanishes for $c_i = 0$ and for $c_i = 1$; for all other permissible values of c_i, $P_i(\theta_i)$ exceeds the probability given by the rule of thumb. Thus, under the logistic model, an item will be maximally informative for examinees whose probability of success is somewhat greater than $\frac{1}{2}(1 + c_i)$. Some typical values for $P_i(\theta_i)$ are

c_i:	0	.1	.15	.2	.25	.333	.5
$\frac{1}{2}(1 + c_i)$:	.500	.55	.575	.60	.625	.667	.75
$P_i(\theta_i)$:	.500	.585	.621	.653	.683	.729	.809

It can be shown by straightforward algebra that the most information that can be provided by a logistic item with specified parameters a_i and c_i is

$$M_i = \frac{D^2 a_i^2}{8(1 - c_i)^2} [1 - 20c_i - 8c_i^2 + (1 + 8c_i)^{3/2}]. \tag{10-6}$$

Typical maximal values can be inferred from the following list:

c_i:	0	.1	.167	.2	.25	.333	.5
$\dfrac{M_i}{a_i^2}$:		.72	.60	.52	.49	.45	.38	.26

If items of optimal difficulty are used to measure an examinee, items with $c_i = .25$ will give only .63 as much information as free-response items ($c_i = 0$). Items with $c_i = .50$ will give only .36 as much information.

Results for the three-parameter normal ogive cannot be written in simple form. The general picture discussed above remains unchanged, however.

10.3. ADMINISTERING THE TAILORED TEST

Consider now the tailored testing of a single examinee. If we know nothing about him, we may administer first an item of middle difficulty from the available item pool. If we have information about the examinee's educational level, or some other relevant fact, we may be able to pick a first item that is better matched to his ability level. Unless the test is very short, a poor choice of the first item will have little effect on the final result.

If the examinee answers the first item incorrectly (correctly), we suppose that it is hard (easy) for him, so we choose an easier (harder) item to administer next. If he answers this incorrectly (correctly) also, we next administer a still easier (harder) item, and so on.

There will be no finite maximum likelihood estimate of the examinee's ability as long as his answers are all correct or all incorrect. Such a situation will not continue very long, however: If successive decrements (increments) in item difficulty are sizable, as they should be, we will soon be administering items at an extreme level of difficulty or easiness.

Once the examinee has given at least one right answer and at least one wrong answer, it is usually possible to solve the likelihood Eq. (5-19) for θ, obtaining a finite maximum likelihood estimate, denoted by $\hat{\theta}$, of the examinee's ability. Since Eq. (5-19) is an equation in just one unknown (θ), it may be readily solved by numerical methods.

Samejima (1973) has pointed out that in certain cases the likelihood equation may have no finite root or may have both a finite and an infinite root (see end of Section 4.13). If this occurs, we can follow Samejima's suggestion (1977) and administer next an extremely easy item if $\hat{\theta} = -\infty$ or an extremely hard item if $\hat{\theta} = +\infty$. This procedure (repeated if necessary) should quickly give a usable ability estimate without danger of further difficulties. Such difficulties are extremely rare, once the number of items administered is more than 10 or 15.

As soon as we have a maximum likelihood estimate $\hat{\theta}$ of the examinee's ability, we can evaluate the information function of each item in the pool at $\theta = \hat{\theta}$. We administer next the item that gives the most information at $\hat{\theta}$. When the examinee has responded to this new item, we can reestimate $\hat{\theta}$ and repeat the procedure. When enough items have been administered, the final $\hat{\theta}$ is the examinee's score. All such scores are on the same scale for all examinees, even though different examinees may have taken totally different sets of items.

10.4. CALIBRATING THE TEST ITEMS

The pool of items available to the computer must be very much larger than the number n of items administered to any one examinee. If the pool contains 200 or more items, it may be impractical to calibrate the items by administering them all simultaneously to a single group of examinees. In certain cases, furthermore, the range of item difficulty may be too great for administration to a single group: Low-ability examinees, for example, who are needed to calibrate the easy items, might find the very hard items intolerable.

When different items are calibrated on different groups of examinees, the calibrations will in general not be comparable, because of the essential indeterminacy of origin and scale from group to group (see Section 3.5). There are many special ways to design test administrations so that the data can be pieced together to place all the estimated parameters on the same scale. A simple design might be as follows.

Divide the entire pool of items to be calibrated into K modules. If a very wide range of item difficulty is to be covered, modules 1, 2, . . . , $\frac{1}{2}K$ should increase in difficulty from module to module; $\frac{1}{2}K$, $\frac{1}{2}K + 1$, . . . , K should decrease in difficulty. Form a subtest by combining modules 1 and 2; another by combining modules 2 and 3; another by combining 3 and 4, . . . ; another by combining $K - 1$ and K. Form a Kth subtest by combining modules K and 1. Administer the K subtests to K nonoverlapping groups of examinees, giving a different subtest to each group.

With this design, each item is taken by two groups of examinees. Each group of examinees shares items with two other groups. This interlocking makes it possible to estimate all item parameters and all ability parameters by maximum likelihood simultaneously in a single computer run (but see Chapter 13 Appendix for a procedure to accelerate iterative convergence). Thus all item parameters are placed on the same scale without any inefficient piecing together of estimates from different sources.

10.5. A BROAD-RANGE TAILORED TEST

Two parallel forms of a tailored test of verbal ability have been built, using the principles outlined in the preceding sections. A main feature is that this test is appropriate at any level of verbal ability from fourth grade up through graduate school.

Many of the test items for grades 4 to 12 were obtained from the *Cooperative School and College Ability Tests* and the *Cooperative Sequential Tests of Educational Progress*. The remaining items were obtained from the College Board's *Preliminary SAT*, their regular *SAT*, and the *Graduate Record Examination.*

A total of more than 1000 verbal items were available from these sources. All items were calibrated and put on the same scale by piecing together scraps of data available from various regular test administrations and from various equating studies. The resulting item parameter estimates are not so accurate as could have been obtained by the procedure outlined in the preceding section; this would have required a large amount of special testing, however.

A very few items with very poor discriminating power a_i were discarded. A better test could have been constructed by keeping only a few hundred of the most discriminating items (as done by Urry, 1974). Here, this was considered undesirable in principle because of the economic cost of discarding hundreds of test items.

Additional items were discarded because they were found to duplicate material covered by other items. The remaining 900 items were arranged in order of difficulty (b_i) and then grouped on difficulty into 10 groups.

All items in the most extreme groups were retained because of a scarcity of very difficult and very easy items. At intermediate difficulty levels, many more items were available than were really needed for the final item pool. Although all items could have been retained, 50 items were chosen at random from each difficulty level for use in the final pool for the broad-range tailored test, thus freeing the other items for other uses. Note again that this selection was made at random and not on the basis of item discriminating power, for the reason outlined in a preceding paragraph.

A total of 363 items were selected by this procedure. Five different item types were represented. Within each of the 10 difficulty levels, items of a given item type were grouped into pairs of approximately equal difficulty (b_i). Two parallel item pools were then formed by assigning one item from each pair at random to each pool. The two pools thus provide two parallel forms for the broad-range tailored test.

Each of the two item pools has exactly 25 items at each difficulty level, except for extreme levels where there are insufficient items. This makes it possible to administer 25 items to an examinee, all or most at a difficulty level appropriate for him. In using the broad-range tailored test, exactly 25 items are administered to each examinee.

If the items given to one examinee were selected solely on the basis of $I\{\theta, \hat{\theta}\}$, it could happen by chance, in an extreme case, that examinee A might receive only items of type C and examinee B might receive only items of type D. If this happened, it would cast considerable doubt on any comparison of the two examinees' "verbal ability" scores. One good way to avoid this problem would be to require that the first item administered to any examinee always be of type

C, the second item always be of type *D*, and so forth. This would assure that all examinees take the same number of items of each type. A practical approximation to this was implemented for the broad-range tailored test. The details need not be spelled out here.

Once a maximum likelihood estimate of the examinee's ability is available, as described in Section 10.3, the item to be administered next is thereafter always the item *of the required item type* that gives the most information at the currently estimated ability level $\hat{\theta}$. If one item in the pool has optimal difficulty level (10.4) at $\hat{\theta}$ but another item is more discriminating, the latter item may give more information at $\hat{\theta}$ and may thus be the one selected to be administered next. Note that this procedure tends to administer the most discriminating items (highest a_i) first and the least discriminating items last or not at all.

10.6. SIMULATION AND EVALUATION

For the flexilevel tests and for the two-stage tests of preceding chapters, it is possible to write formulas for computing the (conditional) mean and variance of the final test score for people at any specified ability level. The information function can then be evaluated from these. Some early theoretical work in tailored testing was done in the same way. The up-and-down branching method (Lord, 1970) and the Robbins–Monro branching method (Lord, 1971) both have formulas for the small-sample conditional mean and variance of the final test score.

The method used here for choosing items, while undoubtedly more efficient than the up-and-down or the Robbins–Monro methods, does not appear to permit calculation of the required mean and variance. Thus, any comparative evaluation of procedures here must depend on Monte Carlo estimates of the required mean and variance, obtained by computer simulation. Monte Carlo methods are more expensive and less accurate than exact formulas. Monte Carlo methods should be avoided whenever formulas can be obtained.

Simulated tailored testing can be carried out as follows. A set of equally spaced ability levels are chosen for study. The following procedure is repeated independently for each ability level θ.

Some way of selecting the first item to be administered is specified. The known parameters of the first items administered are used to compute $P_1(\theta)$, the probability of a correct response to item 1 for examinees at the chosen θ level. A hypothetical observation $u_{1a} = 0$ or $u_{1a} = 1$ is drawn at random with probability of success $P_1(\theta)$. This specifies the response of examinee *a* (at the specified ability level θ) to the first item. The second item to be administered is chosen by the rules of Section 10.3. Then $P_2(\theta)$ is computed, and a value of u_{2a} is drawn at random with probability of success $P_2(\theta)$. The entire process is repeated until $n = 25$ items have been administered to examinee *a*. According to the rules of

Section 10.3, this will involve the computation of many successive maximum likelihood estimates $\hat{\theta}_a$ of the ability of examinee a. The successive $\hat{\theta}_a$ are used to select the items to be administered but not in the computation of $P_i(\theta)$. The final $\hat{\theta}_a$, based on the examinee's responses to all 25 items, is his final test score.

In the simulations reported here, the foregoing procedure was repeated independently for 200 examinees at each of 13 different θ levels. At each θ level, the mean m and variance s^2 of the 200 final scores were computed. In principle, if the θ levels are not too far apart, the information function at each chosen level of θ can be approximated from these results, using the formula (compare Section 5.2)

$$I\{\theta, \hat{\theta}\} \approx \frac{[m(\hat{\theta}|\theta_{+1}) - m(\hat{\theta}|\theta_{-1})]^2}{(\theta_{+1} - \theta_{-1})^2 \, s^2(\hat{\theta}|\theta_0)} \quad , \tag{10-7}$$

where θ_{-1}, θ_0, and θ_{-1} denote successive levels of θ, not too far apart. This formula uses a common numerical approximation to the derivative of $m(\hat{\theta}|\theta)$.

Both $\mu\,(\hat{\theta}|\theta)$ and $\sigma^2(\hat{\theta}|\theta)$ can be estimated by the Monte Carlo method from 200 final scores with fair accuracy. The difference in the numerator of (10-7) is a quite unstable estimator, however, because of loss of significant figures due to cancellation. This is a serious disadvantage of Monte Carlo evaluation of test procedures and designs.

In the present case, it was found that $\mu(\hat{\theta}|\theta)$ was close to θ, showing that $\hat{\theta}$ is a reasonably unbiased estimator of θ. Under such conditions [see Eq. (5-8)], the information function is inversely proportional to the error variance $\sigma^2(\hat{\theta}|\theta)$. Results here are therefore presented in terms of estimated error variance (Fig. 10.7.1) or its reciprocal (Fig. 10.7.2).

10.7.   RESULTS OF EVALUATION

A proper choice of starting point was often an important concern in previous studies of tailored testing (Lord, 1970, 1971). If the first item b_i is too far from the ability level of the examinee, up-and-down and Robbins–Monro branching processes sometimes waste many items before finding the proper ability level. This is especially true whenever a low-ability examinee by lucky guessing answers correctly the first four or five items administered.

Figure 10.7.1[2] shows the effect of starting point on the standard error of measurement $s(\hat{\theta}|\theta)$ for the broad-range tailored test. The points marked + were obtained when the difficulty level of the first item administered was near -1.0 on

---

[2]Figures 10.7.1 and 10.7.2, also the accompanying explanations, are taken with permission from F. M. Lord, A broad-range tailored test of verbal ability. In C. L. Clark (Ed.), *Proceedings of the First Conference on Computerized Adaptive Testing.* Washington, D.C.: United States Civil Service Commission, 1976, pp. 75–78; also *Applied Psychological Measurement,* 1977, *1,* 95–100.

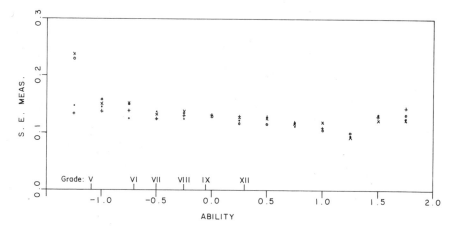

FIG. 10.7.1.   The standard error of measurement at 13 different ability levels for four different starting points for the 25-item broad-range tailored test.

the horizontal scale—about fifth-grade level. The small dots represent the results when the difficulty level of the first item was near 0—about ninth-grade level. For the hexagons, it was near .75—near the average verbal ability level of college applicants taking the College Entrance Examination Board's Scholastic Aptitude Test. For the points marked by an *x*, it was near 1.5. For any given ability level, the standard error of measurement varies surprisingly little, considering the extreme variation in starting item difficulty. We see that the difficulty level of the first item administered is not likely to be a serious problem for the kind of tailored testing recommended here.

It is important to compare the broad-range tailored test with a conventional test. Let us compare it with a 25-item version of the Preliminary Scholastic Aptitude Test of the College Entrance Examination Board. Figure 10.7.2 shows the information function for the Verbal score on each of three forms of the PSAT adjusted to a test length of just 25 items and also the approximate information function for the verbal score on the broad-range tailored test, which administers just 25 items to each examinee. The PSAT information functions are computed from estimated item parameters; the tailored test information function is the reciprocal of the squared standard error of measurement from Monte Carlo results. The tailored test shown in Fig. 10.7.2 corresponds to the hexagons of Fig. 10.7.1.

This tailored test is at least twice as good as a 25-item conventional PSAT at almost all ability levels. This is not surprising: At the same time that we are tailoring the test to fit the individual, we are taking advantage of the large item pool, using the best 25 items available within certain restrictions on item type. Because we are selecting only the best items, the comparison may be called unfair to the PSAT. It is not clear, however, how a "fair" evaluation of the tailored test is to be made.

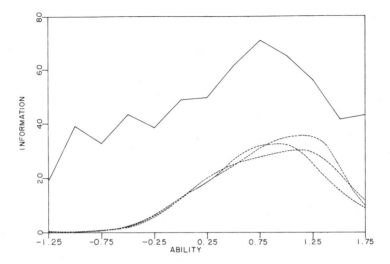

FIG. 10.7.2.   Information function for the 25-item tailored test, also for three forms of the Preliminary Scholastic Aptitude Test (dotted lines) adjusted to a test length of 25 items.

Part of the advantage of the tailored test is due to matching the difficulty of the items administered to the ability level of the examinee. Part is due to selecting the most discriminating items. A study of a hypothetical broad-range tailored test composed of items all having the same discriminating power would throw light on this problem. It would show how much gain could be expected solely from matching item difficulty to ability level.

The advantages of selecting the best items from a large item pool are made clear by the following result. Suppose each examinee answers just 25 items, but these are selected from the combined pool of 363 items rather than from the pool of 183 items used for Fig. 10.7.2. Monte Carlo results show that the tailored test with the doubled item pool will give at least twice as much information as the 25-item tailored test of Fig. 10.7.2. Selecting the best items from a 363-item pool gives a better set of 25 items than selecting from a 183-item pool.

If it is somehow uneconomical to make heavy use of the most discriminating items in a pool, one could require that item selection should be based only on item difficulty and not on information or discriminating power. If this restriction is not accepted, it is not clear how adjustment should be made for size of item pool when comparing different tailored tests.

10.8.   OTHER WORK ON TAILORED TESTS

It is not appropriate here to give a complete list of references on tailored testing. Deserving special attention are work for the U.S. Civil Service Commission by Urry and others and also work for the Office of Naval Research by Weiss and others. Selected reports from these sources and others are included in the list of references. For good recent reviews of tailored testing, see McBride (1976) and Killcross (1976).

REFERENCES

Birnbaum, A. Estimation of an ability. In F. M. Lord & M. R. Novick, *Statistical theories of mental test scores*. Reading, Mass.: Addison-Wesley, 1968.

Clark, C. (Ed.). *Proceedings of the First Conference on Computerized Adaptive Testing*. Professional Series 75-6. Washington, D.C.: U.S. Government Printing Office, 1976.

Cliff, N., Cudeck, R. A., & McCormick, D. *Implied orders as a basis for tailored testing*. Technical Report No. 6. Los Angeles: University of Southern California, 1978.

Davis, C. E., Hickman, J., & Novick, M. R. *A primer on decision analysis for individually prescribed instruction*. Technical Bulletin No. 17. Iowa City, Iowa: Research and Development Division, The American College Testing Program, 1973.

DeWitt, L. J., & Weiss, D. J. *A computer software system for adaptive ability measurement*. Research Report 74-1. Minneapolis: Psychometric Methods Program, Department of Psychology, University of Minnesota, 1974.

Gorham, W. A. (Chair). *Computers and testing: Steps toward the inevitable conquest*. Professional Series 76-1. Washington, D.C.: Research Section, Personnel Research and Development Center, U.S. Civil Service Commission, 1976.

Green, B. F., Jr. Comments on tailored testing. In W. H. Holtzman (Ed.), *Computer-assisted instruction, testing, and guidance*. New York: Harper and Row, 1970.

Killcross, M. C. *A review of research in tailored testing*. Report APRE No. 9/76. Franborough, Hants, England: Ministry of Defense, Army Personnel Research Establishment, 1976.

Koch, W. R., & Reckase, M. D. *A live tailored testing comparison study of the one- and three-parameter logistic models*. Research Report 78-1. Columbia, Mo.: Tailored Testing Research Laboratory, Educational Psychology Department, University of Missouri, 1978.

Lord, F. M. Some test theory for tailored testing. In W. H. Holtzman (Ed.), *Computer-assisted instruction, testing, and guidance*. New York: Harper and Row, 1970.

Lord, F. M. Robbins-Monro procedures for tailored testing. *Educational and Psychological Measurement*, 1971, *31*, 3-31.

McBride, J. R. *Research on adaptive testing, 1973-1976: A review of the literature*. Unpublished report. Minneapolis: University of Minnesota, 1976.

McBride, J. R. *An adaptive test of arithmetic reasoning*. Paper prepared for the Nineteenth Annual Conference of the Military Testing Association, San Antonio, Texas, 1977.

McBride, J. R., & Weiss, D. J. *A word knowledge item pool for adaptive ability measurement*. Research Report 74-2. Minneapolis: Psychometric Methods Program, Department of Psychology, University of Minnesota, 1974.

McBride, J. R., & Weiss, D. J. *Some properties of a Bayesian adaptive ability testing strategy*. Research Report 76-1. Minneapolis: Psychometric Methods Program, Department of Psychology, University of Minnesota, 1976.

Mussio, J. J. *A modification to Lord's model for tailored tests*. Unpublished doctoral dissertation, University of Toronto, 1973.

Samejima, F. A comment on Birnbaum's three-parameter logistic model in the latent trait theory. *Psychometrika*, 1973, *38*, 221-233.

Samejima, F. A use of the information function in tailored testing. *Applied Psychological Measurement*, 1977, *1*, 233-247.

Urry, V. W. *Computer assisted testing: The calibration and evaluation of the verbal ability bank*.

Technical Study 74-3. Washington, D.C.: Research Section, Personnel Research and Development Center, 1974.

Urry, V. W. Tailored testing: A successful application of latent trait theory. *Journal of Educational Measurement,* 1977, *14,* 181–186.

Vale, C. D., & Weiss, D. J. *A simulation study of stradaptive ability testing.* Research Report 75-6. Minneapolis: Psychometric Methods Program, Department of Psychology, University of Minnesota, 1975.

Weiss, D. J. *Strategies of adaptive ability measurement.* Research Report 74-5. Minneapolis: Psychometric Methods of Program, Department of Psychology, University of Minnesota, 1974.

Weiss, D. J. (Ed.). *Computerized adaptive trait measurement: Problems and prospects.* Research Report 75-5. Minneapolis: Psychometric Methods Program, Department of Psychology, University of Minnesota, 1975.

Weiss, D. J. (Ed.). *Applications of computerized adaptive testing.* Research Report 77-1. Minneapolis: Psychometric Methods Program, Department of Psychology, University of Minnesota, 1977.

Weiss, D. J., & Betz, N. E. *Ability measurement: Conventional or adaptive?* Research Report 73-1. Minneapolis: Psychometric Methods Program, Department of Psychology, University of Minnesota, 1973.

11

Mastery Testing

11.1. INTRODUCTION

A primary purpose of mastery testing is to determine whether each examinee has reached a certain required level of achievement. This chapter deals with the problems of (1) designing a test; (2) scoring the test; (3) setting the cutting score, so as to determine mastery or nonmastery for each examinee as accurately as possible. The problem of how to evaluate a mastery test is necessarily covered as part of this development.

It is instructive to see how these problems can be solved in a clear-cut and compelling way, given the assumptions of item response theory. Thus, the line of reasoning is presented here in some detail, for its inherent interest. The development is based on Birnbaum's work (1968, Chapter 19).

When similar groups of examinees are tested year after year, the psychometrician knows, in advance of testing, the approximate distribution of ability in the group to be tested. In this case, a Bayesian approach is appropriate. Any testing procedure may then be evaluated in terms of two numbers: (1) the proportion of rejected masters (those misclassified as nonmasters) and (2) the proportion of accepted nonmasters (those misclassified as masters). Other more complicated evaluation statistics may also be used. The reader is referred to Birnbaum (1969), Davis, Hickman, and Novick (1973), Huynh (1976), Subkoviak (1976), and Swaminathan, Hambleton, and Algina (1975).

In many cases, on the other hand, a single mastery test is to be used by a variety of institutions, each with a different distribution of ability. If the value of the testing procedure to the various institutions depends on a variety of ability distributions unknown to the psychometrician at the time he is developing the test, how can he design a single test that will be appropriate for every institution?

162

What is needed is a way of evaluating the testing procedure that does not depend on the unknown distributions of ability in the groups to be tested. The approach in this chapter makes no use of these unknown ability distributions.

We gain flexibility and generality when we do not require knowledge of the ability distribution in the group tested. At the same time, we necessarily pay a price: An evaluation based on incomplete information cannot have every virtue of an evaluation based on complete information.

11.2. DEFINITION OF MASTERY

We denote level of achievement by θ. It is common to think that there is some cutting point θ_o that divides masters from nonmasters. In practice, when we try to specify the numerical value of such a θ_o, we find it impossible to choose a value that will satisfy everyone and perhaps impossible to choose a value that will satisfy anyone (see Glass, 1978; van der Linden, 1978).

An alternative is to specify two values, θ_2 and θ_1. Let θ_2 be some relatively low level of mastery, preferably the lowest level satisfactory to all judges; let θ_1 denote some relatively high level of nonmastery, preferably the highest level that all judges can agree upon. We consider the problem of discriminating examinees at θ_2 from those at θ_1. Since the judges cannot agree how individuals between θ_2 and θ_1 should be classified, we shall not be concerned with these individuals.

If some test that measures ability θ has already been built and administered, it will be easier to specify mastery levels in terms of true score ξ on this test, rather than in terms of the less familiar θ scale of ability. In this case the judges will choose levels ζ_1 and ξ_2; the required values of θ_1 and θ_2 will then be found from the familiar relationship $\xi \equiv \Sigma_i P_i(\theta)$.

11.3. DECISION RULES

The practical use of any mastery test involves some rule for deciding which examinees are to be classified as masters and which are not. In the case of a test composed of n dichotomous items, each decision is necessarily based on the examinee's n responses. For any one examinee, these responses are denoted by the vector $\mathbf{u} \equiv \{u_1, u_2, \ldots, u_n\}$. Since the decision d depends on $\mathbf{u}$, we may write it as the function $d \equiv d(\mathbf{u})$. The decision to classify an examinee as a master will be denoted by $d = 1$ or "accept"; as a nonmaster, by $d = 0$ or "reject."

The decision rule d may produce two kinds of errors:

$d(\mathbf{u}) = 1$ (accept) when $\theta = \theta_1$,

$d(\mathbf{u}) = 0$ (reject) when $\theta = \theta_2$.

Let α and β denote, respectively, the probabilities of these two kinds of errors, so that

$$\alpha \equiv \text{Prob}[d(\mathbf{u}) = 1|\theta_1],$$
$$\beta \equiv \text{Prob}[d(\mathbf{u}) = 0|\theta_2].$$
(11-1)

We can reduce the probability of error α to 0 by rejecting all examinees regardless of their test performance; but this automatically increases the probability of error β to 1. On the other hand, we could reduce β to 0, but only at the cost of increasing α to 1.

11.4. SCORING THE TEST: THE LIKELIHOOD RATIO[1]

Note that by the definitions already given,

$$\alpha = \sum_{d(\mathbf{u})=1} \text{Prob}(\mathbf{u}|\theta_1),$$
$$\beta = \sum_{d(\mathbf{u})=0} \text{Prob}(\mathbf{u}|\theta_2).$$
(11-2)

The conditional probability of accepting an individual at θ_2 is

$$1 - \beta = \sum_{d=1} \text{Prob}(\mathbf{u}|\theta_2).$$

This can be written

$$1 - \beta = \sum_{d=1} \lambda(\mathbf{u}) \, \text{Prob}(\mathbf{u}|\theta_1),$$
(11-3)

where $\lambda(\mathbf{u})$ is the likelihood ratio

$$\lambda(\mathbf{u}) \equiv \frac{\text{Prob}(\mathbf{u}|\theta_2)}{\text{Prob}(\mathbf{u}|\theta_1)}.$$
(11-4)

This ratio compares the likelihood of the observed response vector $\mathbf{u}$ when the examinee is at θ_2 with the likelihood when he is at θ_1. This is the ratio commonly used to test the hypothesis $\theta = \theta_1$ versus the hypothesis $\theta = \theta_2$. Note that the likelihood ratio for any $\mathbf{u}$ is known from item response theory [see Eq. (4-20) and (11-12)] as soon as the item parameters and the form of the item response function are specified.

The expected value of the likelihood ratio for given θ_1, given the decision to accept, is

---

[1]The problem of how to score the test can be solved by application of the Neyman–Pearson Theorem (R. V. Hogg & A. T. Craig, *Introduction to mathematical statistics* (3rd ed.). New York: Macmillan, 1970, Chapter 9.). An explicit proof is given here in preference to a simple citation of the theorem.

$$\mathscr{E}[\lambda(\mathbf{u})|\theta = \theta_1, d = 1] = \frac{\displaystyle\sum_{d=1} \lambda(\mathbf{u})\,\mathrm{Prob}(\mathbf{u}|\theta_1)}{\displaystyle\sum_{d=1} \mathrm{Prob}(\mathbf{u}|\theta_1)}$$

From this, (11-3), and (11-2), we have

$$1 - \beta = \alpha \mathscr{E}[\lambda(\mathbf{u})|\theta = \theta_1, d(\mathbf{u}) = 1]. \tag{11-5}$$

This is a basic equation for our purposes, since it specifies the essential relationship between the decision rule and the error rates α and β.

Equation (11-5) specifies the restriction that prevents β from going to 0 when α is fixed. To minimize β, for fixed α, we must find the decision rule $d(\mathbf{u})$ that maximizes the right side of (11-5).

For fixed α, maximizing (11-5) means maximizing $\mathscr{E}[\lambda(\mathbf{u})|\theta = \theta_1, d(\mathbf{u}) = 1]$. Now, the value of $\lambda(\mathbf{u})$ depends only on $\mathbf{u}$, not on $d(\mathbf{u})$ or on θ. Thus we can maximize $\mathscr{E}[\lambda(\mathbf{u})|\theta = \theta_1, d(\mathbf{u}) = 1]$ by defining the acceptance rule $d(\mathbf{u}) = 1$ so as to accept only those response patterns $\mathbf{u}$ for which the values of $\lambda(\mathbf{u})$ are largest. This is the way to maximize the expectation of $\lambda(\mathbf{u})$ when $d(\mathbf{u}) = 1$.

We now have an order of preference for accepting the response patterns $\mathbf{u}$. How many patterns should we accept, starting with the most preferred? The answer is given by the first equation in (11-2). Since α is fixed, we must continue accepting response patterns $\mathbf{u}$ until

$$\sum_{d(\mathbf{u})=1} \mathrm{Prob}(\mathbf{u}|\theta_1) = \alpha.$$

For given $\mathbf{u}$, the probabilities on the left are known from Eq. (4-20).

The decision rule for finding the $d(\mathbf{u})$ that minimizes β for any specified α may thus be stated as follows:

1. List the $\lambda(\mathbf{u})$ in order of magnitude.
2. Accept item response patterns $\mathbf{u}$ starting with the pattern with the largest $\lambda(\mathbf{u})$.
3. Continue down the list until the combined probability given θ_1 of all accepted patterns is equal to α.
4. If the combined probability does not exactly equal α, the last pattern must be accepted only a fraction of the time, acceptance being at random and the fraction being chosen so that $\mathrm{Prob}(d = 1|\theta_1) = \alpha$.

To apply this decision rule for fixed α in practical testing, proceed as follows:

1. *Score each answer sheet to obtain* $\lambda(\mathbf{u})$, *the likelihood ratio (11-4) for the pattern of responses given by the examinee* [see Eq. (11-12)].
2. *Accept each examinee whose score* $\lambda(\mathbf{u})$ *is above some cutting score* λ_α^0 *that depends on* α, *as specified in steps 2 and 3 above.*

3. If $\lambda(\mathbf{u}) = \lambda_\alpha^0$ for some examinees, choose among these at random as in step 4 above.

Note that the examinee's score actually is the likelihood ratio for the responses on his answer sheet. The optimal scoring procedure does not require that we know the distribution of ability in the group tested. Simplified scoring methods are considered in Section 11.8.

11.5. LOSSES

Suppose that $A' \geq 0$ is the *loss* of (erroneously) accepting an individual at θ_1 and $B' \geq 0$ is the loss of rejecting an individual at θ_2. If there are N_1 examinees at θ_1 and N_2 examinees at θ_2, the situation is as illustrated in the diagram, which shows the frequencies in the relevant 2×2 table.

	θ_1	θ_2
$d = 1$	$N_1\alpha$	$N_2(1 - \beta)$
$d = 0$	$N_1(1 - \alpha)$	$N_2\beta$
Total	N_1	N_2

The expected loss, to be denoted by C, is $N_1\alpha A' + N_2\beta B'$. Van Ryzin and Susarla (1977) give a practicable empirical Bayes procedure that, in effect, estimates N_1 and N_2 while minimizing C for fixed A' and B'. See also Snijders (1977). We shall not consider such procedures here.

Define $A \equiv N_1 A'$ and $B \equiv N_2 B'$; then the expected loss is

$$C = A\alpha + B\beta. \tag{11-6}$$

Suppose, first, that we are given A and B. We shall find a decision rule that minimizes C.

11.6. CUTTING SCORE FOR THE LIKELIHOOD RATIO

If α is given, Section 11.4 provides the solution to the decision problem posed. The present section deals with the case where α is not known but A and B are specified instead.

For any given α, it is obvious from (11-6) that the expected loss C is minimized by making β as small as possible. Thus here we again want to use the likelihood ratio $\lambda(\mathbf{u})$ as the examinee's score, accepting only the highest scoring examinees. In Section 11.4, we determined the cutting score so as to satisfy the first equation in (11-2) for given α. Here the cutting score that minimizes C, to be denoted now simply by λ^0, will be shown to have a simple relation to A and B.

Let $r = 1, 2, \ldots, R$ index all numerically different scores $\lambda(\mathbf{u})$, arranging them in order so that $\lambda_R > \lambda_{R-1} > \ldots > \lambda_1$. Let $r*$ denote the lowest score to be "accepted" under the decision rule. Consider first the case where it is unnecessary to assign any examinees at random. The expected loss can then be written

$$C_{r*} = A \sum_{r \geq r*} \text{Prob}(\lambda_r | \theta_1) + B \sum_{r < r*} \text{Prob}(\lambda_r | \theta_2). \tag{11-7}$$

We wish to choose α to minimize C. This is the same as choosing $r*$ to minimize C. Since $C \geq 0$, and since each summation in (11-7) lies between 0 and 1, C must have a minimum, to be denoted by C^o, on $0 \leq \alpha \leq 1$, or (equivalently) on $1 \leq r* \leq R$. Denote by r^o the value of $r*$ that minimizes C_{r*}.

If C^o is a minimum, we must have $C_{r^o+1} - C^o \geq 0$ and $C_{r^o-1} - C^o \geq 0$. (If $\alpha = 0$ or $\alpha = 1$, only one of these inequalities is required; for simplicity, we ignore this trivial case.) Substituting into these inequalities from (11-7), we find

$$C_{r^o+1} - C^o = -A \, \text{Prob}(\lambda_{r^o} | \theta_1) + B \, \text{Prob}(\lambda_{r^o} | \theta_2) \geq 0,$$

$$C_{r^o-1} - C^o = A \, \text{Prob}(\lambda_{r^o-1} | \theta_1) - B \, \text{Prob}(\lambda_{r^o-1} | \theta_2) \geq 0.$$

Since A and B are positive, these can be rewritten

$$\frac{\text{Prob}(\lambda_{r^o} | \theta_2)}{\text{Prob}(\lambda_{r^o} | \theta_1)} \geq \frac{A}{B} \geq \frac{\text{Prob}(\lambda_{r^o-1} | \theta_2)}{\text{Prob}(\lambda_{r^o-1} | \theta_1)}. \tag{11-8}$$

If there is only one pattern of scores that has the likelihood ratio $\lambda_{r^o} \equiv \lambda_{r^o}(\mathbf{u})$, we can denote this pattern by $\mathbf{u}_{r^o}$. In this case, $\text{Prob}(\lambda_{r^o} | \theta) \equiv \text{Prob}(\mathbf{u}_{r^o} | \theta)$ and the left side of (11-8) is the likelihood ratio λ_{r^o}. If there is only one pattern of scores that has the likelihood ratio λ_{r^o-1}, the right side of (11-8), similarly, is the likelihood ratio λ_{r^o-1}. Thus (11-8) becomes

$$\lambda_{r^o} \geq \frac{A}{B} \geq \lambda_{r^o-1}. \tag{11-9}$$

This same result is easily found also for the case where there may be several $\mathbf{u}$ with the same $\lambda(\mathbf{u})$. The conclusion is that expected loss is minimized by choosing the cutting score to be

$$\lambda^o = \frac{A}{B}. \tag{11-10}$$

This conclusion was reached for the special case where all examinees with score λ_{r^o} can be accepted (none have to be assigned at random). We now remove this limitation by showing the following: If any examinees have scores exactly equal to the cutting score $\lambda^o \equiv A/B$, there will be no difference in expected loss however these examinees are assigned.

Consider examinees whose score pattern $\mathbf{u}^o$ is such that

$$\lambda(\mathbf{u}^o) \equiv \frac{\text{Prob}(\mathbf{u}^o | \theta_2)}{\text{Prob}(\mathbf{u}^o | \theta_1)} = \frac{A}{B}.$$

If the examinee is accepted, his contribution to the expected loss C will be A $\text{Prob}[\lambda(\mathbf{u}^o)|\theta_1]$; if he is rejected, his contribution to the expected loss will be $B\ \text{Prob}[\lambda(\mathbf{u}^o)|\theta_2]$. We now show that these two contributions are equal:

$$B\ \text{Prob}[\lambda(\mathbf{u}^o)|\theta_2] = B\ \text{Prob}[\lambda(\mathbf{u}^o)|\theta_1]\ \frac{\text{Prob}[\lambda(\mathbf{u}^o)|\theta_2]}{\text{Prob}[\lambda(\mathbf{u}^o)|\theta_1]}$$

$$= B\ \text{Prob}[\lambda(\mathbf{u}^o)|\theta_1]\frac{A}{B}$$

$$= A\ \text{Prob}[\lambda(\mathbf{u}^o)|\theta_1]. \tag{11-11}$$

The fraction on the first right-hand side is evaluated by noting that it is the likelihood ratio for the score pattern $\mathbf{u}^o$ whose likelihood ratio is A/B. Equation (11-11) shows that when the examinee's score is $\lambda(\mathbf{u}^o) = A/B$, the expected loss C will be the same no matter how the examinee is assigned.

In summary, to minimize expected loss:

1. The score assigned to each examinee is the likelihood ratio for his response pattern $\mathbf{u}$.

2. Accept the examinee if his score exceeds the ratio of the two costs, A/B; reject him if his score is less than A/B.

3. If his score equals A/B, either decision is optimal.

Theorem 11.6.1. *The expected loss* C *is minimized by the decision rule* d(**u**) *if and only if*

$$d(\mathbf{u}) = \begin{cases} \text{accept when the examinee's score } \lambda(\mathbf{u}) > \dfrac{A}{B} \\[2mm] \text{reject when the examinee's score } \lambda(\mathbf{u}) < \dfrac{A}{B} \end{cases}.$$

11.7.   ADMISSIBLE DECISION RULES

Usually we do not know the losses A', B', or the weights A and B. In such cases, we can fall back on the fact that any decision rule $d(\mathbf{u})$ obtained from Theorem 11.6.1 for any A and any B is an *admissible* decision rule. In the present context, this means that no other rule $d^*(\mathbf{u})$ can have smaller error probability α unless it also has a larger β, nor can it have a smaller β unless it also has a larger α.

To prove that $d(\mathbf{u})$ of Theorem 11.6.1 is admissible, suppose to the contrary that $\alpha^* \equiv \text{Prob}(d^* = 1|\theta_1) < \alpha$ and that at the same time $\beta^* \equiv \text{Prob}(d^* = 0|\theta_2) \le \beta$. It would follow that $C^* \equiv A\alpha^* + B\beta^* < A\alpha + B\beta \equiv C$. But this contradicts the theorem, which states that d minimizes C; hence the supposition must be false. Any decision rule defined by Theorem 11.6.1 is an admissible rule; there is no other rule that is better both at θ_1 and at θ_2.

If we do not know A and B, we may have to make a somewhat arbitrary decision as to where the cutting score λ^o should be placed. This is not a new difficulty—we are accustomed to making arbitrary decisions as to the dividing line between mastery and nonmastery. Note, however, that we have gained something important: We have found the optimal method of scoring the test. *The optimal scoring method depends on θ_1 and θ_2 but does not depend on knowing $\alpha, \beta, A,$ or B.*

11.8. WEIGHTED SUM OF ITEM SCORES

It will make no difference if we use the logarithm of the likelihood ratio as the examinee's score instead of the ratio itself. From Eq. (4-20), the likelihood ratio for response pattern $\mathbf{u}$ is

$$\lambda(\mathbf{u}) = \prod_{i=1}^{n} \left[\frac{P_i(\theta_2)}{P_i(\theta_1)} \right]^{u_i} \left[\frac{Q_i(\theta_2)}{Q_i(\theta_1)} \right]^{1-u_i} . \tag{11-12}$$

The logarithm of this is

$$\ln \lambda(\mathbf{u}) = \sum_{i=1}^{n} u_i \left[\ln \frac{P_i(\theta_2)}{Q_i(\theta_2)} - \ln \frac{P_i(\theta_1)}{Q_i(\theta_1)} \right] + K. \tag{11-13}$$

where

$$K \equiv \Sigma_i \ln \left[\frac{Q_i(\theta_2)}{Q_i(\theta_1)} \right]. \tag{11-14}$$

Thus, *the examinee's score* y *(say) may be taken to be a weighted sum of item scores:*

$$y \equiv y(\mathbf{u}) \equiv \sum_{i=1}^{n} w_i(\theta_1, \theta_2) u_i \tag{11-15}$$

where the scoring weights are given by

$$w_i(\theta_1, \theta_2) \equiv \ln \frac{P_i(\theta_2)}{Q_i(\theta_2)} - \ln \frac{P_i(\theta_1)}{Q_i(\theta_1)} . \tag{11-16}$$

When θ_1, θ_2, the item parameters, and the form of the item response function are known, K is a known constant and so are the item-scoring weights $w_i(\theta_1, \theta_2)$, which appear in brackets in (11-13).

By Theorem 11.6.1, *all admissible decision rules now have the form*

accept if score $y > y_o$,

reject if score $y < y_o$,

where

$$y_o = \ln A - \ln B - K. \tag{11-17}$$

It does not matter what decision is made if $y = y_o$.

Note that these conclusions hold regardless of the form of the item response function. The form must be known in order to compute the scoring weights $w_i(\theta_1, \theta_2)$, however. If the item response function is logistic with all $c_i = 0$, the optimal scoring weights are not only independent of α, β, A, and B but also are independent of θ_1 and θ_2. (The reader may prove this as an exercise.)

11.9. LOCALLY BEST SCORING WEIGHTS

In general, the item-scoring weights $w_i(\theta_1, \theta_2)$ depend on the choice of θ_1 and θ_2. If we divide all $w_i(\theta_1, \theta_2)$ by $\theta_2 - \theta_1$, and make a corresponding change in the cutting score y_o, this does not change any decision. Let us relabel θ_1 as θ_o and define the *locally best scoring weight* as the limit of $w_i(\theta_o, \theta_2)$ when $\theta_2 \to \theta_o$:

$$w_i^o \equiv w_i(\theta_o) \equiv \lim_{\theta_2 \to \theta_o} \left[\frac{w_i(\theta_o, \theta_2)}{(\theta_2 - \theta_o)} \right]. \tag{11-18}$$

By the definition of a derivative,

$$w_i^o \equiv w_i(\theta_o) = \lim_{\theta_2 \to \theta_o} \frac{\ln [P_i(\theta_2)/Q_i(\theta_2)] - \ln [P_i(\theta_o)/Q_i(\theta_o)]}{\theta_2 - \theta_o}$$

$$= \frac{d}{d\theta_o} \ln \frac{P_i(\theta_o)}{Q_i(\theta_o)} = \frac{P_i'(\theta_o)}{P_i(\theta_o)Q_i(\theta_o)}. \tag{11-19}$$

If we wish to discriminate near some ability level θ_o, then the "locally best" item-scoring weights are given by (11-19).

The scoring weights obtained here are similar to those that maximized the information function in Section 5.6. In the context of Section 5.6, the scoring weights vary from individual to individual, depending on his unknown ability level; this is a serious handicap to practical use there. Here, on the contrary, the scoring weights are the same for everyone. Here, we determine from outside considerations the ability level θ_o that we consider to be the dividing line between mastery and nonmastery; this ability level θ_o determines the locally best scoring weights. *These are the weights to be used for all examinees, regardless of ability level.*

11.10. CUTTING POINT FOR LOCALLY BEST SCORES

The locally best weighted sum Y of item scores is seen from (11-19) to be

$$Y \equiv \sum_{i=1}^{n} w_i(\theta_o) u_i \equiv \sum_{i=1}^{n} \frac{P_i'(\theta_o) u_i}{P_i(\theta_o)Q_i(\theta_o)}. \tag{11-20}$$

If the examinee's score is Y, what is the appropriate cutting score Y_o?

The *locally best score* Y (11-20) is obtained from the optimally weighted sum y (11-15) by the relation

$$Y = \lim_{\theta_2 \to \theta_1} \left. \frac{y}{\theta_2 - \theta_1} \right|_{\theta_0}. \tag{11-21}$$

The cutting score Y_0 is found from (11-21) and (11-17) to be

$$Y_0 = \lim_{\theta_2 \to \theta_1} \left. \frac{\ln A - \ln B - K}{\theta_2 - \theta_1} \right|_{\theta_0}.$$

If $A \neq B$, Y_0 becomes positively (negatively) infinite. This means that all examinees will be accepted (rejected). This case is not of practical use. If $A = B$, however, we can obtain a useful result:

$$\begin{aligned} Y_0 &= \lim_{\theta_2 \to \theta_1} \left. \frac{-K}{\theta_2 - \theta_1} \right|_{\theta_0} \\ &= \lim_{\theta_2 \to \theta_1} \frac{\Sigma_i \, [-\ln Q_i \, (\theta_2) + \ln Q_i \, (\theta_0)]}{\theta_2 - \theta_0} \\ &= -\frac{d}{d\theta_0} \sum_{i=1}^{n} \ln Q_i \, (\theta_0) \\ &= \sum_{i=1}^{n} \frac{P_i' \, (\theta_0)}{Q_i \, (\theta_0)}. \end{aligned} \tag{11-22}$$

If the cost of accepting nonmasters who are just below θ_0 is equal to the cost of rejecting masters who are just above θ_0, then we can use Y_0 in (11-22) as the cutting score against which each person's score Y is compared.

If an examinee's score Y is exactly at the cutting score Y_0, we have from (11-20) and (11-22)

$$Y \equiv \sum_{i=1}^{n} \frac{P_i' \, (\theta_0) u_i}{P_i \, (\theta_0) Q_i (\theta_0)} = \sum_{i=1}^{n} \frac{P_i' \, (\theta_0)}{Q_i \, (\theta_0)}. \tag{11-23}$$

Comparing this with Eq. (5-19), we see that this is the same as the likelihood equation for estimating the examinee's ability from his responses $\mathbf{u}$. This means that if a person's score Y is at the cutting point, then the maximum likelihood estimate of his ability is exactly θ_0, the ability level that divides masters from nonmasters. This result further clarifies the choice of Y_0 as a cutting score.

11.11.   EVALUATING A MASTERY TEST

If we are concerned with two specified ability levels θ_1 and θ_2, as in Sections 11.2–11.8, we obviously should evaluate the mastery test in terms of the expected loss (11-6). For this, we need to know A, B, α, and β.

Given θ_1, θ_2, the item parameters, the form of the item response function, and the cutting score y_o, we can determine misclassification probabilities α and β from the frequency distribution of the weighted sum of item scores

$$y \equiv \Sigma_i w_i(\theta_1, \theta_2)u_i.$$

The required frequency distribution $f_y \equiv f_y(y)$ for any given θ is provided by the generating function

$$\sum_y f_y t^y \equiv \prod_{i=1}^{n} [Q_i(\theta) + P_i(\theta)t^{w_i(\theta_1, \theta_2)}] \tag{11-24}$$

[compare Eq. (4-1)]. In other words, the frequency f_y of any score y appears as the coefficient of t^y on the right side of (11-24) after expansion. To obtain α (or β), (11-24) must be evaluated at $\theta = \theta_1$ (or $\theta = \theta_2$) and the frequencies cumulated as required by (11-2) and by Theorem 11.6.1. For example, if $n = 2$, $w_1(\theta_1, \theta_2) = .9$, $w_2(\theta_1, \theta_2) = 1.2$, then (11-24) becomes

$$Q_1 Q_2 + P_1 Q_2 t^{.9} + Q_1 P_2 t^{1.2} + P_1 P_2 t^{2.1}.$$

Thus $f_y(0) = Q_1 Q_2$, $f_y(.9) = P_1 Q_2$, $f_y(1.2) = Q_1 P_2$, $f_y(2.1) = P_1 P_2$.

If A and B are known, the expected loss can be computed from (11-6). If A and B are not known a priori, but some cutting score λ^o has somehow been chosen, the ratio of A to B can be found from the equation $\lambda^o = A/B$. Together with α and β, this ratio is all that is needed to determine the *relative* effectiveness of different mastery tests.

Although the expected loss can be determined as just described, the procedure is not simple and the formulas are not suitable for needed further mathematical derivations. In view of this, *we shall often evaluate the effectiveness of a mastery test by the test information* $I\{\theta\}$ *at the ability level* $\theta = \theta_o$ *that separates mastery from nonmastery*. The test information at ability θ_o is

$$I_o\{\theta\} = \sum_{i=1}^{n} \frac{P_i'^2}{P_i Q_i} \bigg|_{\theta=\theta_o} \tag{11-25}$$

As discussed in Section 6.3, the value of the information function (11-25) depends on the choice of metric for measuring ability. As in Section 6.4, however, the *relative* effectiveness of two mastery tests, as measured by (11-25), will not be affected by the choice of metric.

11.12.   OPTIMAL ITEM DIFFICULTY

What values of b_i ($i = 1, 2, \ldots, n$) will maximize $I_o\{\theta\}$? We note in Section 5.4 that the contribution of each item to $I\{\theta\}$ is independent of the contribution of every other item. Thus, $I\{\theta\}$ will be maximized by separately maximizing the contribution of each item. This contribution is by definition the item information function, $I\{\theta, u_i\}$.

Many item response functions, including all those considered in Chapter 2, depend on θ and on b_i only through their difference $\theta - b_i$. For such item response functions, the value of b_i that maximizes $I\{\theta, u_i\}$ can be found directly or from the formula for the ability level θ_i that maximizes $I\{\theta, u_i\}$. Some such formulas for θ_i are given in Section 10.2. We can replace θ_i by θ_o in these and solve for b_i.

For the three-parameter logistic function we find from Eq. (10-4), for example, that the item difficulty b_i that maximizes the item information function at $\theta = \theta_o$ is

$$b_i = \theta_o - \frac{1}{Da_i} \ln \frac{1 + \sqrt{1 + 8c_i}}{2}. \tag{11-26}$$

If all items have the same a_i and c_i, then the optimal mastery test will have all items of equal difficulty. Otherwise, the optimal item difficulties b_i will not all be the same.

11.13.   TEST LENGTH

How long does a mastery test need to be? If we are going to evaluate our test in terms of the error rates α and β, a rough answer to this question can be given by using a normal approximation to the distribution of the weighted item score y. This approach is used by Birnbaum (1968, Section 19.5).

If we are going to use the test information at θ_o to evaluate our test, it is natural to think in terms of the length of the asymptotic confidence interval for estimating θ when $\theta = \theta_o$. Suppose our unit of measurement is chosen (see Section 3.5) in some convenient way—for example, so that the standard deviation of θ is 1.0 for some convenient group. Then we can perhaps decide what length confidence interval will be adequate for our purposes.

Alternatively, we may prefer to deal with the more familiar scale of number-right true score ξ. In this case, we can decide on an adequate confidence interval $(\underline{\xi}, \bar{\xi})$ for estimating ξ. We can then transform $\underline{\xi}$ and $\bar{\xi}$ to the θ scale by the relation $\xi = \Sigma_i P_i(\theta)$ and thus find approximately the length of confidence interval needed.

The required information $I_o\{\theta\}$ is then (see Section 5.1) the squared reciprocal of this length multiplied by $[2\Phi^{-1}\{(1 - \gamma)/2\}]^2$, where γ is the confidence level and $\Phi^{-1}\{\ \}$ is the inverse of the cumulative normal distribution function:

$$I_o\{\theta\} = \left[\frac{2\Phi^{-1}\{(1 - \gamma)/2\}}{\text{length of confidence interval}} \right]^2. \tag{11-27}$$

For example, if the confidence level is .95, $\Phi^{-1}\{(1 - \gamma)/2\}$ is the familiar quantity -1.96 that cuts off .025 of the normal curve frequency.

For the three-parameter logistic case, if all items have the same $a_i = a$ and $c_i = c$ and if the b_i are optimal (11-26), then the required number n_o of items is found by dividing the chosen value of $I_o\{\theta\}$ by the maximum item information M given by Eq. (10-6). This gives

$$n_o = \frac{8(1 - c)^2 I_o\{\theta\}}{D^2 a^2 [1 - 20c - 8c^2 + (1 + 8c)^{3/2}]}. \qquad (11\text{-}28)$$

If $c = 0$, the required test length is

$$n_o = \frac{1.384 I_o\{\theta\}}{a^2}. \qquad (11\text{-}29)$$

The number of items required is inversely proportional to the square of the item discriminating power a. If a certain mastery test requires 100 items with $c = 0$, we find from (11-28) that it will require 138 items with $c = .167$, 147 items with $c = .20$, 162 items with $c = .25$, 191 items with $c = .333$, or 277 items with $c = .50$.

11.14. SUMMARY OF MASTERY TEST DESIGN

According to the approach suggested here, the design of a mastery test for a unidimensional skill could proceed somewhat as follows.

1. Obtain a pool of items for measuring the skill of interest.
2. Calibrate the items on some convenient group by determining the parameters a_i, b_i, c_i for each item.
3. Consider the entire item pool as a single test; determine what true-score level ξ_o, or levels ξ_1 and ξ_2, will be used to define mastery. This decision is a matter of judgment for the subject-matter specialist.
4. Using the item parameters obtained in step 2, find θ_o (or θ_1 and θ_2) from ξ_o (or from ξ_1 and ξ_2) by means of the relation $\xi \equiv \Sigma_i P_i(\theta)$.

If a single cutting point θ_o is used:

5. Compute $P_i(\theta_o)$ for each item.
6. Evaluate $I\{\theta, u_i\} \equiv P_i'^2/P_i Q_i$ at θ_o for each item.
7. Decide what length confidence interval for θ will be adequate at θ_o. Find the required $I_o\{\theta\}$ from (11-27).
8. Select items with the highest $I\{\theta, u_i\}$ at θ_o. Continue selecting until the sum $\Sigma^n I_o\{\theta, u_i\}$ equals the required $I_o\{\theta\}$.
9. Compute scoring weights $w_i^o = P_i'/P_i Q_i|_{\theta=\theta_o}$ for each selected item.
10. For each examinee, compute the weighted sum of item scores $Y \equiv \Sigma_i w_i u_i$. (In practice, an unweighted score may be adequate.)

11. Compute the cutting score $Y_o \equiv \Sigma_i^n P_i'(\theta_o)/Q_i(\theta_o)$.

12. Accept each examinee whose score Y exceeds Y_o; reject each examinee whose score is less than Y_o.

The foregoing procedure is appropriate if erroneous acceptance and erroneous rejection of examinees are about equally important for examinees near θ_o. If this is not the case and if the relative importance of such errors can be quantified by some ratio A/B, then steps 5–12 should be replaced by

5. Compute $P_i(\theta_1)$ and $P_i(\theta_2)$ for each item.
6. Compute the item-scoring weights

$$w_i(\theta_1, \theta_2) \equiv \ln \frac{P_i(\theta_2)Q_i(\theta_1)}{P_i(\theta_1)Q_i(\theta_2)}.$$

7. Select the available items with the highest scoring weights.
8. For each examinee, compute the weighted sum of item scores $y = \Sigma_i w_i(\theta_1, \theta_2)u_i$.
9. Compute the cutting score $y_o = \ln A - \ln B - K$.
10. Accept each examinee whose score y exceeds y_o; reject each examinee whose score is less than y_o.

11.15. EXERCISES

11-1 Suppose a mastery test consists of $n = 5$ items exactly like item 2 in test 1 and also that $\theta_1 = -1$, $\theta_2 = +1$. What is α if we accept only examinees who score $x = 5$? (Use Table 4.17.1.) What is β? What if we accept $x \geq 4$? $x \geq 3$? $x \geq 2$? If $A = B = 1$, what is the expected loss C of accepting $x = 5$? $x \geq 4$? $x \geq 3$? $x \geq 2$?

11-2 What is the score (likelihood ratio) of an examinee who gets all five items right ($x = 5$) in Exercise 11-1? What is his score if $x = 4$? 3? 2? 1? 0? Which examinees will be accepted if $A = 5$, $B = 2$?

11-3 Suppose test 1 (see Table 4.17.1) is used as mastery test with $\theta_1 = -1$, $\theta_2 = +1$. What is the score (likelihood ratio) of an examinee with $\mathbf{u} = \{1, 0, 0\}$? $\{0, 1, 0\}$? $\{0, 0, 1\}$? Do these scores arrange these examinees in the order that you would expect? Explain the reason for the ordering obtained.

11-4 What is the optimal scoring weight (11-16) for each of the three items in the test in Exercise 11-3 (be sure to use natural logarithms)? Why does item 3 get the least weight?

11-5 What is the optimally weighted sum of item scores (11-15) for an examinee in Exercise 11-3 with response pattern $\mathbf{u} = \{1, 1, 0\}$? $\{1, 0, 1\}$? $\{0, 1, 1\}$? If $A = B$, what is the cutting score (11-17) for these optimally weighted sums of item scores?

11-6   What are the locally best scoring weights (11-19) for each of the three items in the test in Exercise 11-3 when $\theta_o = 0$? Compare with the weights found in Exercise 11-4. Are the differences important?

11-7   What is the locally best weighted sum of item scores (11-20) for an examinee in Exercise 11-3 with response pattern $\mathbf{u} = \{1, 1, 0\}$? $\{1, 0, 1\}$? $\{0, 1, 1\}$? If $A = B$, what is the locally best cutting score (11-22) for these scores? Compare with the results of Exercise 11-5 and comment on the comparison.

REFERENCES

Birnbaum, A. Some latent trait models and their use in inferring an examinee's ability. In F. M. Lord and M. R. Novick, *Statistical theories of mental test scores.* Reading, Mass.: Addison-Wesley, 1968.

Birnbaum, A. Statistical theory for logistic mental test models with a prior distribution of ability. *Journal of Mathematical Psychology,* 1969, *6,* 258–276.

Davis, C. E., Hickman, J., & Novick, M. R. *A primer on decision analysis for individually prescribed instruction.* Technical Bulletin No. 17. Iowa City, Ia.: Research and Development Division, The American College Testing Program, 1973.

Glass, G. V. Standards and criteria. *Journal of Educational Measurement,* 1978, *15,* 237–261.

Huynh, H. On the reliability of decisions in domain-referenced testing. *Journal of Educational Measurement,* 1976, *13,* 253–264.

Snijders, T. Complete class theorems for the simplest empirical Bayes decision problems. *The Annals of Statistics,* 1977, *5,* 164–171.

Subkoviak, M. J. Estimating reliability from a single administration of a criterion-referenced test. *Journal of Educational Measurement,* 1976, *13,* 265–276.

Swaminathan, H., Hambleton, R. K., & Algina, J. A Bayesian decision-theoretic procedure for use with criterion-referenced tests. *Journal of Educational Measurement,* 1975, *12,* 87–98.

van der Linden, W. J. Forgetting, guessing, and mastery: The Macready and Dayton models revisited and compared with a latent trait approach. *Journal of Educational Statistics,* 1978, *3,* 305–317.

van Ryzin, J., & Susarla, V. On the empirical Bayes approach to multiple decision problems. *The Annals of Statistics,* 1977, *5,* 172–181.

III

PRACTICAL PROBLEMS AND FURTHER APPLICATIONS

12

Estimating Ability and Item Parameters

12.1. MAXIMUM LIKELIHOOD

In its simplest form, the parameter estimation problem is the following. We are given a matrix $\mathbf{U} \equiv \|u_{ia}\|$ consisting of the responses ($u_{ia} = 0$ or 1) of each of N examinees to each of n items. We assume that these responses arise from a certain model such as Eq. (2-1) or (2-2). We need to infer the parameters of the model: a_i, b_i, c_i ($i = 1, 2, \ldots, n$) and θ_a ($a = 1, 2, \ldots, N$).

As noted in Section 4.10 and illustrated for one θ in Fig. 4.9.1, the maximum likelihood estimates are the parameter values that maximize the likelihood $L(\mathbf{U}|\mathbf{\Theta};$ $\mathbf{a}, \mathbf{b}, \mathbf{c})$ given the observations $\mathbf{U}$. Maximum likelihood estimates are usually found from the roots of the likelihood equations (4-30), which set the derivatives of the log likelihood equal to zero. The likelihood equations (4-30) are

$$\sum_{i=1}^{n} \frac{u_{ia} - P_{ia}}{P_{ia} Q_{ia}} \frac{\partial P_{ia}}{\partial \theta_a} = 0 \qquad (a = 1, 2, \ldots, N), \tag{12-1a}$$

$$\left. \begin{aligned} \sum_{a=1}^{N} \frac{u_{ia} - P_{ia}}{P_{ia} Q_{ia}} \frac{\partial P_{ia}}{\partial a_i} &= 0 \qquad (i = 1, 2, \ldots, n), \\ \sum_{a=1}^{N} \frac{u_{ia} - P_{ia}}{P_{ia} Q_{ia}} \frac{\partial P_{ia}}{\partial b_i} &= 0 \qquad (i = 1, 2, \ldots, n), \\ \sum_{a=1}^{N} \frac{u_{ia} - P_{ia}}{P_{ia} Q_{ia}} \frac{\partial P_{ia}}{\partial c_i} &= 0 \qquad (i = 1, 2, \ldots, n). \end{aligned} \right\} \tag{12-1b}$$

For the three-parameter logistic model,

179

$$\frac{\partial P_{ia}}{\partial \theta_a} = \frac{Da_i Q_{ia}(P_{ia} - c_i)}{1 - c_i},$$

$$\frac{\partial P_{ia}}{\partial a_i} = \frac{D(\theta_a - b_i)Q_{ia}(P_{ia} - c_i)}{1 - c_i}, \qquad (12\text{-}2)$$

$$\frac{\partial P_{ia}}{\partial b_i} = \frac{-Da_i Q_{ia}(P_{ia} - c_i)}{1 - c_i},$$

$$\frac{\partial P_{ia}}{\partial c_i} = \frac{Q_{ia}}{1 - c_i}.$$

A similar set of likelihood equations can be obtained in the same way for the three-parameter normal ogive model.

These formulas are given here to show their particular character. The reader need not be concerned with the details. The important characteristic of (12-1a) is that when the item parameters are known, the ability estimate $\hat{\theta}_a$ for examinee a is found from just one equation out of the N equations (12-1a). The estimate $\hat{\theta}_a$ does not depend on the other $\hat{\theta}$. When the examinee parameters are known, the three parameters for item i are estimated by solving just three equations out of (12-1b). The estimates for item i do not depend on the parameters of the other items.

This suggests an iterative procedure where we treat the trial values of $\hat{\theta}_a$ ($a = 1, 2, \ldots , N$) as known while solving (12-1b) for the estimates $\hat{a}_i, \hat{b}_i, \hat{c}_i$ ($i = 1, 2, \ldots , n$); then treat all item parameters ($i = 1, 2, \ldots , n$) as known while solving (12-1a) for new trial values $\hat{\theta}_a$ ($a = 1, 2, \ldots , N$). This is to be repeated until the numerical values converge. Because of the independence within each set of parameter estimates when the other set is fixed, this procedure is simpler and quicker than solving for all parameters at once.

12.2. ITERATIVE NUMERICAL PROCEDURES

The likelihood Eq. (12-1) are of the form $S_r \equiv \partial \ln L / \partial \chi_r = 0$, where χ_r is an arbitrary parameter ($r = 1, 2, \ldots , R$). The following modification of the standard Newton–Raphson interative method for solving equations is very effective in statistical work (Kale, 1962).

Let $I_{qr} \equiv \mathscr{E} S_q S_r$ ($q, r = 1, 2, \ldots , R$), and let a superscript zero distinguish functions of χ_r ($r = 1, 2, \ldots , R$) evaluated at trial values χ_r^0. Solve for Δ^0 the linear equations $\|I_{qr}^0\| \Delta^0 = S^0$, where S^0 is the vector of S_r^0 and $\|I_{qr}^0\|$ is the matrix of I_{qr}^0. Then $\chi^1 = \chi^0 + \Delta^0$ is a vector of improved estimates of the true parameter vector χ.

When the item parameters are fixed (treated as known), the parameter vector χ is simply $\{\theta_1, \theta_2, \ldots \theta_N\}$ and the *information matrix* $\|I_{qr}\|$ is found to be a diagonal matrix. By Eq. (5-4), the diagonal elements of $\|I_{qr}\|$ are the reciprocals of Var $(\hat{\theta}|\theta)$. Thus by Eq. (5-5),

$$I_{rr} = \sum_{i=1}^{n} \frac{P_{ia}'^2}{P_{ia} Q_{ia}} \qquad (r \equiv a = 1, 2, \dots, N).$$ (12-3)

From Eq. (4-30),

$$S_r = \sum_{i=1}^{n} (u_{ia} - P_{ia}) \frac{P_{ia}'}{P_{ia} Q_{ia}} \qquad (r \equiv a = 1, 2, \dots, N).$$ (12-4)

When the item parameters are fixed, the correction Δ_r^0 to $\hat{\theta}_r^0$ is simply $\Delta_r^0 = S_r^0/I_{rr}^0$. Thus $\hat{\theta}_a$ ($a = 1, 2, \dots, N$) can be readily found by the iterative method of the preceding paragraph.

When the ability parameters are fixed (treated as known), the parameter vector χ is $\{a_1, b_1, c_1; a_2, b_2, c_2; \dots; a_n, b_n, c_n\}$. Formulas (see Appendix 12) for the I_{qr} are obtained by the same method used to find Eq. (5-5). The information matrix $\|I_{qr}\|$ is a diagonal supermatrix whose diagonal elements are 3×3 matrices, one for each item. The 3×3 matrices are not diagonal. The corrections Δ_r are obtained separately for each item, by solving three linear equations in three unknown Δ's.

12.3. SAMPLING VARIANCES OF PARAMETER ESTIMATES

If the true item parameters were known, then the asymptotic sampling variance of $\hat{\theta}_a$ would be approximated by $1/I_{aa}$ evaluated at $\theta_a = \hat{\theta}_a$. This is readily obtained from the modified Newton–Raphson procedure after convergence [see Eq. (5-4)]. Ability estimates $\hat{\theta}_a$ and $\hat{\theta}_b$ are uncorrelated with $a \neq b$.

A large sampling variance occurs when the likelihood function has a relatively flat maximum, as in the two curves on the left and the one on the right of Fig. 4.9.1. A small sampling variance occurs when the likelihood function has a well-determined maximum, as in the middle three curves of Fig. 4.9.1.

If the true ability parameters were known, the asymptotic sampling variance–covariance matrix of the $\hat{a}_i$, $\hat{b}_i$, and $\hat{c}_i$ would be approximated by the inverse of the 3×3 matrix of the I_{qr} for item i, evaluated at $\hat{a}_i$, $\hat{b}_i$, and $\hat{c}_i$. Parameter estimates for item i are uncorrelated with estimates for item j when $i \neq j$.

In practice, estimated sampling variances and covariances of parameter estimates are obtained by substituting estimated parameter values for parameters assumed known. When all parameters must be estimated, this substitution underestimates the true sampling fluctuations.

Andersen (1973) argues that when item and person parameters are estimated simultaneously, the estimates do not converge to their true values as the number of examinees becomes large. The relevant requirement, however, is convergence when the number of people and the number of items both become large together. A proof of convergence for this case has been given for the Rasch model by

Haberman (1977). It seems likely that convergence will be similarly proved for the three-parameter model also.

12.4. PARTIALLY SPEEDED TESTS

If an examinee does not respond to the last few items in a test because of lack of time, his (lack of) behavior with respect to these items is not described by current item response theory. Unidimensional item response theory deals with actual responses; it does not predict whether or not a response will occur. Many low-ability students answer all the items in a test well ahead of the allotted time limit. Ability to answer test items rapidly is thus only moderately correlated, if at all, with ability to answer correctly. Item response theory currently deals with the latter ability and not at all with the former. [Models for speeded tests have been developed by Meredith (1970), Rasch (1960, Chapter 3), van der Ven (1976), and others.]

If we knew which items the examinee did not have time to consider, we would ignore these items when estimating his ability. This is appropriate because of the fundamental property that the examinee's ability θ is the same for all items in a unidimensional pool. Except for sampling fluctuations, our estimate of θ will be the same no matter what items in the pool are used to obtain it. Note that our ability estimate for the individual represents what he can do on items that he has time to reach and consider. It does not tell us what he can do in a limited testing time.

In practice, all consecutively omitted items at the end of his answer sheet are ignored for estimating an examinee's ability. Such items are called *not reached* items. If the examinee did not read and respond to the test items in serial order, we may be mistaken in assuming that he did not read such a ''not reached'' item. We may also be mistaken in assuming that he did read all (earlier) items to which he responded. The assumption made here, however, seems to be the best practical assumption currently available.

12.5. FLOOR AND CEILING EFFECTS

If an examinee answers all test items correctly, the maximum likelihood estimate of his ability is $\hat{\theta} = +\infty$. In this case, Bayesian methods would surely give a more plausible result. In maximum likelihood estimation, such examinees may be omitted from the data if desired. Their inclusion, however, will not affect the estimates obtained for the item parameters nor for other ability parameters.

If an examinee answers all items incorrectly, the maximum likelihood estimate of his ability is $\hat{\theta} = -\infty$. Most examinees answer at least a few items correctly, however, if only by guessing. By Eq. (2-1) or (2-2), $P_i(\theta) \geq c_i$. Thus by Eq. (4-5) the number-right true score ξ is always greater than or equal to $\Sigma_i^n c_i$. An examinee's number-right observed score may be less than $\Sigma_i^n c_i$ because he is unlucky in his guessing; in this case we are likely to find an estimate of $\hat{\theta} = -\infty$ for him.

On the other hand, an examinee with a very low number-right score may still have a finite $\hat{\theta}$ provided he has answered the easiest items correctly. This occurs because, as seen in Section 5.6, hard items receive very little scoring weight in determining $\hat{\theta}$ for low-ability examinees. Correspondingly, an examinee with a number-right score above $\Sigma_1^n c_i$ may still obtain $\hat{\theta} = -\infty$. This will happen if he answers some very easy items incorrectly. A person who gets easy items wrong cannot be a high-ability person.

12.6. ACCURACY OF ABILITY ESTIMATION

Figure 3.5.2 compares ability estimates $\hat{\theta}$ for 1830 sixth-grade pupils from a 50-item MAT vocabulary test with estimates obtained independently from a 42-item SRA vocabulary test. Values of $\hat{\theta}$ outside the range -2.5 to $+2.5$ are plotted on the perimeter of the figure. Many of the points on the left and lower boundaries of the figure represent pupils for whom $\hat{\theta} = -\infty$ on one or both tests.

It appears from the figure, as we would anticipate, that $\hat{\theta}$ values between 0 and 1 show much smaller sampling errors than do extreme $\hat{\theta}$ values. Although not apparent from the figure, a pupil might have a $\hat{\theta}$ of -10 on one test and a $\hat{\theta}$ of -50 on the other, simply because of sampling fluctuations. For many practical purposes, the difference between $\hat{\theta} = -10$ and $\hat{\theta} = -50$ for a sixth-grade pupil is unimportant, even if numerically large. In the usual frame of reference, it may not be necessary to distinguish between these two ability levels. If we did wish to distinguish them, we would have to administer a much easier test.

Since some of the $\hat{\theta}$ are negatively infinite in Fig. 3.5.2, we cannot compute a correlation coefficient for this scatterplot. If we simply omit all infinite estimates, the correlation coefficient might be dominated by the large scatter of a few extreme $\hat{\theta}$. If we omit these $\hat{\theta}$ also, the correlation obtained will depend on just which $\hat{\theta}$ we choose to omit and which we retain.

It is helpful to transform the $\hat{\theta}$ scale to a more familiar scale that better represents our interests. A convenient and meaningful scale to use is the proportion-correct score scale. We can transform all $\hat{\theta}$ on to this scale by the familiar transformation [Eq. (4-9)]:

$$\hat{\zeta} \equiv \zeta(\hat{\theta}) \equiv \sum_1^n \frac{P_i(\hat{\theta})}{n} .$$

Figure 12.6.1 is the same as Fig. 3.5.2 except that the points are now plotted on the proportion-correct score scale. The $\hat{\theta}$ obtained from the SRA items have been transformed into SRA proportion-correct estimated true scores; the $\hat{\theta}$ from MAT, to MAT estimated true scores. As noted often before, proportion-correct true scores cannot fall below $\Sigma_1^n c_i/n$. The product-moment correlation between SRA and MAT values of $\hat{\zeta}$ is found to be .914. This is notably higher than the

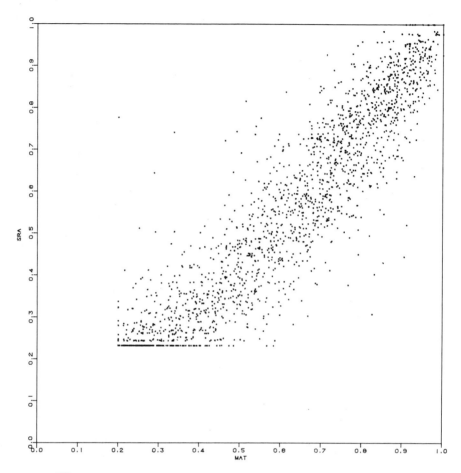

FIG. 12.6.1.   Estimated true scores on a 50-item MAT vocabulary test and a 42-item SRA vocabulary test for 1830 sixth-grade pupils.

reported correlation for these data of .8998 between number-right observed scores on the two tests.

When two tests are at different difficulty levels, their true scores will not be linearly related. Because of this, cubic regressions were fitted to the data in Fig. 12.6.1. The results show that the curvilinear correlation of MAT $\hat{\zeta}$ on SRA $\hat{\zeta}$ is about .920; the curvilinear correlation of SRA on MAT is about .923.

12.7. INADEQUATE DATA AND UNIDENTIFIABLE PARAMETERS

If a parameter value is in principle indeterminate even when we are given the entire population of observable values, then the parameter is called *unidentifiable*.

Actually, all θ, a_i, and b_i (but not c_i) are unidentifiable until we agree on some arbitrary choice of origin and unit of measurement (see Section 3.5). Once this choice is made, all θ and all item parameters will ordinarily be identifiable in a suitable infinite population of examinees and infinite pool of test items.

Just as his θ cannot be estimated from the responses of an examinee who answers all n test items correctly, similarly b_i cannot be estimated from the responses of a sample of N examinees all of whom answer item i correctly. This does not mean that b_i is unidentifiable; it only means that the data are inadequate for our purpose. We need a larger sample of examinees, some examinees will surely get the item wrong if the sample is large enough; or, better, we need a sample of examinees at lower ability levels.

If only a few examinees in a large sample answer item i correctly, $\hat{b}_i$ will have a large sampling error. To make this clearer, consider a special case where $c_i = 0$, $a_i = 1/1.7 = .588$, and all examinees are at $\theta = 0$. The standard error of the proportion p_i of correct answers in a sample of N such examinees is given by the usual binomial formula:

$$SE(p_i) = \sqrt{\frac{P_i Q_i}{N}} \ .$$

Under the logistic model, for the special case considered,

$$P_i = (1 + e^{b_i})^{-1},$$

or

$$b_i = \ln\left(-1 + \frac{1}{P_i}\right).$$

The asymptotic standard error of $\hat{b}_i \equiv \ln(-1 + 1/p_i)$ is easily found by the delta method (Kendall & Stuart, 1969, Chapter 10) to be

$$SE(\hat{b}_i) = \frac{1}{\sqrt{N P_i Q_i}} \ .$$

The two standard errors are compared in the following listing for $N = 1000$.

P_i or Q_i:	.001	.01	.05	.2	.5
b_i:	±6.91	±4.60	±2.94	±1.39	0
SE (p_i):	.001	.003	.007	.013	.016
SE $(\hat{b}_i)$:	1.000*	.318*	.145	.079	.063

*$N = 1000$ may not be large enough for the asymptotic formula to apply when P_i or Q_i is $\leq .01$; for large N, the standard errors will be proportional to those shown here, however.

The listing shows that $\hat{b}_i$ is unstable when P_i or Q_i is small. The situation is much worse when both a_i and b_i must be estimated simultaneously. If only a few examinees answer item i incorrectly, it is obviously impossible to estimate a_i with any accuracy.

The problem is even more obvious for c_i, which represents the performance of low-ability examinees. If we have no such examinees in our sample, we cannot estimate c_i. This is the fault of the sample and not the fault of the estimation method. In such a sample, any reasonable value of $\hat{c}_i$ will be able to fit the data about as well as any other. If we arbitrarily assign some plausible value of c_i and then estimate a_i and b_i accordingly, we shall obtain a good description of our data.

We need not forego practical applications of item response theory just because some of the parameters cannot be estimated accurately from our data, as long as we restrict our conclusions to ranges for which our data are relevant. If we wish to predict far outside these ranges, we must gather data relevant to our problem.

12.8. BAYESIAN ESTIMATION OF ABILITY

In work with published tests, it is usual to test similar groups of examinees year after year with parallel forms of the same test. When this happens, we can form a good picture of the frequency distribution of ability in the next group of examinees to be tested. Such "prior" information can be used to advantage to improve parameter estimation, providing it can be conveniently quantified and conveniently processed numerically.

Suppose each examinee tested is known to be randomly drawn from a population in which the distribution of ability is $g(\theta)$. The joint distribution of examinee ability θ and item response vector $\mathbf{u}$ for a randomly chosen examinee is equal to the conditional probability (4-20) multipled by $g(\theta)$:

$$L(\mathbf{u}, \theta | \mathbf{a}, \mathbf{b}, \mathbf{c}) \equiv L(\mathbf{u} | \theta; \mathbf{a}, \mathbf{b}, \mathbf{c}) g(\theta) = g(\theta) \prod_{i=1}^{n} [P_i(\theta)]^{u_i} [Q_i(\theta)]^{1-u_i}. \tag{12-5}$$

The marginal distribution of $\mathbf{u}$ for a randomly chosen examinee is obtained from the joint distribution by integrating out θ:

$$L(\mathbf{u} | \mathbf{a}, \mathbf{b}, \mathbf{c}) = \int_{-\infty}^{\infty} g(\theta) \prod_{i=1}^{n} [P_i(\theta)]^{u_i} [Q_i(\theta)]^{1-u_i} d\theta. \tag{12-6}$$

The conditional distribution of θ for given $\mathbf{u}$ is obtained by dividing (12-5) by (12-6). This last is the *posterior distribution* of θ given the item response vector $\mathbf{u}$. Since (12-6) is not a function of θ, we can say that the posterior distribution of θ is proportional to (12-5). This distribution contains all the information we have for inferring the ability θ of an examinee whose item responses are $\mathbf{u}$.

If we want a point estimate of θ for a particular examinee, we can use the mean of the posterior distribution (see Birnbaum, 1969) or its mode. There is no convenient mathematical expression for either mean or mode, but both can be determined numerically.

Use of the posterior mean $\bar{\theta}$ to estimate θ from $\mathbf{u}$ is the same as using the regression (conditional expectation) of θ on $\mathbf{u}$. Suppose we have a population of individuals, and for each individual we calculate the posterior mean $\bar{\theta}$. Let $\sigma_{\bar{\theta}}$ denote the standard deviation of these posterior means. By a standard definition, the correlation ratio of θ on $\mathbf{u}$ is

$$\eta_{\theta\mathbf{u}} \equiv \frac{\sigma_{\bar{\theta}}}{\sigma_\theta} \ ,$$

where $\sigma_{\bar{\theta}}^2$ is the prior or marginal variance of θ. Since $\bar{\theta}$ correlates only imperfectly with θ, $\eta_{\theta\mathbf{u}} < 1$ and $\sigma_{\bar{\theta}} < \sigma_\theta$; thus in any group the distribution of the estimates $\bar{\theta}$ will have a smaller variance than does the distribution of true ability θ. The $\bar{\theta}$ exhibit regression toward the mean.

If we define $\bar{\theta}^* \equiv \bar{\theta}/\eta_{\theta\mathbf{u}}$, then $\sigma_{\bar{\theta}_*} = \sigma_\theta$: The estimates have the same variance as the true values. But $\bar{\theta}^*$ is not a type of estimate usually used by Bayesian statisticians. The estimate $\bar{\theta}$ minimizes the mean square error of estimation over all examinees, but, as we have seen, it does not have the same variance as θ; the estimate $\bar{\theta}^*$ has the same variance as θ, but it is a worse estimate in terms of mean square error.

Is $\bar{\theta}$ or $\bar{\theta}^*$ unbiased for a particular person? If $\hat{\theta}$ is an unbiased estimator for every individual in a population of individuals, then the error $\hat{\theta} - \theta$ is uncorrelated with θ, so that in the population $\sigma_{\hat{\theta}}^2 = \sigma_\theta^2 + \sigma_{\hat{\theta}-\theta}^2 > \sigma_\theta^2$. Thus, the unbiased estimates $\hat{\theta}$ have a larger variance than the true ability parameters. They also have a larger variance than $\bar{\theta}$ or $\bar{\theta}^*$. Thus neither $\bar{\theta}$ nor $\bar{\theta}^*$ is unbiased.

The foregoing problems are simply a manifestation of the basic fact that the properties of estimates are never exactly the same as the properties of the true values.

The mode of the posterior distribution of θ is called the *Bayesian modal estimator*. If the posterior distribution is unimodal and symmetric, then the Bayesian modal estimator will be the same as the posterior mean $\bar{\theta}$, whose properties as an estimator have already been discussed.

12.9. FURTHER THEORETICAL COMPARISON OF ESTIMATORS

If $g(\theta)$ is uniform, then [see Eq. (12-5)] the posterior distribution of θ is proportional to the likelihood function (4-20). Thus when $g(\theta)$ is uniform, the maximum likelihood estimator $\hat{\theta}$ that maximizes (4-20) is the same as the Bayesian modal estimator that maximizes (12-5). Since any bell-shaped $g(\theta)$ is surely nearer the truth than a uniform distribution of θ, it has been argued, the Bayesian modal estimator (BME) computed from a suitable bell-shaped prior, $g(\theta)$, must surely be better than the maximum likelihood estimator (MLE), which (it is asserted) assumes a uniform prior.

The trouble with this argument is that it tacitly assumes the conclusion to be proved. If the BME were a faultless estimation procedure, then this line of reasoning would show that the MLE is inferior whenever $g(\theta)$ is not uniform. On the other hand, if the BME is less than perfect as an estimator, then the MLE cannot be criticized on the grounds that under an implausible assumption (uniform distribution of θ) it happens to coincide with the BME.

The MLE is invariant under any continuous one-to-one transformation of the parameter. The same likelihood equations will result whether we estimate θ or $\theta^* \equiv Ke^{k\theta}$, as in Eq. (6-2), or $\xi \equiv \Sigma_1^n P_i(\theta)$. Thus if $\hat{\theta}$ is the MLE of θ, the MLE of θ^* will be $Ke^{k\hat{\theta}}$ and the MLE of ξ will be $\Sigma_1^n P_i(\hat{\theta})$.

If the cited argument proved that the MLE assumes a uniform distribution of θ, then the same argument would prove that the MLE assumes a uniform distribution of θ^* and also of ξ. This is self-contradictory, since if any one of these is uniformly distributed, the others cannot be.

The absurd conclusion stems from the fact that BME is not invariant. It yields a substantively different estimate depending on whether we estimate θ, θ^*, or ξ. The proof of this statement follows.

In simplified notation, the posterior distribution is proportional to $L(\mathbf{u}|\Theta = \theta)g(\theta)$. The BME is the mode of the posterior distribution. If $\theta^* \equiv \theta^*(\theta)$ rather than θ is the parameter of interest, then the prior distribution of θ^* is

$$g^*(\theta^*) = g(\theta)\,\frac{d\theta}{d\theta^*}\ .$$

The posterior distribution of θ^* is thus proportional to

$$L(\mathbf{u}|\Theta^* = \theta^*)g^*(\theta^*) \equiv L(\mathbf{u}|\Theta = \theta)g(\theta)\,\frac{d\theta}{d\theta^*}\ .$$

The posterior for θ^* differs from the posterior for θ by the factor $d\theta/d\theta^*$. Thus the two posterior distributions will in general have different modes and will therefore yield different BME's.

As stated at the beginning, the purpose of this section is not to fault the BME but to point out a fallacy in a plausible line of reasoning, which superficially appears to show that the MLE assumes a uniform distribution of the parameter estimated. As pointed out at the end of Section 12.8, no point estimator, whether Bayesian or non-Bayesian, has all possible desirable properties. If $g(\theta)$ is known approximately, then any inference about θ may properly be based on the posterior distribution of θ given $\mathbf{u}$ (but not necessarily on the mode of this distribution). The MLE, on the other hand, is of interest in situations where we cannot or do not wish to restrict our attention to any particular $g(\theta)$.

It is often argued in other applications of Bayesian methods that the choice of prior distribution, here $g(\theta)$, does not matter much when the number n of observations is large. This fact is not helpful here, since n here is the number of items. Mental test theory exists only because the observed score on n items differs nonnegligibly from the true score that would be found if n were infinite.

12.10. ESTIMATION OF ITEM PARAMETERS

Bayesian estimation of item parameters might start by assuming that b_i has a normal or logistic prior distribution, that a_i has a gamma distribution, and that c_i has a beta distribution. Assuming all item parameters are distributed independently (there is some evidence to the contrary), one could try to work out convenient formulas for Bayesian estimation. So far, this seems not to have been attempted.

The following approach to item parameter estimation has been devised and used successfully by Bock and Lieberman (1970). Equation (12-6) gives the (marginal) probability of response vector $\mathbf{u}$. Denote this probability by $\pi_{\mathbf{u}}$ and the corresponding sample frequency of the response pattern (vector) by $f_{\mathbf{u}}$. There are 2^n possible different response patterns $\mathbf{u}$. The joint distribution of all possible pattern frequencies (response vectors) is the multinomial distribution

$$L \equiv \frac{N!}{\prod_{\mathbf{u}} f_{\mathbf{u}}} \cdot \prod_{\mathbf{u}} (\pi_{\mathbf{u}})^{f_{\mathbf{u}}} \tag{12-7}$$

Since the $\pi_{\mathbf{u}}$ are functions of the item parameters (but not of any θ), maximum likelihood estimates may be obtained by finding the item parameter values that maximize (12-7). Further details are given by Bock and Lieberman (1970).

12.11. ADDENDUM ON ESTIMATION

It is likely that new and better methods will be found for estimating both item parameters and ability parameters. Illustrative data in this book have mostly been obtained by certain modified maximum likelihood methods (Wood & Lord, 1976; Wood, Wingersky, & Lord, 1976). It is not the purpose of this book to recommend any particular estimation method, however, since such a recommendation is likely to become quickly out of date. The practical applications outlined in these chapters are useful regardless of whatever effective estimation method is used.

Anderson (1978) and Maurelli (1978) report studies comparing maximum likelihood estimates with Bayesian estimates. The interested reader is referred to Urry (1977) for a description of an alternative estimation procedure.

12.12. THE RASCH MODEL

Rasch's item response theory (Rasch 1966a, 1966b; Wright, 1977) assumes that all items are equally discriminating and that items cannot be answered correctly by guessing. The Rasch model is the special case of the three-parameter logistic model arising when $c_i = 0$ and $a_i = a$ for all items. If the Rasch assumptions are satisfied for some set of data, then sufficient statistics (Section 4.12) are available for estimating both item difficulty and examinee ability. If, as is usually the case, however, the Rasch assumptions are not met, then use of the Rasch model does not provide estimators with optimal properties. This last statement seems obvious, but it is often forgotten.

In any comparison of results from use of the Rasch model with results from the use of the three-parameter logistic model, it is important to remember the following. If the Rasch model holds, we are comparing the results of two statistical estimation procedures; we are *not* comparing two different models, since the Rasch model is included in the three-parameter model. If the Rasch model does not hold, then its use must be justified in some way. If sample size is small, for example, Rasch estimates may be more accurate than three-parameter-model estimates, even when the latter model holds and the Rasch model does not.

12.13.   EXERCISES

12-1   Given that $a = 1/1.7$, $b = 0$, $c = 0$, the logistic item response function is $P(\theta) = (1 + e^{-\theta})^{-1}$. If $\mathbf{u} = \{1, 0\}$ on a test with just $n = 2$ equivalent items, the likelihood function is $L(\mathbf{u}|\Theta = \theta) = P(\theta)Q(\theta)$. By trial and error, find numerically the MLE of θ, the value of θ that maximizes $P(\theta)Q(\theta)$.

12-2   If $\theta^* \equiv e^{\theta}$, the likelihood function for the situation in Exercise 12-1 is $P(\ln \theta^*)Q(\ln \theta^*)$. Find numerically the MLE of θ^*. Compare with the MLE of θ.

12-3   Suppose $g(\theta) = .1$ for $-5 \leqslant \theta \leqslant 5$, $g(\theta) = 0$ elsewhere. If $\mathbf{u} = \{1, 0\}$ on a test with just $n = 2$ equivalent items, the posterior distribution of θ is proportional to

$$L(\mathbf{u}|\Theta = \theta) = \begin{cases} 0.1 \ P(\theta)Q(\theta), \ (-5 \leqslant \theta \leqslant 5), \\ 0 \quad \text{elsewhere.} \end{cases}$$

Find the BME of θ for the test in Exercise 12-1. Compare with the MLE found there.

12-4   If $\theta^* = e^{\theta}$, the posterior distribution of θ^* for the situation in Exercise 12-3 is proportional to

$$L(\mathbf{u}|\Theta^* = \theta^*) = \begin{cases} \dfrac{.1 \ P(\theta)Q(\theta)}{e_{\theta}} \quad (e^{-5} \leqslant \theta^* \leqslant e^{5}), \\ 0 \quad \text{elsewhere.} \end{cases}$$

Show that $P(\theta)Q(\theta)/e^{\theta} \equiv Q^2(\theta)$. Find numerically the BME of θ^*. What is the corresponding value of $\theta \equiv \ln \theta^*$? Compare this with the estimates obtained in Exercise 12-2 and 12-3.

APPENDIX

Listed here for convenient reference are formulas for I_{qr} $(q, r = a, b, c)$ for the three-parameter logistic function. These formulas are used in the modified Newton–Raphson iterations (Section 12.2) and for computing sampling variances of maximum likelihood estimators (Section 12.3).

$$I_{aa} = \frac{D^2}{(1 - c_i)^2} \sum_{a=1}^{N} (\theta_a - b_i)^2 (P_{ia} - c_i)^2 \frac{Q_{ia}}{P_{ia}} . \qquad (12\text{-}8)$$

$$I_{bb} = \frac{D^2 a_i^2}{(1 - c_i)^2} \sum_{a=1}^{N} (P_{ia} - c_i)^2 \frac{Q_{ia}}{P_{ia}} . \qquad (12\text{-}9)$$

$$I_{cc} = \frac{1}{(1 - c_i)^2} \sum_{a=1}^{N} \frac{Q_{ia}}{P_{ia}} . \qquad (12\text{-}10)$$

$$I_{ab} = - \frac{D^2 a_i}{(1 - c_i)^2} \sum_{a=1}^{N} (\theta_a - b_i)(P_{ia} - c_i)^2 \frac{Q_{ia}}{P_{ia}} . \qquad (12\text{-}11)$$

$$I_{ac} = \frac{D}{(1 - c_i)^2} \sum_{a=1}^{N} (\theta_a - b_i)(P_{ia} - c_i) \frac{Q_{ia}}{P_{ia}} . \qquad (12\text{-}12)$$

$$I_{bc} = - \frac{D a_i}{(1 - c_i)^2} \sum_{a=1}^{N} (P_{ia} - c_i) \frac{Q_{ia}}{P_{ia}} . \qquad (12\text{-}13)$$

REFERENCES

Andersen, E. B. Conditional inference for multiple-choice questionnaires. *The British Journal of Mathematical and Statistical Psychology*, 1973, 26, 31–44.

Anderson, M. R. *The robustness of two parameter estimation methods for latent trait models.* Doctoral dissertation, University of Kansas, 1978.

Birnbaum, A. Statistical theory for logistic mental test models with a prior distribution of ability. *Journal of Mathematical Psychology*, 1969, 6, 258–276.

Bock, R. D., & Lieberman, M. Fitting a response model for n dichotomously scored items. *Psychometrika*, 1970, 35, 179–197.

Haberman, S. J. Maximum likelihood estimates in exponential response models. *The Annals of Statistics*, 1977, 5, 815–841.

Kale, B. K. On the solution of likelihood equations by iteration processes. The multiparametric case. *Biometrika*, 1962, 49, 479–486.

Kendall, M. G., & Stuart, A. *The advanced theory of statistics* (Vol. 1) (3rd ed.). New York: Hafner, 1969.

Maurelli, V. A., Jr. *A comparison of Bayesian and maximum likelihood scoring in a simulated stradaptive test.* Master's thesis, St. Mary's University, San Antonio, Texas, 1978.

Meredith, W. Poisson distributions of error in mental test theory. *British Journal of Mathematical and Statistical Psychology*, 1970, 24, 49–82.

Rasch, G. *Probabilistic models for some intelligence and attainment tests.* Copenhagen: Nielsen and Lydiche, 1960.

Rasch, G. An individualistic approach to item analysis. In P. F. Lazarsfeld & N. W. Henry (Eds.), *Readings in mathematical social science*. Chicago: Science Research Associates, 1966. (a)

Rasch, G. An item analysis which takes individual differences into account. *The British Journal of Mathematical and Statistical Psychology, 1966, 19,* 49–57. (b)

Urry, V. Tailored testing: A successful application of latent trait theory. *Journal of Educational Measurement, 1977, 14,* 181–196.

van der Ven, Ad H. G. S. An error score model for time-limit tests. *Tijdschrift voor Onderwijs-research, 1976, 1,* 215–226.

Wood, R L, & Lord, F. M. *A user's guide to LOGIST*. Research Memorandum 76-4. Princeton, N.J.: Educational Testing Service, 1976.

Wood, R L, Wingersky, M. S., & Lord, F. M. *LOGIST–A computer program for estimating examinee ability and item characteristic curve parameters*. Research Memorandum 76-6. Princeton, N.J.: Educational Testing Service, 1976.

Wright, B. D. Solving measurement problems with the Rasch model. *Journal of Educational Measurement, 1977, 14,* 97–116.

13

Equating

13.1. EQUATING INFALLIBLE MEASURES

Consider a situation where many people are being selected to do typing. All applicants have been tested before applying for employment. Some come with test record x showing typing speed in words per second; others come with test record y showing typing speed in seconds per word. We assume for this section that all typing tests are perfectly reliable ("infallible").

There is a one-to-one correspondence between the two measures x and y of typing speed. The hiring official will undoubtedly wish to express all typing speeds in the same terms for easy comparison of applicants. Perhaps he will replace all y scores by their reciprocals. In general, we denote such a transformation by $x_y \equiv x(y)$. In the illustration, $x(y) = 1/y$. Clearly x and x_y are comparable values.

[Note on notation: In practical test work, a new test is commonly equated to an old test. It seems natural to call the old test x and the new test y. The function $x_y \equiv x(y)$ may seem awkward, since we habitually think of y as a function of x. An alternative notation would write $y^*(y)$ instead of $x(y)$; this would fail to emphasize the key fact that $x_y \equiv x(y)$ is on the same scale as x.]

In mental testing, we may believe that two tests, x and y, measure the same trait without knowing the mathematical relation between the score scale for x and the score scale for y. Suppose the hiring officer knew that both x and y were perfectly reliable measures of typing speed but did not know how each was expressed. Could he without further testing find the mathematical relation $x(y)$ between x and y, so as to use them for job selection? If many applicants have both x and y, it is easy to find $x(y)$ approximately. But suppose that the hiring officer never obtains both x and y on the same individual.

The true situation, not known to the hiring officer, is illustrated schematically in Fig. 13.1.1. The points falling along the curve represent corresponding values of x and y for various individuals. The frequency distributions of x and y for the combined population (of all applicants regardless of test taken) are indicated along the two axes (the y distribution is shown upside down).

It should be clear from Fig. 13.1.1 that when y and x have a one-to-one monotonic relation, any cutting score Y_0 on y implies a cutting score $X_0 \equiv x(Y_0)$ on x. Moreover, the people who lie to the right of Y_0 are the same people as the people who lie below X_0. Thus the percentile rank of Y_0, counted from right to left in the distribution of y, is the same as the percentile rank of X_0 counting upward in the distribution of x. The cutting scores X_0 and Y_0 are said to have an *equipercentile relationship*.

If $G(y)$ denotes the cumulative distribution of y cumulated from right to left and $F(x)$ denotes the cumulative distribution of x cumulated from low to high, then $F(X_0) \equiv G(Y_0)$ for any pair of corresponding cutting points (Y_0, X_0). Since F is monotonic, we can solve this equation for X_0, obtaining $X_0 \equiv F^{-1}[G(Y_0)]$, where F^{-1} is the inverse function of F. Thus, the transformation $x(y)$ is given by

$$x_y \equiv x(y) \equiv F^{-1}[G(y)]. \tag{13-1}$$

It is generally more convenient to express this relationship by the parametric equations

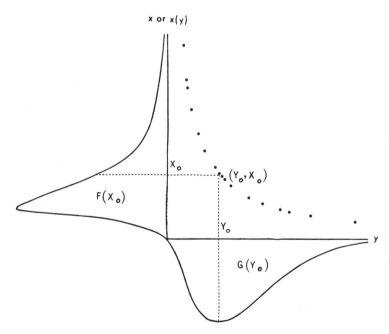

FIG. 13.1.1.   Equipercentile relation of X_0 to Y_0.

$$F(x_y) = p \atop G(y) = p, \Bigg\} \qquad\qquad\qquad (13\text{-}2)$$

where p is the percentile rank of both y and x_y. This last pair of equations is a direct statement of the *equipercentile relationship* of x_y to y.

In the present application where $y = 1/x$, y decreases as x increases. In most typical applications, x and y increase together, in which case we define $G(y)$ in the usual way, cumulated from left to right. If x and y increase together, (13-2) still applies, using the appropriate definition of $G(y)$.

Suppose, now, that the hiring officer in our illustration knows that applicants with x are a random sample from the same population as applicants with y. This information will allow him to estimate the mathematical relation of x to y. His sample cumulative distribution of y values is an estimate of $G(y)$; his sample distribution of x values is an estimate of $F(x)$. He can therefore estimate the relationship $x(y)$ from (13-1) or (13-2).

When this has been done, the transformed or "equated" score x_y is on the x scale of measurement, and test y is said to have been *equated* to test x. To summarize, *if (1)* x(y) *is a one-to-one function of* y *and (2) the* X *group has the same distribution of ability as the* Y *group, then (3) equipercentile equating will transform* y *to the same scale of measurement as* x; *and (4) the transformed* y, *denoted by* $x_y \equiv$ x(y), *will have the same frequency distribution as* x. Two perfectly reliable tests measuring the same trait can be equated by administering them to equivalent populations of examinees and carrying out an equipercentile equating by (13-2). *The equating will be the same no matter what the distribution of ability in the two equivalent populations.*

13.2. EQUITY

If an equating of tests x *and* y *is to be equitable to each applicant, it must be a matter of indifference to applicants at every given ability level* θ *whether they are to take test* x *or test* y. More precisely, equity requires that for applicants at every ability level θ, the (conditional) frequency distribution $f_{x\mid\theta}$ of score x should be the same as the (conditional) frequency distribution $f_{x(y)\mid\theta}$ of the (transformed) score $x(y)$:

$$f_{x\mid\theta} \equiv f_{x(y)\mid\theta}, \qquad\qquad\qquad (13\text{-}3)$$

where $x(y)$ is a one-to-one function of y. Note that if $f_{x\mid\theta}$ [or $f_{x(y)\mid\theta}$] has nonzero variance, as will be assumed hereafter, this implies that x (or y) is an imperfectly reliable ("fallible") measurement.

It is not sufficient for equity that $f_{x\mid\theta}$ and $f_{x(y)\mid\theta}$ have the same means. Suppose they have the same means but different variances. Competent applicants can be confident that a test score with small conditional variance will make their competence evident; a score with large conditional variance (large errors of measurement) may not do so. Thus, if the variances are unequal, it is not a matter of indifference to them whether they take test x or test y.

Note that if the equity requirement holds over a certain range of ability, it necessarily holds for all groups within that range of ability. This statement is true no matter how the groups are defined; for example, by sex, by race, or by educational or social characteristics.

If an X group and a Y group have the same distribution of ability, $g^*(\theta)$, then the unconditional distribution of x in the X group is

$$\phi_X(x) = \int_{-\infty}^{\infty} g^*(\theta) f_{x|\theta} \, d\theta; \tag{13-4}$$

the unconditional distribution of $x(y)$ in the Y group is

$$\phi_Y(x_y) = \int_{-\infty}^{\infty} g^*(\theta) f_{x(y)|\theta} \, d\theta.$$

By (13-3), if equity holds, the conditional frequency distributions are the same, so that

$$\phi_X(\ ) \equiv \phi_Y(\ ). \tag{13-5}$$

Consequently, x and y have an equipercentile relationship; equipercentile equating using (13-2) will discover the relation $x(y)$.

A similar result is shown in the preceding section for perfectly reliable scores; the present result applies to imperfectly reliable scores *provided* the equity requirement holds. Unfortunately, as we shall see, the equity requirement cannot hold for fallible tests unless x and y are parallel tests, in which case there is no need for any equating at all.

13.3. CAN FALLIBLE TESTS BE EQUATED?

From Eq. (4-1), the conditional frequency distribution $f_{x|\theta}$ of number-right test score x is given by the identity

$$\sum_{x=0}^{n} f_{x|\theta} t^x \equiv \prod_{i=1}^{n} (Q_i + P_i t), \tag{13-6}$$

where the symbol t serves only to determine the proper grouping of terms on the right. For $n = 3$, for example, (13-6) becomes

$$\begin{aligned}
f_{0|\theta} + f_{1|\theta} t + f_{2|\theta} t^2 + f_{3|\theta} t^3 &\equiv Q_1 Q_2 Q_3 \\
&+ (Q_1 Q_2 P_3 + Q_1 P_2 Q_3 + P_1 Q_2 Q_3)t + (Q_1 P_2 P_3 + P_1 Q_2 P_3 \\
&+ P_1 P_2 Q_3)t^2 + P_1 P_2 P_3 t^3,
\end{aligned}$$

which holds for all values of t.

If m is the number of items in test y, we have similarly for the conditional distribution $g_{y|\theta}$ of number-right score y

$$\sum_{y=0}^{m} g_{y|\theta} t^{y} \equiv \prod_{j=1}^{m} (Q_j + P_j t).$$

It should not matter which test is labeled x, so we choose the labeling to make $n \geq m$. Since $x(y)$ is a function of y, it follows that the conditional distribution $h_{x(y)|\theta}$ of the equated score $x(y)$ is given by

$$\sum_{y=0}^{m} h_{x(y)|\theta} t^{y} \equiv \prod_{j=1}^{m} (Q_j + P_j t). \tag{13-7}$$

Equity, however, requires that the distribution of the function $x(y)$ be the same as that of x. Substituting $x(y)$ for x in (13-6), we have

$$\sum_{x(y)=0}^{n} f_{x(y)|\theta} t^{x(y)} \equiv \prod_{i=1}^{n} (Q_i + P_i t). \tag{13-8}$$

Since each $f_{x(y)|\theta} > 0$, the $h_{x(y)|\theta}$ in (13-7) must be the same as the $f_{x(y)|\theta}$ in (13-8). Thus $m = n$. From (13-3), (13-7), and (13-8),

$$\prod_{i=1}^{n} (Q_i + P_i t) \equiv \prod_{j=1}^{n} (Q_j + P_j t) \tag{13-9}$$

for all θ and for all t.

We now prove (under regularity conditions) that (13-9) will hold only if tests x and y are strictly parallel. Since t in (13-9) is arbitrary, replace t by $t + 1$ to obtain $\Pi_i(1 + P_i t) \equiv \Pi_j(1 + P_j t)$. Taking logarithms, we have $\Sigma_i \ln (1 + P_i t) \equiv \Sigma_j \ln (1 + P_j t)$. Expanding each logarithm in a power series, we have for $t^2 < 1$ and for all θ that

$$\Sigma_i(P_i t - \tfrac{1}{2}P_i^2 t^2 + \tfrac{1}{3}P_i^3 t^3 - \cdots) \equiv \Sigma_j(P_j t - \tfrac{1}{2}P_j^2 t^2 + \tfrac{1}{3}P_j^3 t^3 - \cdots).$$

$$\tag{13-10}$$

After dividing by n, this may be rewritten

$$\sum_{r=1}^{\infty} \frac{\mu_r (-t)^r}{r} \equiv \sum_{r=1}^{\infty} \frac{\nu_r (-t)^r}{r}, \tag{13-11}$$

where (for any given θ) $\mu_r \equiv n^{-1}\Sigma^n P_i^r$ is the rth (conditional) moment about the origin of the P_i for n items in test x, and ν_r is the rth (conditional) moment about the origin of the P_j for the n items in test y. Because a convergent Taylor series is unique, it follows that $\mu_r \equiv \nu_r$. Since the distribution of a bounded variable is determined by its moments [Kendall & Stuart, 1969, Section

4.22(c)], it follows under realistic regularity conditions[1] that for each item in test *x* there is an item in test *y* with the same item response function $P(\theta)$, and vice versa.

Since it contradicts common thinking and practice, it is worth stating this result as a theorem:

Theorem 13.3.1.   Under realistic regularity conditions, *scores* x *and* y *on two tests cannot be equated unless either (1) both scores are perfectly reliable or (2) the two tests are strictly parallel [in which case* x(y) $\equiv$ y].

13.4. REGRESSION METHODS

Since test users are frequently faced with a real practical need for equating tests from different publishers, what can be done in the light of Theorem 13.3.1, which states that such tests cannot be equated? A first reaction is typically to try to use some prediction approach based on regression equations.

If we were to try to predict *x* from *y*, we would clearly be doing the wrong thing. From the point of view of the examinee, *x* and *y* are symmetrically related. *A basic requirement of equating is that the result should be the same no matter which test is called* x *and which is called* y. This requirement is not satisfied when we predict one test from the other.

Suppose we have some criterion, denoted by ω, such as grade-point average or success on the job. Denote by $R_x(\omega|x)$ the value of ω predicted from *x* by the usual (linear or nonlinear) regression equation and by $R_y(\omega|y)$ the value predicted from *y*. A sophisticated regression approach will determine $x(y)$ so that $R_x[\omega|x(y)] = R_y(\omega|y)$. For example, if ω is academic grade-point average, a person scoring *y* on test *y* and a person scoring *x* on test *x* will be treated as equal whenever their predicted grade-point averages are equal.

By Theorem 13.3.1, however, it is clear that such an $x(y)$ will ordinarily not satisfy the equity requirement. Other difficulties follow. We state here a general conclusion reached in the appendix at the end of this chapter: *Suppose* x(y) *is defined by* $R_x[\omega|x(y)] \equiv R_y(\omega|y)$. *The transformation* x(y) *found typically will vary from group to group unless* x *and* y *are equally correlated with the criterion* ω. This is not satisfactory: An equating should hold for all subgroups of our total group (for men, women, blacks, whites, math majors, etc.).

Suppose that *x* is an accurate predictor of ω and that *y* is not. Competent

---

[1]The need for regularity conditions has been pointed out by Charles E. Davis. For example, let test *x* consist of the two items illustrated in Fig. 3.4.1. Let θ† denote the value of θ where these two response functions cross. Let the first (second) item in test *y* have the same response function as item 1 (2) in test *x* up to θ† and the same response function as item 2 (1) in test *x* above θ†. Test *x* can be equated to this specially contrived test *y*. Since such situations are not realistic, the mathematical regularity conditions required to eliminate them are not detailed here.

examinees are severely penalized if they take test y: Their chance of selection may be little better than under random selection. Regression methods may optimize selection from the point of view of the selecting institution; they may not yield a satisfactory solution to the equity problem from the point of view of the applicants.

13.5.   TRUE-SCORE EQUATING

Three important requirements are mentioned in preceding sections for equating two unidimensional tests that measure the same ability:

1. Equity: For every θ, the conditional frequency distribution of $x(y)$ given θ must be the same as the conditional frequency distribution of x.

2. Invariance across groups: $x(y)$ must be the same regardless of the population from which it is determined.

3. Symmetry: The equating must be the same regardless of which test is labeled x and which is labeled y.

We have seen that in practice these seemingly indispensable requirements in general cannot be met for fallible test scores. An equating of true scores, on the other hand, can satisfy the listed requirements. We therefore proceed to consider how item response theory can be used to equate true scores.

If test x and test y are both measures of the same ability θ, then their number-right true scores are related to θ by their test characteristic functions [Eq. (4-5)]:

$$\xi \equiv \sum_{i=1}^{n} P_i(\theta), \qquad \eta \equiv \sum_{j=1}^{m} P_j(\theta). \qquad (13\text{-}12)$$

Equations (13-12) are parametric equations for the relation between η and ξ. A single equation for the relationship is found (in principle) by eliminating θ from the two parametric equations. In practice, this relationship can be estimated by using estimated item parameters to approximate the $P_i(\theta)$ and $P_j(\theta)$ and then substituting a series of arbitrary values of θ into (13-12) and computing ξ and η for each θ. The resulting paired values define ξ as a function of η (or vice versa) and constitute an equating of these true scores. Note that the relation between ξ and η is mathematical and not statistical (not a scatterplot). Since ξ and η are each monotonic increasing functions of θ, it follows that ξ is a monotonic increasing function of η.

Figure 13.5.1 shows the estimated test characteristic curves of two calculus tests: AP with 45 five-choice items and CLEP with 50 five-choice items. The broken line in Fig. 13.5.1 graphically illustrates the meaning of true-score equating. The broken line shows that a true score of 35 on CLEP is equivalent to a true

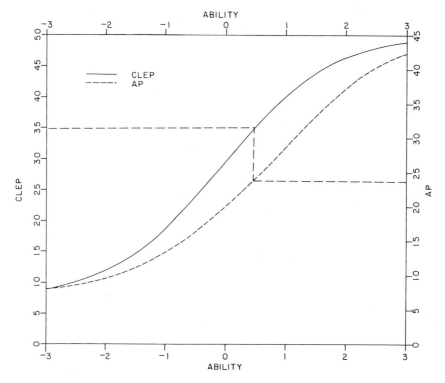

FIG. 13.5.1.   Equating AP and CLEP using test characteristic curves.

score of approximately 24 on AP. The estimated equating relation between true scores on CLEP and AP, obtained in this way from Fig. 13.5.1 or directly from (13-12), is shown by the dashed curve in Fig. 13.5.2.

13.6.   TRUE-SCORE EQUATING WITH AN ANCHOR TEST

If test x and test y are both given to the same examinees, the test administered second is not being given under typical conditions because of practice effects, for example, fatigue. If, on the other hand, each of the two tests is given to a different sample of examinees, the equating is impaired by differences between the samples.

Differences between the two samples of examinees can be measured and controlled by administering to each examinee an *anchor test* measuring the same ability as x and y. *When an anchor test is used, equating may be carried out even when the* x *group and the* y *group are not at the same ability level.* The anchor test may be a part of both test x and test y; such an anchor test is called *internal*.

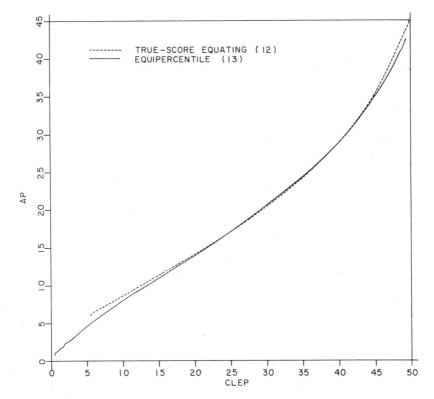

FIG. 13.5.2.   Two estimates of the line of relationship between AP and CLEP.

If the anchor test is a separate test, it is called *external*. An external anchor test is administered second, after x or y, to avoid any practice effect on the scores being equated. If the difference between the two groups is small, any difference between test x and test y in their practice effect on the anchor test is a second-order effect, assumed to be negligible.

Data from such an administration are readily used for the equating procedure of the preceding section. All item response data of all examinees are analyzed simultaneously to obtain estimates of all item parameters. The fact that each examinee takes only part of the items is no problem for the parameter estimation procedure; the procedure simply ignores items not administered to a particular examinee, just as the "not reached" items are ignored in Section 12.4. This is appropriate and effective, in view of the presumed invariance of an examinee's ability θ from test to test.

In the case of Fig. 13.5.2, the two groups did differ substantially in ability. The equating was made possible by the fact that 17 items appeared in both tests, providing an internal anchor test.

If the anchor test is external to the two regular tests, the item parameters for the anchor items are not used in the equating procedure of Section 13.5. They have served their purpose by tying the data together so that all parameters are expressed on the same scale. Without such anchor items, equating would be impossible unless the x group and the y group had the same distribution of ability.

13.7.   RAW-SCORE "EQUATING" WITH AN ANCHOR TEST

The true-score equating of the preceding section is straightforward and effective. How else could you estimate the curvilinear relation between true scores on two nonparallel tests when no person has taken both?

The problem is that there is no really appropriate way to make use of the true-score equating obtained. We do not know an examinee's true score. We can estimate his true score from his responses: $\hat{\xi} = \Sigma_i \hat{P}_i(\hat{\theta})$ is such an estimate. However, an estimated true score does not have the properties of true scores; an estimated true score, after all, is just another kind of fallible observed score. As proved in Section 13.3, fallible scores cannot be strictly equated unless the two tests are strictly parallel.

We consider here a possible approximate equating for raw scores. We start with an estimate $\hat{\gamma}(\theta)$ of the distribution $\gamma(\theta)$ of θ in some specified group (often this group will be all the examinees in the equating study). The actual distribution of $\hat{\theta}_a$ in the group is an approximation to $\gamma(\theta)$. A better approximation is given in Chapter 16.

As in Eq. (4-12), the distribution of observed score x for the specified group can be estimated by

$$\hat{\phi}_x(x) = \frac{1}{N} \sum_{a=1}^{N} \hat{\phi}_x(x|\hat{\theta}_a), \qquad (13\text{-}13)$$

where $a = 1, 2, \ldots, N$ indexes the examinees in the specified group. If $\hat{\gamma}(\theta)$ is continuous as in Chapter 16, however, the estimated $\phi(x)$ is obtained by numerical integration from

$$\hat{\phi}_x(x) = \int_{-\infty}^{\infty} \hat{\phi}_x(x|\theta)\hat{\gamma}(\theta) \, d\theta. \qquad (13\text{-}14)$$

The function $\hat{\phi}_x(x|\hat{\theta}_a)$ is given by Eq. (4-1), using estimated item parameters for test x items in place of their true values.

Similar equations apply for test y. Furthermore, since x and y are independently distributed when θ is fixed, the joint distribution of scores x and y for the specified group is estimated by

$$\hat{\phi}(x, y) = \frac{1}{N} \sum_{a=1}^{N} \hat{\phi}_x (x|\hat{\theta}_a) \hat{\phi}_y (y|\hat{\theta}_a), \tag{13-15}$$

or by

$$\hat{\phi}(x, y) = \int_{-\infty}^{\infty} \hat{\phi}_x (x|\theta) \hat{\phi}_y (y|\theta) \hat{\gamma}(\theta) \, d\theta. \tag{13-16}$$

Note that, thanks to the anchor test, it is possible to estimate the joint distribution of x and y even though no examinee has taken both tests.

The integrand of (13-16) is the trivariate distribution of θ, x, and y. Since θ determines the true scores ξ and η, this distribution also represents the joint distribution of the four variables ξ, η, x, and y. *The joint distribution contains all possible information about the relation of* x *to* y. *Yet, by Section 13.3, it cannot provide an adequate equating of* x *and* y *unless the two tests are already parallel.*

A plausible procedure is to determine the equipercentile relationship between x and y from (13-15) or (13-16) and to treat this as an approximate equating. Is this better than applying the true-score equating of Section 13.5 to observed scores x and y or to estimated true scores $\hat{\xi} \equiv \sum \hat{P}_i(\hat{\theta})$ and $\hat{\eta}$?

At present, we have no criterion for evaluating the degree of inadequacy of an imperfect equating. Without such a criterion, the question cannot be answered. At least the equipercentile equating of x and y covers the entire range of observed scores, whereas the equating of ξ and η cannot provide any guide for scores below the "chance" levels represented by $\sum c_i$.

The solid line of relationship in Fig. 13.5.2 is obtained by the methods of this section. The result agrees very closely with the true-score equating of Section 13.6. Further comparisons of this kind need to be made before we can safely generalize this conclusion.

13.8. ILLUSTRATIVE EXAMPLE[2]

Figure 13.5.2 is presented because it deals with a practical equating problem. For just this reason, however, there is no satisfactory way to check on the accuracy of the results obtained. The results obtained by conventional methods cannot be justified as a criterion.

The following example was set up so as to have a proper criterion for the equating results. Here, unknown to the computer procedure, test X and test Y are actually the same test. Thus we know in advance what the line of relation should be.

[2]This section is taken with special permission from F. M. Lord, Practical applications of item characteristic curve theory. *Journal of Educational Measurement,* Summer 1977, *14,* No. 2, 117–138. Copyright 1977, National Council on Measurement in Education, Inc., East Lansing, Mich.

Test X is the 85-item verbal section of the College Board SAT, Form XSA, administered to a group of 2802 college applicants in a regular SAT administration. Test Y is the same test administered to a second group of 2763 applicants. Both groups also took a 39-item verbal test mostly, but not entirely, similar to the regular 85-item test. The 39-item test is used here as an anchor test for the equating.

The two groups differed in ability level (otherwise the outcome of the equating would be a foregone conclusion). The proportion of correct answers given to typical items is lower by roughly 0.10 in the first group than in the second.

The equating was carried out exactly as described in Section 13.6. One computer run was made simultaneously for all $85 + 85 + 39 = 209$ items and for all 5565 examinees. The resulting line of relationship between true-scores on test

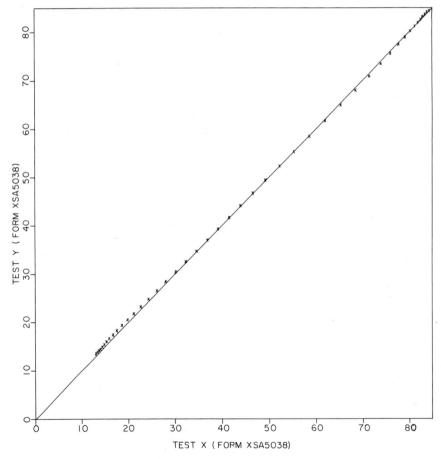

FIG. 13.8.1. Estimated equating (crosses) between "Test X" and "Test Y," which are actual y identical.

X and test Y is shown by the crosses in Fig. 13.8.1. It agrees very well with the 45-degree line, also shown, that should be found when a test is equated to itself.

Results like this have been obtained for many sets of data. It is the repeated finding of such results that encourages confidence in the item response function model used.

13.9. PREEQUATING

Publishers who annually produce several forms of the same test have a continual need for good equating methods. Conventional methods may properly require 1000 or more examinees for each test equated. If the test to be equated is a secure test used for an important purpose, a special equating administration is likely to impair its security. The reason is that coaching schools commonly secure detailed advance information about the test questions from such equating administrations.

In preequating, by use of item response theory, each new test form is equated to previous forms before it is administered. In preequating, a very large pool of calibrated test items is maintained. New forms are built from this pool. The method of Section 13.5 is used to place all true scores on the same score scale. Scaled observed scores on the various test forms are then treated as if they were interchangeable. A practical study of preequating is reported by Marco (1977).

Preequating eliminates special equating administrations for new test forms. It requires instead special calibration administrations for new test items to be included in the pool. Each final test form is drawn from so many calibration administrations that its security is not seriously compromised.

Figure 13.9.1 shows a plan for a series of administrations for item calibration. Rows in the table represent sets of items; columns represent groups of examinees. An asterisk represents the administration of an item set to a particular group. The column labeled n shows the number of items in each item set; the row labeled n shows the number of items taken by each group. The row labeled N shows the number of examinees in each group; the column labeled N shows the number of examinees taking each item set.

A total of 399 items are to be precalibrated using a total of 15,000 examinees. The total number of responses is approximately 938,000; thus an examinee takes about 62 items on the average, and an item is administered to about 2350 examinees on the average. The table is organized to facilitate an understanding of the adequacy of linkages tying the data together.

Item set F72 consists of previously calibrated items taken from the precalibrated item pool. The remaining items are all new items to be calibrated. The item parameters of the new items will be estimated from these data while the b_i for the 20 precalibrated items are held fixed at their precalibrated values. This will place all new item parameters on the same scale as the precalibrated item pool. All new item and examinee parameters will be estimated simultaneously by maximum likelihood from the total data set consisting of all 958,000 responses (see Appendix).

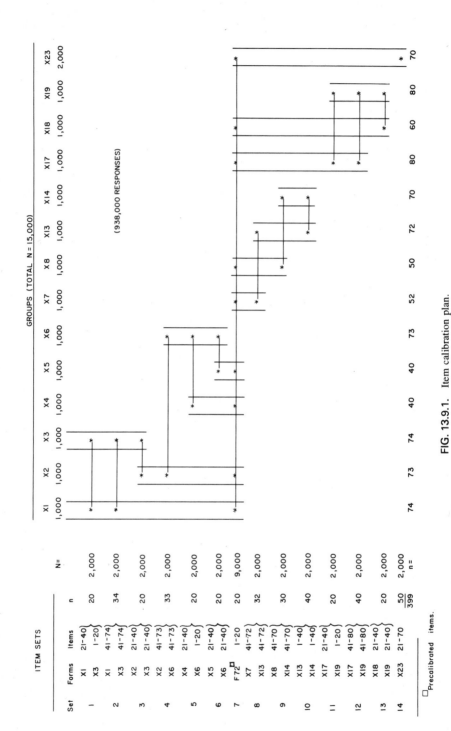

FIG. 13.9.1. Item calibration plan.

13.10. CONCLUDING REMARKS

Since practical pressures often require that tests be "equated" at least approximately, the procedures suggested in Sections 13.5–13.7 may be used. What is really needed is a criterion for evaluating approximate procedures, so as to be able to choose from among them. *If you can't be fair (provide equity) to everyone, what is the next best thing?*

There is a parallel here to the problem of determining an unbiased selection procedure (Hunter & Schmidt, 1976; Thorndike, 1971). Some procedures are fair from the point of view of the selecting institutions. Usually, however, no procedure can be simultaneously fair, even from a statistical point of view, both to the selecting institutions and to various subgroups of examinees.

In the present problem, the equating needs of a particular selecting institution could be satisfied by regression methods (Section 13.4). If regression methods of "equating" are used, however, examinees could properly complain that they had been disadvantaged (denied admission to college, for example) because they had taken test y instead of test x or test x instead of test y. It seems important to avoid this.

An equipercentile "equating" of raw scores has the convenient property that when a cutting score is used, the proportion of selected examinees will be the same for those taking test x *and for those taking test* y, *except for sampling fluctuations.* This will be true regardless of where the institution sets its cutting score. Thus equipercentile "equating" of raw scores gives an appearance of being fair to everyone.

Most practical equatings are carried out between "parallel" test forms. In such cases, forms x and y are so nearly alike that equipercentile equating, or even conventional mean-and-sigma equating, should yield excellent results. This chapter does not discourage such practical procedures. This chapter tries to clarify the implications of equating as a concept. Such clarification is especially important for any practical equating of tests from two different publishers or of tests at two different educational levels.

The reader is referred to Angoff (1971) for a detailed exposition of conventional equating methods. Woods and Wiley (1978) give a detailed account of their application of item response theory to a complicated practical equating problem involving the equating of 60 different reading tests, using available data from 31 states and the District of Columbia.

13.11. EXERCISES

13-1   The test characteristic function for test 1 was computed in Exercise 5.9.1. Compute for $\theta = -3, -2, -1, 0, 1, 2, 3$ the test characteristic function of a test composed of $n = 3$ items just like the items in Table 4.17.2. From these two test characteristic functions, determine equated true scores for these two tests. Plot seven points on the equating function $x(y)$ and connect by a smooth curve.

13-2 Suppose that test x is a perfectly reliable test with scores $x \equiv T$. Suppose test y is a poorly reliable test with scores $y \equiv T + E$, where E is a random error of measurement, as in Section 1.2. Make a diagram showing a scatterplot for x and y and also the regressions of y on x and of x on y. Discuss various functions $x(y)$ that might be used to try to "equate" scores on test y to scores on test x.

APPENDIX

"Equating" by Regression Methods Is Not Invariant Across Groups

This appendix points out one disadvantage of determining $x(y)$ so that the regression R_x of criterion ω on $x(y)$ is the same as the regression R_y of the criterion on y (see Section 13.4):

$$R_x[\omega|x(y)] = R_y(\omega|y). \tag{13-17}$$

We shall work with the usual linear regression coefficients $\beta_{x\omega}$, $\beta_{\omega x}$, $\beta_{y\omega}$, and $\beta_{\omega y}$. Suppose that all regressions are actually linear; that the standard error of estimate, denoted here by $\sigma_{x\cdot\omega}$, is the same for all ω; and that $\sigma_{y|\omega} = \sigma_{y\cdot\omega}$ likewise.

A standard formula for the effect of explicit selections on ω (Gulliksen, 1950, Chapter 11) shows how the correlation $\rho_{x\omega}$ (likewise $\rho_{y\omega}$) changes as the variance of ω is changed:

$$\rho_{x\omega}'^2 = \frac{1}{1 + \dfrac{\sigma_\omega^2}{\sigma_\omega'^2}\dfrac{1 - \rho_{x\omega}^2}{\rho_{x\omega}^2}}, \tag{13-18}$$

where the prime denotes a statistic for the selected group. For any group

$$\beta_{x\omega}\beta_{\omega x} = \rho_{x\omega}^2. \tag{13-19}$$

From (13-18) and (13-19) we have

$$\beta_{x\omega}'\beta_{\omega x}' = \frac{1}{1 - (\sigma_\omega^2/\sigma_\omega'^2)[1 - (1/\rho_{x\omega}^2)]} \tag{13-20}$$

and similarly for y

$$\beta_{y\omega}'\beta_{\omega y}' = \frac{1}{1 - (\sigma_\omega^2/\sigma_\omega'^2)[1 - (1/\rho_{y\omega}^2)]}. \tag{13-21}$$

If the equating (13-17) is to hold for the selected group, we must have $R'_x[\omega|x(y)]$ $\equiv R'_y(\omega|y)$ and consequently $\beta'_{\omega x} = \beta'_{\omega y}$. Dividing (13-21) by (13-20) to eliminate $\beta'_{\omega y} = \beta'_{\omega x}$, we have

$$\frac{\beta'_{y\omega}}{\beta'_{x\omega}} = \frac{\sigma_\omega'^2 - \sigma_\omega^2[1 - (1/\rho_{x\omega}^2)]}{\sigma_\omega'^2 - \sigma_\omega^2[1 - (1/\rho_{y\omega}^2)]} . \tag{13-22}$$

We assume, as is usual, that the (linear) regressions on ω are the same before and after selection: $\beta'_{x\omega} = \beta_{x\omega}$ and $\beta'_{y\omega} = \beta_{y\omega}$. Thus, finally

$$\frac{\beta_{y\omega}}{\beta_{x\omega}} = \frac{\sigma_\omega'^2 - \sigma_\omega^2[1 - (1/\rho_{x\omega}^2)]}{\sigma_\omega'^2 - \sigma_\omega^2[1 - (1/\rho_{y\omega}^2)]} . \tag{13-23}$$

Consider what happens when $\sigma_\omega'^2$ varies from group to group. All unprimed statistics in (13-23) refer to a fixed group and do not vary. The ratio on the left stays the same, but the ratio on the right can stay the same only if $\rho_{y\omega} = \rho_{x\omega}$. This is an illustration of a more general conclusion:

Suppose x(y) *is defined by* $R_x[\omega|x(y)] \equiv R_y(\omega|y)$. *The transformation* x(y) *that is found will typically vary from group to group unless* x *and* y *are equally correlated with the criterion* ω.

Numerical Estimation Procedures to Accelerate Convergence

If all item and examinee parameters were estimated simultaneously, the estimation problem for Fig. 13.9.1 would not differ significantly from typical problems discussed in Chapter 12, except for the very large number of parameters to be estimated. Actually, item parameters and person parameters must be estimated alternately (see Section 12.1) rather than simultaneously, in order to keep the information matrix $\|I_{qr}\|$ diagonal, or nearly so. In practice, convergence is slow whenever, as illustrated in Fig. 13.9.1, the item–person matrix is poorly internally interconnected (that is, when several changes of direction may be required to get from one part of the matrix to another following the marked straight paths from asterisk to asterisk).

In such cases, the iterative estimation process reaches a condition where the estimates no longer fluctuate up and down; instead, each estimate moves consistently in the same direction iteration after iteration. The estimates will converge, but only slowly. The following extrapolation procedure, suggested by Max Woodbury, has been found very successful in such cases. One application is often sufficient.

Let χ_t denote the tth approximation to the maximum likelihood estimate $\hat{\chi} \equiv \chi_\infty$ of parameter χ. Assume that the discrepancy $\chi_t - \chi_\infty$ is proportional to some positive constant r raised to the tth power:

$$\chi_t - \chi_\infty = kr^t, \tag{13-24}$$

where k is the constant of proportionality. Then

$$\chi_{t-1} - \chi_t = kr^{t-1}(1 - r) \tag{13-25}$$

and

$$\chi_{t-1} - \frac{\chi_{t-1} - \chi_t}{1 - r} = \chi_\infty ,$$

so that

$$\chi_\infty = \frac{\chi_t - r\chi_{t-1}}{1 - r} . \tag{13-26}$$

The rate r can thus be found from

$$r = \frac{\chi_t - \chi_{t-1}}{\chi_{t-1} - \chi_{t-2}} . \tag{13-27}$$

In practice, r is computed from (13-27), using the results of three successive iterations. Then (13-26) provides an extrapolated approximation to the maximum likelihood estimate χ_∞.

In the situation illustrated by Fig. 13.9.1, the b_i for all items in each subtest may be averaged and this average substituted for χ in (13-27) to find the rate r. The same rate r may then be used in (13-26) separately for each item to approximate the maximum likelihood estimator $\hat{b}_i$.

These $\hat{b}_i$ for all items are then held fixed and the θ_a are estimated iteratively for all individuals. The $\hat{\theta}_a$ are then held fixed while reestimating all item parameters by ordinary estimation methods. Additional applications of (13-26) and (13-27) may be carried out after further iterations that provide new values of χ_{t-2}, χ_{t-1}, and χ_t. One application of (13-26) and (13-27), however, will often sufficiently accelerate convergence.

True-Score "Equating" Below the Chance Level

The raw-score "equating" of Section 13.7 is rather complicated to be done routinely in the absence of any clear indication that it is superior to true-score equating. Yet, we cannot use true-score equating of Section 13.5 without some way to deal with observed scores below $\Sigma_j c_j$. This appendix suggests a convenient practical procedure.

Consider applying the method of Section 13.7 just to a hypothetical group of examinees all at ability level $\theta = -\infty$. According to Eq. (4-2) and (4-3), the observed scores for such a group of examinees have a mean of $\Sigma_j c_j$ and a variance of $\Sigma_j c_j(1 - c_j)$. For y scores below $\Sigma_j c_j$, let us take the equating function $x(y)$ to be a linear function of y chosen so that both x and $x(y)$ have the same mean and also the same variance in our hypothetical subgroup of examinees. This means we shall use a conventional "mean and sigma" linear equation based on this subgroup of examinees. This equating requires that

$$\frac{x(y) - \Sigma_i c_i}{\sqrt{\Sigma_i c_i (1 - c_i)}} = \frac{y - \Sigma_j c_j}{\sqrt{\Sigma_j c_j (1 - c_j)}} \; ,$$

where i indexes the items in test x and j indexes the items in test y. The desired equating function $x(y)$ is thus seen to be

$$x(y) = \frac{\sqrt{\Sigma_i c_i (1 - c_i)}}{\sqrt{\Sigma_j c_j (1 - c_j)}} (y - \Sigma_j c_j) + \Sigma_i c_i . \tag{13-28}$$

We use (13-28) for test y scores below $\Sigma_j c_j$; we use true-score equating (13-12) above $\Sigma_j c_j$. The equating relationship so defined is continuous: When $y = \Sigma_j c_j$, we find that $x(y) = \Sigma_i c_i$ whether we use the true-score equating curve of (13-12) or the raw-score "equating" line of (13-28). We cannot defend (13-28) as uniquely correct, but it is a good practical solution to an awkward problem.

REFERENCES

Angoff, W. H. Scales, norms, and equivalent scores. In R. L. Thorndike, *Educational measurement* (2nd ed.). Washington, D.C.: American Council on Education, 1971.

Gulliksen, H. *Theory of mental tests.* New York: Wiley, 1950.

Hunter, J. E., & Schmidt, F. L. Critical analysis of the statistical and ethical implications of various definitions of *test bias. Psychological Bulletin,* 1976, *83,* 1053–1071.

Kendall, M. G., & Stuart, A. *The advanced theory of statistics* (Vol. 1, 3rd ed.). New York: Hafner, 1969.

Marco, G. L. Item characteristic curve solutions to three intractable testing problems. *Journal of Educational Measurement,* 1977, *14,* 139–160.

Thorndike, R. L. Concepts of cultural-fairness. *Journal of Educational Measurement,* 1971, *8,* 63–70.

Woods, E. M., & Wiley, D. E. *An application of item characteristic curve equating to item sampling packages or multi-form tests.* Paper presented at the annual meeting of the American Educational Research Association, Toronto, March 1978.

14
Study of Item Bias

14.1. INTRODUCTION

It is frequently found that certain disadvantaged groups score poorly on certain published cognitive tests. This raises the question whether the test items may be unfair or biased against these groups.

Suppose a set of items measures one ability or skill for one group and a different ability or skill for another. Such a test would in general be unfair, since one ability or skill will in general be more relevant for the purposes of the test than the other. Such a situation is best detected by factor analytic methods and is not considered further here. Instead, we consider a situation where most of the test items measure about the same dimension for all groups tested, but the remaining items may be biased against one group or another.

If each test item in a test had exactly the same item response function in every group, then people at any given level θ of ability or skill would have exactly the same chance of getting the item right, regardless of their group membership. Such a test would be completely unbiased. This remains true even though some groups may have a lower mean θ, and thus lower test scores, than another group. In such a case, the test results would be reflecting an actual group difference and not item bias.

If, on the other hand, an item has a different item response function for one group than for another, it is clear that the item is biased. If the bias is substantial, the item should be omitted from the test.

If the item response function for one group is above the function for another group at all θ levels, then people in the first group at a given ability level have a better chance of answering the item correctly than people of equal ability in the other group. This situation is the simplest and most commonly considered case of item bias.

If the item response functions for the two groups cross, as is frequently found in practice, the bias is more complicated. Such an item is clearly biased for and against certain subgroups.

It seems clear from all this that item response theory is basic to the study of item bias. Mellenbergh (1972) reports an unsuccessful early study of this type, using the Rasch model. A recent report, comparing item response theory and other methods of study, is given by Ironson (1978). Before applying item response theory here, let us first consider a conventional approach in current use.

14.2.   A CONVENTIONAL APPROACH[1]

For illustrative purposes, we shall compare the responses of about 2250 whites with the responses of about 2250 blacks on the 85-item Verbal section of the April 1975 College Board SAT.[2] Each group is about 44% male. All items are five-choice items.

For each item, Fig. 14.2.1 plots p_i, the proportion of correct answers, for blacks against p_i for whites. Items (crosses) falling along the diagonal (dashed) line in the figure are items that are as easy for blacks as for whites. Items below this line are easier for whites. The solid oblique line is a straight line fitted to the scatter of points. The solid line differs from the diagonal line because whites score higher on the test than blacks. If all the items fell directly on the solid line, we could say that the items are all equally biased or, conceivably, equally unbiased.

It has been customary to look at the scatter of items about the solid line and to pick out the items lying relatively far from the line and consider them as atypical and undesirable. In the middle of Fig. 14.2.1 there is one item lying far below the line that appears to be strongly biased in favor of whites and also another item far above the line that favors blacks much more than other items. A common judgment would be that both of these items should be removed from the test.

In Fig. 14.2.1 the standard error of a single proportion is about .01, or less. Thus, most of the scattering of points is not attributable to sampling fluctuations. Unfortunately, the failure to fall along a straight line is not necessarily attributable to differences among items in bias. This statement is true for several different reasons, discussed below.

---

[1]Most of this section is taken, by permission, from F. M. Lord, A study of item bias, using item characteristic curve theory. In Y. H. Poortinga (Ed.), *Basic problems in cross-cultural psychology.* Amsterdam: Swets and Zeitlinger, 1977, pp. 19–29.

[2]Thanks are due to Gary Marco and to the College Entrance Examination Board for permission to present some of their data and results here.

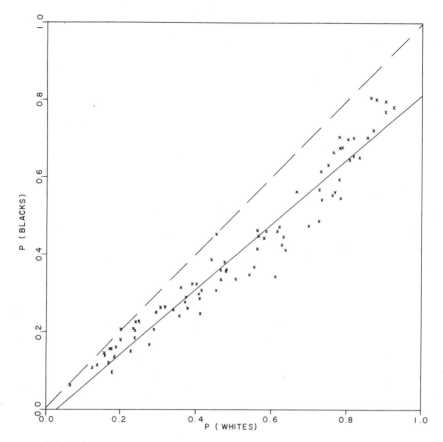

FIG. 14.2.1.   Proportion of right answers to 85 items, for blacks and for whites.

In the first place, we should expect the scatter in Fig. 14.2.1 to fall along a curved and not a straight line. If an item is easy enough, everyone will get it right, and the item will fall at (1, 1). If the item is hard enough, everyone will perform at some "chance" level c, so the item will fall at (c, c). Logically, the items must fall along some line passing through the points (c, c) and (1, 1). If the groups performed equally well on the test, the points could fall along the diagonal line. But since one group performs better than the other, most of the points must lie to one side of the diagonal line, so the relationship must be curved.

Careful studies attempt to avoid this curvature by transforming the proportions. If an analysis of variance is to be done, the conventional transformation is the arcsine transformation. The real purpose of the arcsine transformation is to equalize sampling variance. Whatever effect it may have in straightening the line of relationship is purely incidental.

The transformation usually used to straighten the line of relationship is the inverse normal transformation. The proportion of correct answers is replaced by the relative deviate that would cut off the same upper proportion of the area under the standard normal curve. The result of this transformation is shown in Fig. 14.2.2. Indeed, the points in Fig. 14.2.2 fall about a line that is more nearly straight than is the case in Fig. 14.2.1. Unfortunately, there are theoretical objections to the inverse normal transformation.

Let π_i denote the proportion of correct answers to item i in the population: $\pi_i \equiv \mathrm{Prob}(u_i = 1)$. A superscript o will be used to denote the special case where there is no guessing. By a standard formula

$$\pi_i = \mathscr{E}_\theta \,\mathrm{Prob}(u_i = 1|\theta) \equiv \mathscr{E}_\theta P_i(\theta), \qquad (14\text{-}1)$$

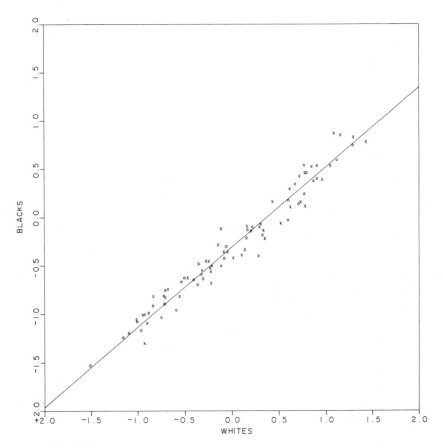

FIG. 14.2.2   Inverse normal transformation of proportion of correct answers for 85 items.

the expectation being taken over θ. Now, by Eq. (2-2), $P_i(\theta) \equiv c_i + (1 - c_i)\, P_i^o(\theta)$, so, by (14-1),

$$\pi_i = c_i + (1 - c_i)\mathscr{E}_\theta P_i^o(\theta)$$
$$= c_i + (1 - c_i)\pi_i^o. \tag{14-2}$$

Solving for π_i^o, we find

$$\pi_i^o = \frac{\pi_i - c_i}{1 - c_i}. \tag{14-3}$$

If $P_i(\theta)$ is the three-parameter normal-ogive response function (2-2), and if θ happens to be normally distributed, then by Eq. (3-9) (adding a superscript o to accord with the present notation),

$$\pi_i^o = 1 - \Phi(\gamma_i) \equiv \Phi(-\gamma_i), \tag{14-4}$$

where Φ is the cumulative normal distribution function and $\gamma_i = \rho_i' b_i$, where ρ_i' is the biserial correlation between item score and ability. Substituting this into (14-2), we have

$$\pi_i = c_i + (1 - c_i)\Phi(-\rho_i' b_i). \tag{14-5}$$

It appears from (14-5) that an inverse normal transformation Φ^{-1} of π_i (as done for Fig. 14.2.2) does not seem to yield anything that is theoretically meaningful.

More interesting results are obtained by applying the inverse normal transformation to the "corrected item difficulty" (14-3). By (14-4), since $\gamma_i = \rho_i' b_i$, the useful result is that

$$\Phi^{-1}\!\left(\frac{\pi_i - c_i}{1 - c_i}\right) = \Phi^{-1}[\Phi(-\gamma_i)] = -\rho_i' b_i. \tag{14-6}$$

Now all the b_i are invariant from group to group except for an indeterminate origin and unit of measurement. Suppose now that ρ_i' is approximately the same for all items. In this special case, the inverse normal transformation of the *corrected* conventional item difficulty is invariant from group to group except for an undetermined linear transformation.

It seems as if Fig. 14.2.2 should have been based on "corrected item difficulties" (14-3) rather than on actual π_i; but there are obvious reasons why this is not totally satisfactory either:

1. Equation (14-6) holds only if θ is normally distributed in both groups.
2. The value of c_i must be known for each item.
3. The value of ρ_i' must be the same for each item.
4. Because of sampling fluctuations, and because examinees sometimes do systematically worse than chance on some items, sample estimates of π_i^o are too often zero or negative, in which case the transformation cannot be carried out.

In practice, items differ from each other in discriminating power (ρ_i' or, equivalently, a_i). Use of (14-2) may make items of the same discriminating power lie along the same straight line; but items of a different discriminating power will then lie along a different straight line. The more discriminating items will show more difference between blacks and whites than do the less discriminating items; thus use of (14-2) cannot make all items fall along a single straight line. All this is a reflection of the fact, noted earlier (Section 3.4), that π_i is really not a proper measure of item difficulty. Thus the π_i, however transformed, are not really suitable for studying item bias.

14.3. ESTIMATION PROCEDURES

Suppose we plan to study item bias with respect to several groups of examinees. A possible practical procedure is as follows:

1. Estimate approximately the item parameters for all groups combined, standardizing on the b_i and not on θ (see below).
2. Fixing the c_i at the values obtained in step 1, reestimate a_i and b_i separately for each group, standardizing on the b_i.
3. For each item, compare across groups the item response functions or parameters obtained in step 2.

Standardizing on the b_i means that the scale is chosen so that the mean of the b_i is 0 and the standard deviation is 1.0 (see Section 3.5). Except for sampling fluctuations, this automatically places all parameters for all groups on the same scale. If the usual method of standardizing on θ were used, the item parameters for each group would be on a different scale.

Before standardizing on the b_i, it would be best to look at all b_i values and exclude very easy and very difficult items both from the mean and the standard deviation. Items with low a_i should also be omitted. The reason in both cases is that the b_i for such items have large sampling errors. Such items are omitted only from the mean and standard deviation used for standardization; they are treated like other items for all other purposes.

Following the outlined procedure, a given item response function will be compared across groups on $\hat{a}_i$ and $\hat{b}_i$ only. We are acting as if a given item has the same c_i in all groups. The reason for doing this is that many $\hat{c}$'s are so indeterminate (see Chapter 12) that they are simply set at a typical or average value; this makes tests of statistical significance among $\hat{c}_i$ impossible in many or most cases. If there are differences among groups in c_i, they cannot be found by the recommended procedure; however, this should not prevent us from observing differences in a_i and b_i. The null hypothesis states that a_i, b_i, and c_i do not vary across groups. If the recommended procedure discovers significant differences, it is clear that the null hypothesis must be rejected.

14.4.   COMPARING ITEM RESPONSE FUNCTIONS
ACROSS GROUPS

Figure 14.4.1 compares estimated item response functions for an antonym item. The data are the same as for Fig. 14.2.1 and 14.2.2. The top and bottom 5% of individuals in each group are indicated by individual dots, except that the lowest 5% of the black group fall outside the limits of the figure. Clearly, this item is much more discriminating among whites than it is among blacks.

Figure 14.4.2 shows an item on which blacks as a whole do worse than whites; nevertheless at every ability level blacks do better than whites! Such results are possible because there are more whites than blacks at high values of θ and more blacks than whites at low values of θ. The item is a reading comprehension item from the SAT. This is the only item out of 85 for which the item response function of blacks is consistently so far above that of whites. The reason for this result will be suggested by the following excerpts from the reading passage on which the item is based:

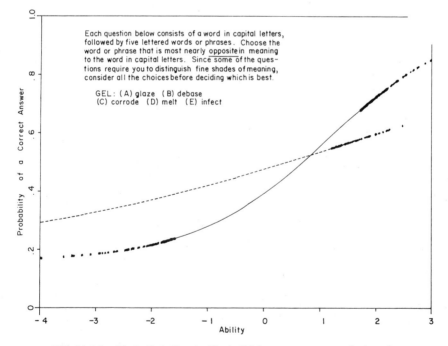

Each question below consists of a word in capital letters, followed by five lettered words or phrases. Choose the word or phrase that is most nearly opposite in meaning to the word in capital letters. Since some of the questions require you to distinguish fine shades of meaning, consider all the choices before deciding which is best.

GEL: (A) glaze (B) debase
(C) corrode (D) melt (E) infect

FIG. 14.4.1.   Black (dashed) and white (solid) item response curves for item 8. (From F. M. Lord, Test theory and the public interest. In *Proceedings of the 1976 ETS Invitational Conference—Testing and the Public Interest.* Princeton, N.J.: Educational Testing Service, 1977.)

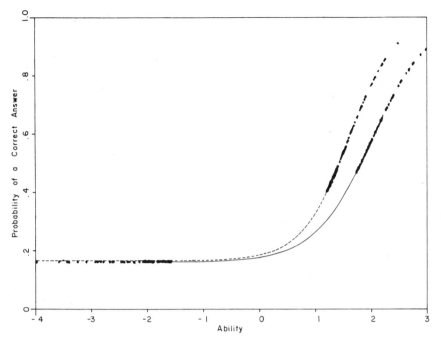

FIG. 14.4.2.   Item response curves for item 59. (From F. M. Lord, *Test theory and the public interest. Proceedings of the 1976 ETS Invitational Conference— Testing and the Public Interest.* Princeton, N.J.: Educational Testing Service, 1977.)

American blacks have been rebelling in various ways against their status since 1619. Countless Africans committed suicide on the passage to America. . . . From 1955 to the present, the black revolt has constituted a true social movement.

It is often difficult or impossible to judge from figures like the two shown whether differences between two response functions may be due entirely to sampling fluctuations. A statistical significance test is very desirable. An obvious procedure is to compare, for a given item, the difference between the black and the white $\hat{b}_i$ with its standard error

$$\text{SE} \, (\hat{b}_{i1} - \hat{b}_{i2}) = \sqrt{\text{Var} \, \hat{b}_{i1} + \text{Var} \, \hat{b}_{i2}}. \tag{14-17}$$

The same can be done with the $\hat{a}_i$.

If the $\hat{b}_i$ and the $\hat{a}_i$ are maximum likelihood estimates, the necessary sampling variances can be approximated by standard asymptotic formulas (see Section 12.3); if the b_i are the only parameters estimated,

$$\text{Var} \, \hat{b}_i = \frac{1}{\mathscr{E}\left[\left(\dfrac{\partial \ln L}{\partial b_i}\right)^2\right]} \, ,$$

and similarly for $\hat{a}_i$. As shown for Eq. (5-5), we can carry out the differentiation and expectation operations. In the case of the three-parameter logistic function, after substituting estimated parameters for their unknown true values, we obtain

$$\text{Var } \hat{b}_i \doteq \left[\frac{D^2 \hat{a}_i^2}{(1 - \hat{c}_i)^2} \sum_{a=1}^{N_i} (\hat{P}_{ia} - \hat{c}_i)^2 \frac{\hat{Q}_{ia}}{\hat{P}_{ia}} \right]^{-1}, \tag{14-8}$$

$$\text{Var } \hat{a}_i \doteq \left[\frac{D^2}{(1 - \hat{c}_i)^2} \sum_{a=1}^{N_i} (\hat{\theta}_a - \hat{b}_i)^2 (\hat{P}_{ia} - \hat{c}_i)^2 \frac{\hat{Q}_{ia}}{\hat{P}_{ia}} \right]^{-1}. \tag{14-9}$$

The summation is only over the N_i examinees who reached item i.

Equations (14-8) and (14-9) assume that the ability parameters θ_a are known. Although the θ_a are actually estimated, available evidence shows that this usually increases Var $(\hat{b}_i)$ and Var $(\hat{a}_i)$ only slightly.

Using (14-7) and (14-8) or (14-9), and assuming asymptotic normality of $\hat{b}_i$, one can readily make a simple asymptotic significance test of the null hypothesis that $b_{i1} = b_{i2}$. A separate significance test can be made of the null hypothesis that $a_{i1} = a_{i2}$. It is preferable, however, to test both these hypotheses simultaneously. This can be done by a chi-square test. The method used is described in the Appendix at the end of this chapter.

14.5. PURIFICATION OF THE TEST

If many of the items are found to be seriously biased, it appears that the items are not strictly unidimensional: The θ obtained for blacks, for example, is not strictly comparable to the θ obtained for whites. This casts some doubt on the results obtained when all items are analyzed together. A solution (suggested by Gary Marco) is

1. Analyze the total test, as described in the preceding sections.
2. Remove all items that have significantly different response functions in the groups under study. The remaining items may now be considered to be a unidimensional pool, even when the groups are combined.
3. Combine all groups and estimate θ for each individual. These θ will all be comparable.
4. For each group separately, while *holding θ fixed for all individuals* at the values obtained in step 3, estimate the a_i and the b_i for each item. Do this for all items, including those previously removed.
5. Compare estimated item response functions or parameters by the methods of Section 14.4.

The resulting comparisons should be legitimate since an appropriate θ scale is presumably being used across all groups. Table 14.5.1 shows some illustrative

TABLE 14.5.1
Approximate Significance Test for the Hypothesis That Blacks and
Whites Have Identical Item Response Functions

Item No.	a_i Whites	a_i Blacks	b_i Whites	b_i Blacks	Chi Square	Significance Level
1	.87	.66	−1.5	−1.6	14.6	.00
2	.28	.02	−3.3	−31.3	51.6	.00
3	.63	.45	−1.1	−1.4	9.7	.01
4	.85	.61	.1	.2	12.7	.00
5	.35	.24	−1.9	−1.3	50.6	.00
6	.82	.74	−.4	−.4	1.6	.45
7	.56	.67	−.6	−.2	18.6	.00
8	.50	.17	1.2	1.8	40.1	.00
9	1.43	1.74	.5	.5	4.8	.09
10	1.09	.88	.7	.8	3.4	.18
11	1.64	1.39	1.7	1.7	.9	.63
12	.49	.41	1.9	1.9	2.8	.24
13	1.63	2.17	1.7	1.7	1.2	.55
14	1.27	1.04	2.6	2.9	.2	.91
15	.68	.89	3.4	2.7	1.5	.47

final results for the first 15 verbal items for the data described in Section 14.2.[3]

Does the SAT measure the same psychological trait for blacks as for whites? If it measured totally different traits for blacks and for whites, Fig. 14.2.2 would show little or no relationship between the item difficulty indices for the two groups. In view of this, the study shows that the test does measure approximately the same skill for blacks and whites.

The item characteristic curve techniques used here can pick out certain atypical items that should be cut out from the test. It is to be hoped that careful study will help us understand better why certain items are biased, why certain groups of people respond differently than others on certain items, and what can be done about this.

14.6. CHECKING THE STATISTICAL SIGNIFICANCE TEST

The significance test used in Section 14.5 has been questioned on the grounds that if some items are biased, unidimensionality and local independence are

---

[3]The remainder of this section is taken, by permission, from F. M. Lord, A study of item bias, using item characteristic curve theory. In Y. H. Poortinga (Ed.), *Basic problems in cross-cultural psychology*. Amsterdam: Swets and Zeitlinger, 1977, pp. 19–29.

violated; hence the item parameter estimates are not valid. This objection is not compelling if the test has been purified. Statistical tests of a null hypothesis (in this case the hypothesis of no bias) are typically made by assuming that the null hypothesis holds and then looking to see if the data fit this assumption. If not, then the null hypothesis is rejected.

The statistical significance tests used are open to several other criticisms, however:

1. They are asymptotic.
2. They assume that the θ_a are known rather than estimated.
3. They only apply to maximum likelihood estimates. Data containing omitted responses (see Chapter 15) do not fit the usual dichotomous item response model; this difficulty is dealt with by modifying the estimation procedures.

In view of these difficulties, it is wise to make some check on the adequacy of the statistical method, such as that described below.

For the data discussed in this chapter, an empirical check was carried out. All 4500 examinees, regardless of color, were divided at random into two groups, "reds" and "blues." The entire item bias study was repeated step by step for these two new groups.

TABLE 14.6.1
Distribution of Significance Levels
Testing the Difference Between the
Item Response Functions for Two
Randomly Selected Groups of
Subjects*

Significance Level	No. of Items
.00– .05	3 } 9
.05– .10	6
.10– .20	6
.20– .30	6
.30– .40	11
.40– .50	9
.50– .60	7
.60– .70	5
.70– .80	12
.80– .90	10
.90–1.00	10

*Taken, by permission, from F. M. Lord, A study of item bias, using item characteristic curve theory. In Y. H. Poortinga (Ed.), *Basic problems in cross-cultural psychology*. Amsterdam: Swets and Zeitlinger, 1977, pp. 19–29.

Table 14.6.1 shows the 85 significance levels obtained for the 85 SAT Verbal items. Since the groups were random groups, the significance levels should be approximately rectangularly distributed from 0 to 1, with about 8½ items for each interval of width .10. The actual results are very close to this.

Although Table 14.6.1 is not a complete proof of the adequacy of the statistical procedures of Section 14.4, a comparison with the complete SAT results abstracted for Table 14.5.1 makes it very clear that blacks and whites are quite different from random groups for present purposes. The final SAT results show a significant difference at the 5% level between blacks and whites for 38 out of 85 items, this is quite different from the 9 out of 85 shown in Table 14.6.1 for a comparison of random groups.

It is not claimed here that the suggested statistical significance tests are optimal, nor that the parameter estimates are valid for those items that are biased. A good additional check on the foregoing statistical analysis could be obtained by repeating the entire comparison separately for independent samples of blacks and whites.

APPENDIX

This appendix describes the chi-square test used in Section 14.4 for the null hypothesis that for given i both $b_{i1} = b_{i2}$ and $a_{i1} = a_{i2}$. The procedure is based on the chi-square statistic

$$\chi_i^2 \equiv \mathbf{v}_i' \Sigma_i^{-1} \mathbf{v}_i \tag{14-10}$$

where $\mathbf{v}'$ is the vector $\{\hat{b}_{i1} - \hat{b}_{i2}, \hat{a}_{i1} - \hat{a}_{i2}\}$ and Σ_i^{-1} is the inverse of the asymptotic variance–covariance matrix for $\hat{b}_{i1} - \hat{b}_{i2}$ and $\hat{a}_{i1} - \hat{a}_{i2}$.

Since $\hat{a}_{i1}$ and $\hat{b}_{i1}$ for whites are independent of $\hat{a}_{i2}$ and $\hat{b}_{i2}$ for blacks, we have

$$\Sigma_i = \Sigma_{i1} + \Sigma_{i2}, \tag{14-11}$$

where Σ_{i1} is the sampling variance–covariance matrix of $\hat{a}_{i1}$ and $\hat{b}_{i1}$ in group 1, and similarly for Σ_{i2}. These latter matrices are found for maximum likelihood estimators from the formulas $\Sigma_{i1} = I_{i1}^{-1}$ and $\Sigma_{i2} = I_{i2}^{-1}$, where I_i is the 2 × 2 information matrix for $\hat{a}_i$ and $\hat{b}_i$ [Eq. (12-8), (12-9), (12-11)]. The diagonal elements of I_i are the reciprocals of (14-8) and (14-9).

The significance test is carried out separately for each item by computing χ_i^2 and looking up the result in a table of the chi-square distribution. If the null hypothesis is true, χ_i^2 has a chi-square distribution with 2 degrees of freedom (Morrison, 1967, p. 129, Eq. 1).

When there are more than two groups, a simultaneous significance test for differences across groups on a_i and b_i can be made by multivariate analysis of variance.

REFERENCES

Ironson, G. H. *A comparative analysis of several methods of assessing item bias.* Paper presented at the annual meeting of the American Educational Research Association, Toronto, March 1978.

Mellenbergh, G. J. Applicability of the Rasch model in two cultures. In L. J. Cronbach & P. J. D. Drenth (Eds.), *Mental tests and cultural adaptation.* The Hague: Mouton, 1972.

Morrison, D. F. *Multivariate statistical methods.* New York: McGraw-Hill, 1967.

15

Omitted Responses and Formula Scoring

15.1. DICHOTOMOUS ITEMS

The simpler item response theories consider only two kinds of response to an item. Such theories are not directly applicable if the item response can be right, wrong, or omitted.

More complex theories deal with cases where the item response may be *A, B, C, D,* or *E,* for example. Although these more complex theories have sometimes been used to deal with omitted responses, it is not always obvious that the mathematical models used are appropriate or effective for this use.

15.2. NUMBER-RIGHT SCORING

When test score is number of right answers, it is normally to the examinee's advantage to answer every item, even if his response must be at random. If examinees are convincingly instructed as to their best strategy, as they properly should be, and if they act in their own best interests, there will then be no omitted or "not-reached" responses on such tests.

Although superficially this situation seems appropriate for dichotomous-item response theory, it is actually inappropriate whenever examinees do not have time to finish the test. In his own best interest, an examinee who runs short of time on a number-right scored test should quickly answer all unread items at random. Such responses violate the item response theory model: They do not depend on the examinee's θ.

In principle, item response theory can be applied to number-right scored tests only if they are unspeeded. In practice, some deviation from this rule can doubt-less be tolerated.

15.3.   TEST DIRECTIONS

If a test is to measure fairly or effectively, examinees at a given ability level must all follow the same strategy. Thus, test directions must convincingly explain to the examinee how to act in his own self-interest. In particular, in the case of a number-right scored test, we should *not* tell the examinee never to respond at random, since it is clearly in his best interest to do so.

When a test is *formula scored,* the examinee's score is

$$y \equiv x - \frac{w}{A - 1} \qquad\qquad (15\text{-}1)$$

where x is the number-right score, w is the number of wrong answers, and A is the number of alternative choices per item. When formula scoring is used, we may discourage the examinees from responding *purely* at random, since in the long run their scores will not be improved by purely random guessing. If an examinee does not have time to finish the test, he can, if he wishes, increase the random error in his score by answering unread items at random. If examinees understand the test directions fully, however, many will probably refrain from doing this.

15.4.   NOT-REACHED RESPONSES

If most examinees read and respond to items in serial order, a practical procedure for formula-scored tests is to ignore the "not-reached" responses of each exam-inee when making statistical inferences about examinee and item parameters. Such treatment of not-reached responses is discussed in Section 12.4.

To summarize: If item response theory is to be applied, tests should be unspeeded. If many examinees do not have time to finish the test, purely random responses may be discouraged by using formula scoring and giving appropriate directions to the examinee. The not-reached responses that appear in formula-scored tests should be ignored during parameter estimation.

15.5.   OMITTED RESPONSES

If (1) number-right scores are used, (2) proper test directions are given, (3) the examinees understand the directions, and (4) they act in their own self-interest, then there will be no omitted responses. If formula scoring is used with appropriate directions, there will be a scattering of omitted responses by many examinees, in addition to any not-reached responses at the end of the test.

For the remainder of this chapter, the term *omitted response,* or simply *omit,* implies that the examinee read the item and decided not to answer it, so that *omit* and *not reached* are mutually exclusive categories. As a practical expedient, we assume that omitted and not-reached responses can be distinguished by the fact that all not-reached responses fall in a block at the end of the test. The remainder of the chapter is concerned with the treatment of omitted responses.

15.6. MODEL FOR OMITS UNDER FORMULA SCORING

If an examinee's chance of answering a particular item correctly is better than $1/A$, under formula scoring he should answer the item—he should not omit it. The test directions to the examinee should be constructed to ensure this. In the remainder of this chapter, we assume formula scoring, together with appropriate test directions, unless otherwise specified.

If an examinee's chance of answering a particular item correctly is only $1/A$, we cannot predict whether he will respond or not. We can make inferences in the other direction, however. If the test directions are effective, we can say that when an examinee omits an item, his chance of success, were he to answer the item, should be approximately $1/A$.

Of course, an examinee may not be a completely accurate judge of his own chance of success. Empirical studies bearing on this assumption have been carried out by Ebel (1968), Sax and Collet (1968), Slakter (1969), Traub and Hambleton (1972), Waters (1967), and others. None of these studies is really definitive. Other references are cited by Diamond and Evans (1973).

15.7. THE PRACTICAL MEANING OF AN ITEM RESPONSE FUNCTION

Before proceeding, we need to clarify a definition whose inadequacy may have escaped the reader's attention. Suppose examinee S and examinee T both omit the same item. If forced to respond, each would have a probability of $1/A$ of answering correctly. Since $\text{Prob}(u_i = 1|\theta_S) = \text{Prob}(u_i = 1|\theta_T) = 1/A$, it apparently follows that $\theta_S = \theta_T$.

But this is absurd in practice. Two examinees who omit the same item need not be of equal ability, even approximately. Where is the fallacy?

Another paradox arising from the same source is the following. Suppose item i and item j measure the same ability θ and have identical item response functions with $c_i = c_j = 0$. Suppose examinee A knows the answer to item i but does not know the answer to item j; examinee B knows item j but does not know item i.

Such situations occur constantly in practice. Since apparently $P_i(\theta_A) > P_i(\theta_B)$, θ_A must be greater than θ_B. But also apparently $P_j(\theta_A) < P_j(\theta_B)$, so θ_A must be less than θ_B. What is the source of this absurdity?

The trouble comes from an unsuitable interpretation of the practical meaning of the item response function $P_i(\theta_A) \equiv \text{Prob}(u_{iA} = 1|\theta_A)$. If we try to interpret $P_i(\theta_A)$ as the probability that a particular examinee A will answer a particular item i correctly, we are likely to reach absurd conclusions. To obtain useful results, we may properly

1. Interpret $P_i(\theta_A)$ as the probability that a particular examinee A will give the right answer to a randomly chosen item whose parameters are a_i, b_i, and c_i.

2. Interpret $P_i(\theta_A)$ as the probability that a randomly chosen examinee at ability level θ_A will answer a particular item i correctly.

3. Make both of these interpretations simultaneously.

15.8.   IGNORING OMITTED RESPONSES

A complete mathematical model for item response data with omits would involve many new parameters: for example, a parameter for each examinee, representing his behavior when faced with a choice of omitting or guessing at random. Such complication might make parameter estimation impractical; we therefore avoid all such complicated models here.

Since "not-reached" responses can be ignored in parameter estimation, why not ignore omitted responses? Two lines of reasoning make it clear that we cannot do this:

1. "Not-reached" responses contain no readily quantifiable information about the examinee's ability θ. On the other hand, according to our model, omitted responses specifically imply that the examinee's ability is limited: If the examinee were required to answer, his responses to a group of such items would be correct only $1/A$ of the time in the long run.

2. If we ignore omitted responses, the examinee can obtain as high a $\hat\theta$ as he pleases, simply by answering only those items he is sure he can answer correctly and omitting all others.

The last argument is a compelling one.

15.9.   SUPPLYING RANDOM RESPONSES

A simple solution to our problem might seem to be to require each examinee to answer every item. If an examinee failed to follow this requirement, we could presumably supply random responses in place of those he could have chosen. (Note that not-reached items should *not* be assigned random responses: The examinee would often do better than random if he had time to read and respond to such items.)

If number-right scoring is used, as already noted, omitted responses should not occur. If formula scores are used, as we assume here, a requirement to answer all items would be unfair and unreasonable. Suppose a student, needing a formula score of 7 to pass a course, finds that he knows the answers to exactly 8 of the 10 true–false final examination questions. We cannot properly force him to answer the other two questions, thereby running a substantial risk of flunking the course with a formula score of $8 - 2 = 6$. Neither can we properly supply the random responses ourselves, for the same reason.

15.10. PROCEDURE FOR ESTIMATING ABILITY

Supplying random responses in place of omits does not introduce a bias into the examinee's formula score: His expected formula score is the same whether he omits or responds at random. The objection to requiring him to respond is that the required (random) responses would reduce the accuracy of measurement.

Although we can obtain unbiased estimates of ability by supplying random responses in place of omits, introduction of random error degrades the data. There should be some way to obtain unbiased estimates of the same parameters without degrading the data.

A method for doing this is described in Lord (1974). The usual likelihood function

$$\Pi_i \Pi_a P_{ia}^{u_{ia}} Q_{ia}^{1-u_{ia}} \tag{4-21}$$

is replaced by

$$\Pi_i \Pi_a P_{ia}^{v_{ia}} Q_{ia}^{1-v_{ia}}, \tag{15-2}$$

where $v_{ia} = u_{ia}$ if the examinee responds to the item and $v_{ia} = 1/A$ if the examinee omits the item. The product Π_a is to be taken only over the examinees who actually reached item i. It should be noted that (15-2) is not a likelihood function. Nevertheless, if the item parameters are known, the value of θ_a that maximizes (15-2) is a better estimate of θ than the maximum likelihood estimate obtained from Eq. (4-21) after replacing omits by random responses.

15.11. FORMULA SCORES

If an examinee answers all n items, the number of wrong answers is $w = n - x$, and his formula score (15-1) can be rewritten

$$y \equiv x - \frac{n-x}{A-1} = \frac{Ax}{A-1} - \frac{n}{A-1} .$$ (15-3)

If there are no omits, formula score y is a specified linear transformation of number-right score x.

There are two ways we can predict a person's formula score from his ability θ and from the item parameters. If we know which items examinee a answered, his number-right true score is

$$\xi_a = \Sigma^{(a)} P_i(\theta_a)$$ (15-4)

where the summation is over the items answered by examinee a. From this and (15-1), the examinee's true formula score η_a is

$$\eta_a = \Sigma^{(a)} P_i(\theta_a) - \frac{\Sigma^{(a)} Q_i(\theta_a)}{A-1} .$$ (15-5)

We can estimate the examinee's observed formula score from his $\hat{\theta}_a$ by substituting y_a for η_a and $\hat{\theta}_a$ for θ_a in (15-5).

If examinee a answered all the items in the test, (15-5) becomes

$$\eta_a = \frac{A \sum_{}^{n} P_i(\theta_a) - n}{A-1} .$$ (15-6)

This can also be derived directly from (15-3). Again, the examinee's formula score can be estiamted from his $\hat{\theta}_a$ by substituting $\hat{\theta}_a$ for θ_a and y_a for η_a in (15-6).

An examinee's formula score has the same expected value whether he omits items or whether he answers them at random. If we do not know which items the examinee omitted, we cannot use (15-5) but we can still use (15-6) if the examinee finished the test.

If the examinee did not finish the test, we can use (15-5) or (15-6) to estimate his actual formula score on the partly speeded test from his $\hat{\theta}$, provided we know which items he did not reach: The not-reached items are simply omitted from the summations in (15-5) and (15-6). If we do not know which items he reached, we can still use (15-6) to estimate the formula score that he would get if given time to finish the test.

REFERENCES

Diamond, J., & Evans, W. The correction for guessing. *Review of Educational Research*, 1973, *43*, 181–191.

Ebel, R. L. Blind guessing on objective achievement tests. *Journal of Educational Measurement*, 1968, *5*, 321–325.

Lord, F. M. Estimation of latent ability and item parameters when there are omitted responses. *Psychometrika*, 1974, *39*, 247–264.

Sax, G., & Collet, L. The effects of differing instructions and guessing formulas on reliability and validity. *Educational and Psychological Measurement*, 1968, *28*, 1127–1136.

Slakter, M. J. Generality of risk taking on objective examinations. *Educational and Psychological Measurement*, 1969, *29*, 115–128.

Traub, R. E., & Hambleton, R. K. The effect of scoring instructions and degree of speededness on the validity and reliability of multiple-choice tests. *Educational and Psychological Measurement*, 1972, *32*, 737–758.

Waters, L. K. Effect of perceived scoring formula on some aspects of test performance. *Educational and Psychological Measurement*, 1967, *27*, 1005–1010.

IV ESTIMATING TRUE-SCORE DISTRIBUTIONS

16

Estimating True-Score Distributions[1]

16.1. INTRODUCTION

We have already seen [Eq. (4-5) or (4-9)] that true-score ζ or ξ on a test is simply a monotonic transformation of ability θ. The transformation is different from test to test. If we know the distribution $g(\zeta)$ of true score, the joint distribution of true score and observed score is

$$\phi(x, \zeta) = g(\zeta)h(x|\zeta), \tag{16-1}$$

where $h(x|\zeta)$ is the conditional distribution of observed score for given true score. The form of the conditional distribution $h(x|\zeta)$ is usually known [see Eq. (4-1), (11-24)]; its parameters (the a_i, b_i, and c_i) can be estimated. If we can estimate $g(\zeta)$ also, then we can estimate the joint distribution of true score and observed score. As noted in Section 4.5, *this joint distribution contains all relevant information for describing and evaluating the properties of observed score* x *as a measure of true score* ζ *or as a measure of ability* θ. An estimated true-score distribution is thus essential to understanding the measurement process, the effects of errors of measurement, and the properties of observed scores as fallible measurements.

In addition, an estimated true-score distribution can be used for many other purposes, to be explained in more detail:

1a. To estimate the population frequency distribution of observed scores.
1b. To smooth the sample frequency distribution of observed scores.

---

[1]Much of the material in this chapter was first presented in Lord (1969).

2. To estimate the frequency distribution of observed scores for a shortened or lengthened form of the test.

3. To estimate the bivariate distribution of observed scores on two parallel test forms when only one has been administered. This is useful in many ways, for example, for determining how many of the people who failed one test form would have passed the other.

4. To estimate the bivariate distribution of observed scores on two different tests of the same ability.

5. To estimate national norms for a full-length test when only a short form has been administered to the norms sample.

6. To estimate the effect of selecting on observed score instead of on true score.

7. By using observed scores, to match two groups on true score.

8. To equate two tests.

9. To investigate whether two tests measure the same psychological trait.

10. To estimate item-test regressions and item response functions.

If $h(x|\zeta)$ is given by Eq. (4-1) or (11-24), then the estimation of a true-score distribution is a branch of item response theory. In this chapter, we use approximations to Eq. (4-1) that do not depend on item-response-function parameters. The latent trait theory developed here is closely related to many problems encountered in earlier chapters, as is apparent from the foregoing list. The theory and its applications are presented here because of their relevance to practical applications of item response theory.

16.2.   POPULATION MODEL

If we integrate (16-1) over all true scores, we obtain the marginal distribution of observed scores:

$$\phi(x) = \int_0^1 g(\zeta)h(x|\zeta)\,d\zeta \qquad (x = 0, 1, 2, \ldots, n). \qquad (16\text{-}2)$$

Our first problem is to infer the unknown $g(\zeta)$ from $\phi(x)$, the distribution of observed scores in the population, presumed known, and from $h(x|\zeta)$, also known.

If observed score x were a continuous variable, (16-2) would be a Fredholm integral equation of the first kind. In this case it may be possible to solve (16-2) and determine $g(\zeta)$ uniquely. Here we deal only with the usual case where x is number-right score, so that (16-2) need hold only for $x = 0, 1, 2, \ldots, n$.

Suppose temporarily that $h(x|\zeta)$ is binomial (see Section 4.1). Let us multiply both sides of (16-2) by $x^{[r]} \equiv x(x - 1) \cdots (x - r + 1)$, where r is a positive integer. Summing over all x, we have

$$\sum_{x=0}^{n} x^{[r]}\phi(x) = \int_{0}^{1} g(\zeta) \sum_{x=0}^{n} x^{[r]} h(x|\zeta) \, d\zeta.$$

Now, the sum on the left is by definition the rth factorial moment of $\phi(x)$, to be denoted by $M_{[r]}$; the sum on the right is the rth factorial moment of the binomial distribution, which is known (Kendall & Stuart, 1969, Eq. 5.8) to be $n^{[r]}\zeta^r$. The foregoing equation can now be written

$$\frac{M_{[r]}}{n^{[r]}} = \int_{0}^{1} \zeta^r g(\zeta) \, d\zeta \equiv \mu_r' \qquad (r = 1, 2, \ldots, n), \qquad (16\text{-}3)$$

where μ_r' is the rth ordinary moment of the true-score distribution $g(\zeta)$. This equation shows that when $h(x|\zeta)$ is binomial, the first n moments of $g(\zeta)$ can be easily determined from the first n moments of the distribution of observed scores. This last statement is still true when $h(x|\zeta)$ has the generalized binomial distribution [Eq. (4-1)] appropriate for item response theory.

Since only n mathematically independent quantities can be determined from the n mathematically independent values $\phi(1), \phi(2), \ldots, \phi(n)$, it follows that the higher moments, above order n, of the true-score distribution cannot be determined from $\phi(x)$. Indeed, any $g(\zeta)$ with appropriate moments up through order n will satisfy (16-3) exactly, regardless of the value of its higher moments. Since the frequency distribution of a bounded integer-valued variable (x) is determined by its moments, it follows that any $g(\zeta)$ with the appropriate moments up through order n will be a solution to (16-2). Thus, *the true-score distribution for an infinite population of examinees in principle cannot be determined exactly from their* $\phi(x)$ *and* $h(x|\zeta)$ ($x = 0, 1, \ldots, n$).

If two different true-score distributions have the same moments up through order n, they have the same best fitting polynomial of degree n in the least-squares sense (Kendall & Stuart, 1969, Section 3.34). If the distributions oscillate more than n times about the best fitting polynomial, they could differ noticeably from each other. If the true-score distributions are reasonably smooth, however, without many peaks and valleys, they will be closely fitted by the same degree n polynomial. Since they each differ little from the polynomial, they cannot differ much from each other. Thus any smooth $g(\zeta)$ with the required moments up through order n will be a good approximation to the true $g(\zeta)$ whenever the latter is smooth.

It is common experience in many diverse areas that sample frequency distributions of continuous variables become smooth as sample size is increased. We therefore assume here that the true $g(\zeta)$ is smooth.

16.3. A MATHEMATICAL SOLUTION FOR THE POPULATION

There is no generally accepted unique way of measuring smoothness. Mathematical measures of smoothness generally depend on a constant and on a weight function to be specified by the user.

A function with many sharp local fluctuations is not well fitted by any smooth function. Thus we could take

$$\int [g(\zeta) - \gamma(\zeta)]^2 \, d\zeta$$

as a convenient measure of smoothness, where $\gamma(\zeta)$ is some smooth density function specified by the user. Actually, we shall use instead the related measure

$$\int_0^1 \frac{[g(\zeta) - \gamma(\zeta)]^2}{\gamma(\zeta)} \, d\zeta \,. \tag{16-4}$$

This measure of smoothness is the same as an ordinary chi square between $g(\zeta)$ and $\gamma(\zeta)$ except that summation is replaced by integration.

The need for the user to choose $\gamma(\zeta)$ may seem disturbing. For most practical purposes, however, it has been found satisfactory to choose $\gamma(\zeta) \equiv 1$ or $\gamma(\zeta) \propto \zeta(1 - \zeta)$. The choice usually makes little difference in practice. Remember that we are finding one among many $g(\zeta)$, all of which produce an exact fit to the population $\phi(x)$. Any smooth solution to our problem will be very close to any other smooth solution.

Given $\gamma(\zeta)$, $h(x|\zeta)$, and $\phi(x)$, what we require is to find the $g(\zeta)$ that minimizes (16-4) subject to the restriction that $g(\zeta)$ must satisfy (16-2) exactly for $x = 0, 1, 2, \ldots, n$. This is a problem in the calculus of variations. The solution (Lord, 1969) is

$$g(\zeta) = \gamma(\zeta) \sum_{X=0}^{n} \lambda_X h(X|\zeta), \tag{16-5}$$

the values of the λ_X being chosen so that (16-2) is satisfied for $x = 0, 1, 2, \ldots, n$.

To find the λ_X, substitute (16-5) in (16-2):

$$\sum_{X=0}^{n} \lambda_X \int_0^1 \gamma(\zeta) h(X|\zeta) h(x|\zeta) \, d\zeta = \phi(x) \qquad (x = 0, 1, \ldots, n). \tag{16-6}$$

These are $n + 1$ simultaneous linear equations in the $n + 1$ unknowns λ_X. If $h(x|\zeta)$ is binomial and if $\gamma(\zeta)$ is constant or a beta distribution with integer parameters, then the integral in (16-6) can be evaluated exactly for X, $x = 0, 1, 2, \ldots, n$. If $h(x|\zeta)$ is the generalized binomial of Eq. (4-1), we replace it by a two- or four-term approximation (see Lord, 1969), after which the integral in (16-1) can again be evaluated exactly. The required values of λ_X are then found by inverting the resulting matrix of coefficients and solving linear equations (16-6).

To be a valid solution, the $g(\zeta)$ found from (16-5) in this way must be nonnegative for $0 \leq \zeta \leq 1$. This requirement could be imposed as part of the calculus of variations problem; however, the resulting solution might still be intuitively unsatisfactory because of its angular character. A practical way of dealing with this condition is suggested at the end of Section 16.5.

16.4.   THE STATISTICAL ESTIMATION PROBLEM

The problem solved in the last section has no direct practical application since we never know the $\phi(x)$ exactly. Instead, we have sample frequencies $f(x)$ that are only rough approximations to the $\phi(x)$. In most statistical work, the substitution of sample values for population values provides an acceptable approximation, but not in the present case, as we shall see.

It is clear from (16-2) that $\phi(x)$ is a weighted average of $h(x|\zeta)$, averaged over $0 \leq \zeta \leq 1$ with weight $g(\zeta)$. Likewise, the first difference $\Delta_\phi(x) \equiv \phi(x + 1) - \phi(x)$ is a weighted average of conditional first differences $h(x + 1|\zeta) - h(x|\zeta)$. Since an average is never more than its largest component, $\Delta_\phi(x)$ can never be greater than $\max_\zeta [h(x + 1|\zeta) - h(x|\zeta)]$. This proves that sufficiently sharp changes in $\phi(x)$ are incompatible with (16-2). A similar argument holds for second- and higher-order differences. Thus any sample frequency distribution $f(x)$ may be incompatible with (16-2) simply because of local irregularities due to sampling fluctuations. In such cases, any $g(\zeta)$ obtained by the methods of Section 16.3 are negative somewhere in the range $0 \leq \zeta \leq 1$ and thus not an acceptable solution to our problem. This is what usually happens when $f(x)$ is substituted for $\phi(x)$ in (16-5) and (16-6).

The statistical estimation problem under discussion is characterized by the fact that a small change in the observed data produces a large change in the solution. Such problems are important in many areas of science where the scientist is trying to infer unobservable, causal variables from their observed effects. Recently developed methods for dealing with this class of problems are discussed by Craven and Wahba (1977), Franklin (1970, 1974), Gavurin and Rjabov (1973), Krjanev (1974), Shaw (1973), Varah (1973) and Wahba (1977).

16.5.   A PRACTICAL ESTIMATION PROCEDURE

The difficulties discussed in Section 16.4 arise because of sampling irregularities in the observed-score frequency distribution. The simplest way to reduce such irregularities is to group the observed scores into class intervals. When this has been done, the observations are now the grouped frequencies

$$f_u \equiv \sum_{x:u} f(x) \qquad (u = 1, 2, \ldots, U), \tag{16-7}$$

where the notation indicates that the summation is to be taken over all integers x in class interval u.

The reasoning of Section 16.3 can now be applied to the grouped frequencies. The basic equation specifying the model is now

$$\phi_u = \int_0^1 g(\zeta) \sum_{x:u} h(x|\zeta) \, d\zeta \qquad (u = 1, 2, \ldots, U). \tag{16-8}$$

The "smoothest" solution to this equation is now

$$g(\zeta) = \gamma(\zeta) \sum_{u=1}^{U} \lambda_u \sum_{X:u} h(X|\zeta). \tag{16-9}$$

The λ_u are the parameters of the observed-score distribution ϕ_u. If we follow the reasoning in Section 16.3, the U observed values of f_u are just enough to determine the U unknown parameters λ_u exactly. If the λ_u were determined from the ϕ_u in this way, the model (16-8) would fit the grouped sample frequencies f_u exactly ($u = 1, 2, \ldots, U$). The ungrouped sample frequencies $f(x)$, of course, would not be fitted exactly.

A still better procedure is to use all $n + 1$ sample frequencies $f(x)$ to estimate the parameters λ_u ($u = 1, 2, \ldots, U$). The $f(x)$ ($x = 0, 1, \ldots, n$) are jointly multinominally distributed: Their likelihood function is proportional to

$$\prod_{x=0}^{n} [\phi(x)]^{f(x)}. \tag{16-10}$$

Assuming that the true-score distribution is given by (16-9), substitution of (16-9) into (16-2) expresses each $\phi(x)$ as a known function of the parameters λ_u:

$$\phi(x) = \sum_{u=1}^{U} \lambda_u a_{xu} \qquad (x = 0, 1, \ldots, n)$$

where

$$a_{xu} \equiv \sum_{X:u} \int_0^1 \gamma(\zeta) h(X|\zeta) h(x|\zeta) \, d\zeta. \tag{16-11}$$

If $\gamma(\zeta)$ is a constant or a beta distribution with integer exponents and $h(x|\zeta)$ is binomial or a suitable approximation to a generalized binomial, the integration in (16-11) can be carried out algebraically.

It is now a straightforward matter (see Lord, 1969; Stocking, Wingersky, Lees, Lennon, & Lord, 1973) to find the values of λ_u ($u = 1, 2, \ldots, U$) that maximize the likelihood (16-10) for any given observed frequencies $f(x)$ ($x = 0, 1, \ldots, n$). The maximizing values are the maximum likelihood estimators $\hat{\lambda}_u$ ($u = 1, 2, \ldots, U$). Notice that the λ_u are the parameters of the true-score distribution (16-9) as well as of the observed-score distribution (16-11).

Given an appropriate grouping into class intervals, our estimated true-score distribution is therefore

$$\hat{g}(\zeta) \equiv \gamma(\zeta) \sum_{u=1}^{U} \hat{\lambda}_u \sum_{X:u} h(X|\zeta), \tag{16-12}$$

provided $\hat{g}(\zeta) \geq 0$ for $0 \leq \zeta \leq 1$. If $\gamma(\zeta)$ is constant or a beta distribution, then the estimated true-score distribution is a weighted sum of beta distributions.

If $\hat{g}(\zeta)$ turns out to be negative in the range $0 \leq \zeta \leq 1$, it is not an acceptable solution to our problem. In principle, maximization of the likelihood should be carried out subject to the restriction that $\hat{g}(\zeta) \geq 0$ for $0 \leq \zeta \leq 1$. Instead, it seems to be satisfactory and is much simpler to require that $\hat{\lambda}_u \geq 0$ for all u. This requirement is too restrictive, but it seems beneficial in practice. It automatically guarantees that $\hat{g}(\zeta)$ will be nonnegative for $0 \leq \zeta \leq 1$.

Our estimated observed-score distribution is simply

$$\hat{\phi}(x) \equiv \sum_{u=1}^{U} \hat{\lambda}_u a_{xu} \qquad (x = 0, 1, \ldots, n). \tag{16-13}$$

16.6. CHOICE OF GROUPING

The main problem not already dealt with is the choice of class intervals for grouping the number-right scores. Arbitrary grouping frequently fails to provide a good fit to the data, as measured by a chi square between actual and estimated frequencies $f(x)$ and $\hat{\phi}(x)$. A possible automatic method for finding a successful grouping is as follows.

1. Group the tails of the sample distribution to avoid very small values of $f(x)$.

2. Arbitrarily group the remainder of the score range, starting in the middle and keeping the groups as narrow as possible, until the total number of groups is reduced to some practical number, perhaps $U = 25$.

3. Estimate $\hat{\lambda}_u$ ($u = 1, 2, \ldots, 25$) by maximum likelihood, subject to the restriction that $\hat{\lambda}_u \geq 0$.

4. As a by-product of step 3, obtain the asymptotic variance–covariance matrix of the nonzero $\hat{\lambda}_u$ (the inverse of the Fisher information matrix).

5. Compute $\hat{\phi}(x)$ from (16-13).

6. Compute the empirical chi square comparing $\hat{\phi}(x)$ with $f(x)$:

$$X^2 = \sum_{x=1}^{n} \frac{[f(x) - \hat{\phi}(x)]^2}{\hat{\phi}(x)}. \tag{16-14}$$

7. Determine the percentile rank of X^2 in a standard chi square table with $U^* - U$ degrees of freedom, where U^* is the number of class intervals at the end of step 1.

8. If $\hat{\lambda}_u$ and $\hat{\lambda}_{u+1}$ were identical for some u, it would make no difference if we combined intervals u and $u + 1$ into a single class interval (the reader may check this assertion for himself). If $\hat{\lambda}_u$ and $\hat{\lambda}_{u+1}$ are nearly the same, it makes little difference if we combine the two intervals.

    (a) For each $u = 0, 1, \ldots, U - 1$, compute the asymptotic variance of $\hat{\lambda}_{u+1} - \hat{\lambda}_u$.

(b) Divide $\hat{\lambda}_{u+1} - \hat{\lambda}_u$ $(u = 1, 2, \ldots, U - 1)$ by its asymptotic standard error.

(c) Find the value of u for which the resulting quotient is smallest $(u = 1, 2, \ldots, U - 1)$; for this value of u, combine interval u and interval $u + 1$ into a single interval.

9. Repeat steps 3 through 8, reducing U by 1 at each repetition.

10. At first, the percentile rank of X^2 will decrease at each repetition, due to the increase in degrees of freedom. When the percentile rank of X^2 no longer decreases, stop the process and use $\hat{g}(\zeta)$ from (16-12) as the estimated true-score distribution.

Under the procedure suggested above, the grouping is determined by the data. Thus, strictly speaking, the resulting X^2 no longer has a chi square distribution with $U^* - U$ degrees of freedom. If an accurate chi square test of significance is required, the data should be split into random halves and the grouping determined from one half as described above. A chi-square test of significance can then be properly carried out, using this grouping, on the other half of the data.

Chi-square significance levels quoted in this chapter and in the next chapter are computed as in step 10. Thus the significance levels quoted are only nominal; they are numerically larger (less "significant") than they should be.

16.7.   ILLUSTRATIVE APPLICATION

Seven estimated true-score distributions, obtained by the methods of this chapter, are seen in Fig. 6.8.1. A different illustration is presented and considered here in more detail. Figure 16.7.1 shows the estimated true-score distribution and the estimated observed-score distribution obtained for a nationally known test of vocabulary administered to a nationally representative sample of 1715 sixth-grade pupils. The test consists of 42 four-choice items. These data were chosen for the illustration because of the interesting results. For most data, the true-score distribution is similar in shape to the observed-score distribution, except that it has a slightly smaller variance, because observed scores contain errors of measurement. These data show an interesting exception.

Before discussing the true-score distribution, some special features in the treatment of the data will be noted. There is no provision in the mathematical model (16-2) for dealing with omitted item responses or with examinees who fail to finish the test. Each omitted item response in the present data was replaced by a randomly chosen response. This procedure is adequate for dealing with items that the examinee has considered and then omitted. It is not appropriate for dealing with items that the examinee did not reach in the allowed testing time; for this reason, examinees who did not answer the last item in the test were simply excluded from the data.

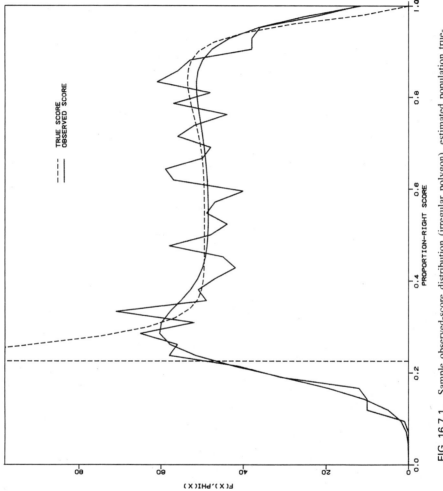

FIG. 16.7.1. Sample observed-score distribution (irregular polygon), estimated population true-score and observed-score distributions, sixth-grade vocabulary test, $N = 1715$.

We know from item response theory that true score ζ can never be less than $\Sigma_1^n c_i / n$. In the case of Fig. 16.7.1, estimated c_i were available. These values were utilized by setting a lower limit of $\Sigma_1^n \hat{c}_i / n = .225755$ to the range of ζ, requiring that $g(\zeta) = 0$ when $\zeta < .225755$. This requirement was imposed by replacing the lower limit 0 in the integrals of (16-8) and (16-11) by .225755. The integral in (16-11), now an incomplete beta function, can be evaluated by recursive procedures (Jordan, 1947, Section 25, Eq. 5) without using approximate methods, as long as $\gamma(\zeta)$ is either a constant or a beta function with integer exponents.

In the case of Fig. 16.7.1, $\gamma(\zeta)$ was taken as constant. The figure shows the resulting estimated true- and observed-score distributions. The estimated true-score distribution has $U - 1 = 3$ independent parameters λ_u. The chi square (16-14) is 23.5; nominally, the degrees of freedom are 30, suggesting a good fit. The results are considered further in the next section.

16.8. BIMODALITY

The sample observed-score distribution shown in Fig. 16.7.1 has an unusual shape. One wonders if this shape results from a rectangular or bimodal distribution of ability θ in the group tested. (Note that unimodality of the distribution of θ does not necessarily imply unimodality of the true-score distribution; the relation between the two distributions depends on the test characteristic curve.)

It is intuitively obvious, regardless of the distribution of θ, that a "peaked" test, consisting of items all of equal difficulty, can produce a bimodal distribution of observed scores providing the items are sufficiently highly intercorrelated (see Section 4.4). It is an important question in general whether a bimodal observed-score distribution should be attributed to the characteristics of the group tested or simply to distortions introduced by the measuring instrument (Section 4.4).

When there is no guessing and the ability θ is normally distributed, the tetrachoric item intercorrelations must be at least .50 to produce a bimodal observed-score distribution, according to the normal ogive item characteristic curve model (Lord, 1952, Section D). This is a much higher correlation than is ordinarily ever attained for multiple-choice items. When there is guessing, however, as in the present situation where the test is composed of four-choice items, it is not so easy to reach a conclusion.

Some computer runs, using the three-parameter normal ogive model with all $c_i = .25$, throw light on this matter. The computer runs simulate the administration of various medium-difficulty tests, each composed of 40 four-choice items all of equal difficulty, to a group of examinees in which ability θ is normally distributed. The various tests differ only in a_i, assumed to be the same for all items within a test. Figure 16.8.1 shows the frequency distribution of number-right scores obtained for three such tests. As item-ability correlation increases,

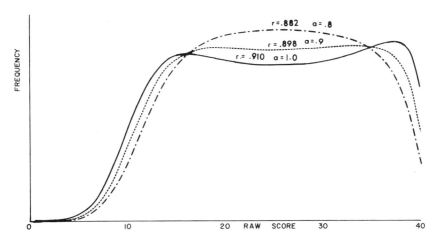

FIG. 16.8.1.   Frequency distribution and reliability (r) of number-right observed score for three hypothetical peaked tests differing only in item discriminating power (a).

bimodality appears when the KR-20 reliability of number-right scores reaches $r = .895$ ($a_i = .9$), approximately.

When adjusted to a standard length of 40 items, the actual Kuder–Richardson formula-20 test reliability computed from the data used to obtain Fig. 16.7.1 was $r = .925$. It thus appears that the bimodal distribution in that figure may be attributable to the measuring instrument rather than to some special characteristic of the group tested.

16.9.   ESTIMATED OBSERVED-SCORE DISTRIBUTION

The estimated observed-score distribution $\hat{\phi}(x)$ is sometimes of interest for its own sake. Equation (16-13) is a complicated but effective way of smoothing a sample distribution of observed scores. Unlike many other methods, it has the advantage that the smoothing (1) does not introduce negative frequencies; (2) preserves a total relative frequency of exactly 1; (3) does not introduce any frequencies outside the permissible range $0 \leq x \leq n$; and (4) is compatible with relevant mental test theory. Equations (16-8), (16-9), and (16-13) can be used also to estimate ungrouped frequencies of test scores when the only available data are grouped.

16.10.   EFFECT OF A CHANGE IN TEST LENGTH

If a test is lengthened by adding parallel forms of the test, the true score of each person remains unchanged; thus $g(\zeta)$ is also unchanged. Any change in test

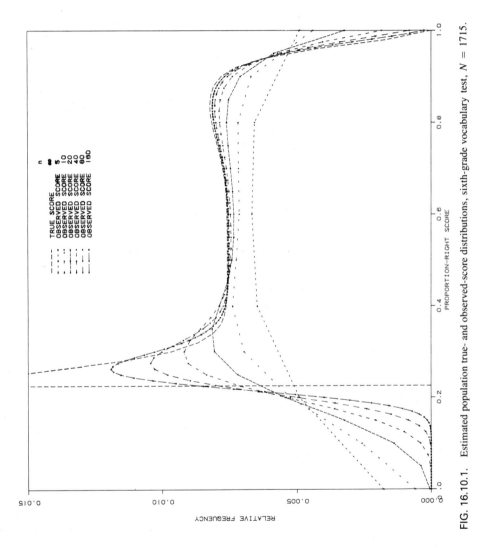

FIG. 16.10.1. Estimated population true- and observed-score distributions, sixth-grade vocabulary test, $N = 1715$.

length n changes $h(x|\zeta)$ in a known way. Thus the theoretical effect of test length on $\phi(x)$ can be determined from (16-2).

In practical applications, we have the estimated true-score distribution (16-12). In this case, the effect of test length on $\hat{\phi}(x)$ can be determined by varying n in (16-11) and (16-13). The a_{xu} defined by (16-11) must be determined from (16-10) each time n is changed; the estimates of λ_u are supposed to be unaffected by changes in n.

Figure 16.10.1 shows estimated proportion-correct observed-score frequency distributions when the 42-item vocabulary test of Fig. 16.7.1 is shortened or lengthened to $n = 5, 10, 20, 40, 80, 160$, or ∞. As n becomes large, the distribution of proportion-correct score $z \equiv x/n$ approaches $g(\zeta)$. For small n, observed- and true-score distributions may have very different shapes, as illustrated.

16.11.   EFFECTS OF SELECTING ON OBSERVED SCORE: EVALUATION OF MASTERY TESTS

Typically, we would like to select individuals on true score rather than on observed score. What is the effect of selecting on observed score? This question can be answered using the estimated joint distribution (16-1) of true score ζ and observed score x, determining from this distribution the effect of selecting on x.

The general principles are illustrated by discussing the evaluation of a mastery test. Chapter 11 develops a theory of mastery testing without requiring knowledge of the distribution of ability or of true scores in the group tested. Such a theory is particularly useful when a particular test with a predetermined cutting score is to be used in many different groups having different distributions of ability. In contrast, we see here a little of what can be done once the frequency distribution of true scores has been estimated for a particular group.

Figure 16.11.1 shows the observed-score distribution $f(x)$ for a nationwide sample of 2395 high school seniors taking a 65-item Basic Skills Reading test. The figure also shows the corresponding estimated population observed-score distribution $\hat{\phi}(x)$ and the estimated true-score distribution $\hat{g}(\zeta)$. The chi square is 6.33 with 12 degrees of freedom, showing a good fit of the model to the data. Since the test is intended to determine whether high school seniors can do the kind of reading required in adult life (reading medicine labels, guarantees, employment application forms, and so forth), it is not surprising that most high school seniors obtain high scores on the test.

Table 16.11.1 shows the estimated bivariate cumulative frequency distribution of true score and observed score for all students tested. The cumulative frequencies are shown only for values of ζ that are multiples of .05. The table is obtained by applying the trapezoidal rule to ordinates of the noncumulative distribution (16-1) of ζ and x and then cumulating across rows. The table entry at (ζ_o, x_o) shows the number of cases out of 1000 for whom $\zeta \le \zeta_o$ and $x \le x_o$.

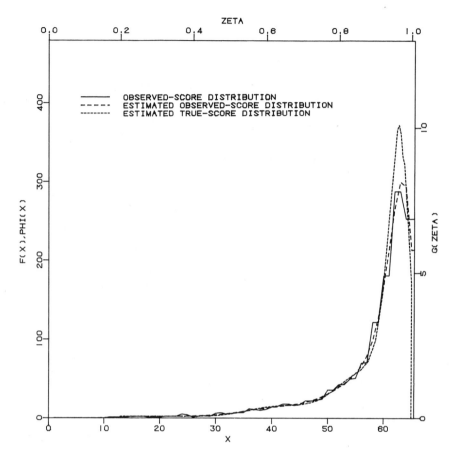

FIG. 16.11.1. Sample observed-score distribution and estimated population observed-score and true-score distributions for the Basic Skills Reading test.

Table 17.5.1 compares observed-score and true-score distributions for a re-jected group ($x \leq 38$). The Test x column of Table 17.5.1 is the same as the lower part of the last column of Table 16.11.1 except that Table 17.5.1 is noncumulative. The number-right true-score distribution shown in Table 17.5.1 corresponds to the cumulative distribution of proportion-correct true scores in row 38 of Table 16.11.1. Table 17.5.1 illustrates the effect of selecting on observed score instead of on true score. Because of the regression effect, the two distributions are rather different in this example.

To illustrate another use of Table 16.11.1, suppose it is decided that a true score above $\zeta = .60$ represents satisfaction of minimal qualifications and that a true score below $\zeta = .60$ represents failure to meet minimal qualifications. The top row of the table shows that about .046 of all students are unqualified. If we

TABLE 16.11.1
Students at or below a Given Observed Score and a Given True
Score (Proportion of All Students Multiplied by 1000) Basic Skills
Assessment Program, Reading Test

Observed Score	True Score													
	.35	.40	.45	.50	.55	.60	.65	.70	.75	.80	.85	.90	.95	1.00
65	9	12	15	20	30	46	66	89	117	160	228	325	584	1000
64	9	12	15	20	30	46	66	89	117	160	228	325	582	911
63	9	12	15	20	30	46	66	89	117	160	228	325	571	788
62	9	12	15	20	30	46	66	89	117	160	228	325	542	663
61	9	12	15	20	30	46	66	89	117	160	228	323	497	552
60	9	12	15	20	30	46	66	89	117	160	228	317	441	462
59	9	12	15	20	30	46	66	89	117	160	227	308	386	392
58	9	12	15	20	30	46	66	89	117	160	225	294	338	339
57	9	12	15	20	30	46	66	89	117	160	221	276	297	298
56	9	12	15	20	30	46	66	89	116	159	215	255	265	265
55	9	12	15	20	30	46	66	89	116	158	207	233	237	237
54	9	12	15	20	30	46	66	89	116	155	196	212	213	213
53	9	12	15	20	30	46	66	89	115	152	183	192	192	192
52	9	12	15	20	30	46	66	89	113	147	169	173	174	174
51	9	12	15	20	30	46	66	89	111	140	155	157	157	157
50	9	12	15	20	30	46	66	88	108	133	142	143	143	143
49	9	12	15	20	30	46	66	88	104	124	129	130	130	130
48	9	12	15	20	30	46	66	87	99	115	118	118	118	118
47	9	12	15	20	30	46	66	85	94	107	108	108	108	108
46	9	12	15	20	30	46	65	83	88	98	99	99	99	99
45	9	12	15	20	30	46	64	79	88	90	91	91	91	91
44	9	12	15	20	30	45	63	76	81	83	83	83	83	83
43	9	12	15	20	30	45	61	71	75	76	76	76	76	76

(continued)

TABLE 16.11.1
(continued)

Observed Score	True Score													
	.35	.40	.45	.50	.55	.60	.65	.70	.75	.80	.85	.90	.95	1.00
42	9	12	15	20	29	44	58	66	68	69	69	69	69	69
41	9	12	15	20	29	43	55	61	62	62	62	62	62	62
40	9	12	15	20	29	42	52	56	56	56	56	56	56	56
39	9	12	15	20	29	40	48	50	51	51	51	51	51	51
38	9	12	15	20	28	38	44	45	45	45	45	45	45	45.5
37	9	12	15	19	27	36	39	40	40	40	40	40	40	40.6
36	9	12	15	19	26	33	35	36	36	36	36	36	36	36.1
35	9	12	15	19	25	30	32	32	32	32	32	32	32	32.1
34	9	12	15	18	24	27	28	28	28	28	28	28	28	28.5
33	9	12	15	18	22	25	25	25	25	25	25	25	25	25.4
32	9	12	15	17	21	22	23	23	23	23	23	23	23	22.7
31	9	12	14	17	19	20	20	20	20	20	20	20	20	20.4
30	9	11	14	16	18	18	18	18	18	18	18	18	18	18.4
29	9	11	14	15	16	17	17	17	17	17	17	17	17	16.7
28	9	11	13	14	15	15	15	15	15	15	15	15	15	15.2
27	9	11	13	13	14	14	14	14	14	14	14	14	14	13.9
26	8	11	12	12	13	13	13	13	13	13	13	13	13	12.7
25	8	10	11	11	12	12	12	12	12	12	12	12	12	11.6
24	8	10	11	10	11	11	11	11	11	11	11	11	11	10.6
23	8	9	10	10	10	10	10	10	10	10	10	10	10	9.7
22	7	8	9	9	9	9	9	9	9	9	9	9	9	8.7
...	...	...	...	...	...	...	...	...	...	...	...	...	...	...

reject all students with $x \leq 38$ (refuse to graduate them from high school), the right-hand column shows that we shall be rejecting .045 of all students. The table entry at (.60, 38) shows that .038 of all students lie at or below $\zeta = .60$ and also at or below $x = 38$; these students are all rightly rejected.

From the foregoing numbers we can compute the following 2×2 table:

	unqualified	qualified		
accepted	(.046 − .038 =).008	(.954 − .007 =).947	(1 − .045 =).955	$x = 38.5$
rejected	.038	(.045 − .038 =).007	.045	
	.046	(1 − .046 =).954		
		$\zeta = .60$		

This shows that .008 of the total group were accepted even though they were really unqualified and that .007 of the total group were rejected even though they were really qualified. These two proportions are useful for summarizing the effectiveness of the minimum qualifications reading test, since they represent the proportion of students erroneously classified. The foregoing procedure is described and implemented by Livingston (1978).

16.12. ESTIMATING ITEM TRUE-SCORE REGRESSION

An item-test regression (Section 3.1) can be computed for each observed score x as follows: Divide the number of examinees at x who answer the item correctly by the total number of examinees at x. An item–true-score regression can in principle be obtained similarly. If $g_i(u_i, \zeta)$ denotes the bivariate density function of u_i (item score) and ζ (proportion-correct true score), and if $g(\zeta)$ is the (marginal) density of ζ, then the item–true-score regression may be found from

$$\mathscr{E}(u_i|\zeta) = \frac{g_i(1, \zeta)}{g(\zeta)} . \tag{16-15}$$

The denominator on the right of (16-15) can be estimated by (16-12). If we apply (16-12) to the subgroup of examinees who answer item i correctly, we obtain an estimate of $g_i(\zeta|u_i = 1)$, the conditional distribution of true score for examinees who answer item i correctly. The numerator in (16-15) is $g_i(1, \zeta) = \pi_i g_i(\zeta|u_i = 1)$, where π_i is the proportion of all examinees who answer item i correctly. Since π_i can be approximated by the observed proportion of correct answers in the total group, we can use (16-12) to estimate both the numerator and the denominator of (16-15) and thus to estimate the item–true-score regression.

Let ζ_n denote true score on an n-item test; let ζ_{n-1} denote true score on the same test excluding item i. This use of (16-12) is appropriate only if item i is excluded from the items used to determine number-right score x. Thus, (16-12) and (16-15) yield an estimate of the regression of u_i on ζ_{n-1}.

If the item response function parameters are known, then ζ_n is a known monotonic function of ζ_{n-1}. This functional relation is given by the parametric equations

$$
\left.
\begin{aligned}
\zeta_n &\equiv \frac{1}{n} \sum_j P_j(\theta), \\
\zeta_{n-1} &= \frac{1}{n-1} \sum_{j \ne i} P_j(\theta).
\end{aligned}
\right\}
\tag{16-16}
$$

By eliminating θ from (16-16) numerically, any value of ζ_{n-1} can be transformed to the corresponding value of ζ_n. Thus any regression of u_i on ζ_{n-1} can be used to write the regression of u_i on ζ_n. This is done simply by replacing ζ_{n-1} in $\mathscr{E}(u_i|\zeta_{n-1})$ by the corresponding value of ζ_n.

If the numerator and denominator of (16-15) are each independently estimated by (16-12), chance fluctuations may allow the estimate of the numerator to be larger than the estimate of the denominator when ζ is near 1.0. This can result in an estimated item–true-score regression that is larger than 1.0 when ζ is near 1.0. Such an awkward result of sampling fluctuations can be avoided by estimating the item–true-score regression using the following equivalent of (16-15):

$$
\mathscr{E}(u_i|\zeta) = \frac{g_i(1, \zeta)}{g_i(1, \zeta) + g_i(0, \zeta)} .
\tag{16-17}
$$

The distribution $g_i(0, \zeta)$ is estimated by applying (16-12) to the group of examinees who answered item i incorrectly.

16.13.   ESTIMATING ITEM RESPONSE FUNCTIONS

The relation

$$
\zeta_{n-1} \equiv \zeta_{n-1}(\theta) \equiv \frac{1}{n-1} \Sigma_{j \ne i} P_j(\theta),
\tag{16-18}
$$

transforms ζ_{n-1} to θ. Since $P_i(\theta) \equiv \mathscr{E}(u_i|\theta)$, (16-18) can be used to convert an estimated item–true-score regression into an estimated item response function (regression of item score on ability). Thus the item response function can be written

$$
P_i(\theta) = \frac{g_i[1, \zeta_{n-1}(\theta)]}{g_i[1, \zeta_{n-1}(\theta)] + g_i[0, \zeta_{n-1}(\theta)]} .
\tag{16-19}
$$

In practice, the item–true-score regression is estimated by (16-17). Then the base scale is transformed from true score to ability, using (16-18), to obtain the estimated item response function (16-19).

Results obtained by this method are illustrated by the dashed curves in Fig. 2.3.1. The solid curves are three-parameter logistic functions computed by Eq. (2-1) from maximum likelihood estimates $\hat{a}_i$, $\hat{b}_i$, and $\hat{c}_i$. The agreement between the two methods of estimation is surprisingly close, especially so when one considers that the methods of this chapter are based on data and on assumptions very different from the data and assumptions used to obtain the logistic curves (solid lines) in Fig. 2.3.1. An explicit listing and contrasting of the data and assumptions used by the two methods is given in Lord (1970), along with further details of the procedure used. Assuming they are confirmed on other sets of data, results such as shown in Fig. 2.3.1 suggest that the three-parameter logistic function is quite effective for representing the response functions of items in published tests.

REFERENCES

Craven, P., & Wahba, G. *Smoothing noisy data with spline functions: Estimating the correct degree of smoothing by the method of generalized cross-validation*. Technical Report No. 445. Madison, Wis.: Department of Statistics, University of Wisconsin, 1977.

Franklin, J. N. Well-posed stochastic extensions of ill-posed linear problems. *Journal of Mathematical Analysis and Applications*, 1970, *31*, 682–716.

Franklin, J. N. On Tikhonov's method for ill-posed problems. *Mathematics of Computation*, 1974, *28*, 889–907.

Gavurin, M. K., & Rjabov, V. M. Application of Čebyšev polynomials in the regularization of ill-posed and ill-conditioned equations in Hilbert space. (In Russian) *Žurnal Vyčislitel'noĭ Matematiki i Matematičeskoĭ Fiziki*, 1973, *13*, 1599–1601, 1638.

Jordan, C. *Calculus of finite differences* (2nd ed.). New York: Chelsea, 1947.

Kendall, M. G., & Stuart, A. *The advanced theory of statistics* (Vol. 1). New York: Hafner, 1969.

Krjanev, A. V. An iteration method for the solution of ill-posed problems. (In Russian) *Žurnal Vyčislitel'noĭ Matematiki i Matematičeskoĭ Fiziki*, 1974, *14*, 25–35, 266.

Livingston, S. *Reliability of tests used to make pass–fail decisions: Answering the right questions*. Paper presented at the meeting of the National Council on Measurement in Education, Toronto, March 1978.

Lord, F. M. A theory of test scores. *Psychometric Monograph No. 7*. Psychometric Society, 1952.

Lord, F. M. Estimating true-score distributions in psychological testing (An empirical Bayes estimation problem). *Psychometrika*, 1969, *34*, 259–299.

Lord, F. M. Item characteristic curves estimated without knowledge of their mathematical form—a confrontation of Birnbaum's logistic model. *Psychometrika*, 1970, *35*, 43–50.

Shaw, C. B., Jr. Best accessible estimation: Convergence properties and limiting forms of the direct and reduced versions. *Journal of Mathematical Analysis and Applications*, 1973, *44*, 531–552.

Stocking, M., Wingersky, M. S., Lees, D. M., Lennon, V., & Lord, F. M. *A program for estimating the relative efficiency of tests at various ability levels, for equating true scores, and for predicting bivariate distributions of observed scores*. Research Memorandum 73-24. Princeton, N.J.: Educational Testing Service, 1973.

Varah, J. M. On the numerical solution of ill-conditioned linear systems with applications to ill-posed problems. *SIAM Journal on Numerical Analysis*, 1973, *10*, 257–267.

Wahba, G. Practical approximate solutions to linear operator equations when the data are noisy. *SIAM Journal on Numerical Analysis*, 1977, *14*, 651–667.

17

Estimated True-Score Distributions for Two Tests

17.1. MATHEMATICAL FORMULATION

This chapter considers problems involving two or more tests of the same trait. In every discussion of tests x and y here, it is assumed that the ability θ is the same for both tests.

The trivariate distribution of x, y, and θ for any population may be written [compare Eq. (16-1)]

$$\phi(x, y, \theta) = g^*(\theta)h_1^*(x|\theta)h_2^*(y|\theta), \tag{17-1}$$

where g^* is the distribution of θ and h_1^* and h_2^* are the conditional distributions of observed scores x and y for given θ. The bivariate distribution of x and y is thus

$$\phi(x, y) = \int_{-\infty}^{\infty} g^*(\theta)\, h_1^*(x|\theta)\, h_2^*(y|\theta)\, d\theta. \tag{17-2}$$

Now, the proportion-correct true scores ζ and η are related to θ by the formulas

$$\zeta \equiv \frac{1}{n_x} \sum_{i=1}^{n_x} P_i(\theta), \qquad \eta \equiv \frac{1}{n_y} \sum_{j=1}^{n_y} P_j(\theta), \tag{17-3}$$

where i indexes the n_x items in test x, and j indexes the n_y items in test y. Thus after a transformation of variables, (17-2) can now be written [compare Eq. (16-2)]

$$\phi(x, y) = \int_0^1 g(\zeta)h_1(x|\zeta)h_2[y|\eta(\zeta)]\, d\zeta, \tag{17-4}$$

254

where $g(\zeta)$ is the same as in Chapter 16, $h_1(x|\zeta)$ is the same as $h(x|\zeta)$ in Chapter 16, $h_2(y|\eta)$ is the conditional distribution of y, and $\eta \equiv \eta(\zeta)$ is the transformation relating η to ζ, obtained from (17-3) by elimination of θ.

If the item parameters are known, then h_1^* and h_2^* are known and it should be possible in principle to estimate $g^*(\theta)$ from $\phi(x, y)$ using (17-2); equivalently, it should be possible to estimate $g(\zeta)$ from $\phi(x, y)$ using (17-4). Full-length numerical procedures for doing this would be complicated and have not been implemented. Some short-cut procedures (using a series approximation to the generalized binomial) are the subject of this chapter. Illustrative results are presented.

17.2. BIVARIATE DISTRIBUTION OF OBSERVED SCORES ON PARALLEL TESTS

If x and y are parallel test forms, then ζ and η are identical and also h_1 and h_2 are identical. In this case, (17-4) becomes

$$\phi(x, y) = \int_0^1 g(\zeta)h(x|\zeta)h(y|\zeta) \, d\zeta. \qquad (17\text{-}5)$$

As in Chapter 16, the conditional distribution h is considered known: It is binomial or the generalized binomial of Section 4.1. When h is known or approximated and g is estimated by the methods of Chapter 16, then the bivariate distribution of x and y can be obtained from (17-5) by numerical integration. Thus the bivariate distribution of observed scores on two parallel forms can be deduced from a single administration of just one of the forms.

Table 17.2.1 shows part of the estimated bivariate cumulative distribution of observed scores on two parallel forms of the Basic Skills Reading test discussed in Section 16.11. It would be desirable to check this estimated distribution against actual frequencies of scores on two parallel forms. This has not been done since actual scatterplots for parallel forms are not available.

Reading down the right-hand column in Table 17.2.1, we see that an estimated 45 examinees out of 1000 will be rejected by a cutting score of 38.5 on form x. Reading down column 38, we see that an estimated 34 of these 45 examinees would have been rejected if they had taken parallel test form y instead of x and 11 of these 45 examinees would not have been rejected by form y. This provides one way to describe the consistency of basic skills assessment without having to talk about unobservable true scores.

17.3. TRUE-SCORE EQUATING

If test x and test y are different measures of the same trait, their proportion-correct true scores, ζ and η, have a mathematical relationship. This relation

TABLE 17.2.1
Estimated Joint Cumulative Distribution of Number-Right
Observed Scores on Two Parallel Test Forms, x and y, of the Basic
Skills Assessment Reading Test

x \	y = 23	26	29	32	35	38	41	44	47	50	53	56	59	62	65
65	10	13	17	23	32	45	62	83	108	143	192	265	392	663	1000
62	10	13	17	23	32	45	62	83	108	143	192	264	377	550	663
59	10	13	17	23	32	45	62	83	108	143	190	250	319	377	392
56	10	13	17	23	32	45	62	83	108	140	179	220	250	264	265
53	10	13	17	23	32	45	62	82	105	132	159	179	190	192	192
50	10	13	17	23	32	45	62	80	99	118	132	140	143	143	143
47	10	13	17	23	32	45	60	76	89	99	105	108	108	108	108
44	10	13	17	23	32	43	56	67	76	80	82	83	83	83	83
41	10	13	17	22	30	40	49	56	60	62	62	62	62	62	62
38	10	13	16	21	27	34	40	43	45	45	45	45	45	45	45
35	10	12	16	20	24	27	30	32	32	32	32	32	32	32	32
32	9	12	15	17	20	21	22	23	23	23	23	23	23	23	23
29	9	11	13	15	16	16	17	17	17	17	17	17	17	17	17
26	9	10	11	12	12	13	13	13	13	13	13	13	13	13	13
23	8	9	9	9	10	10	10	10	10	10	10	10	10	10	10

could be determined by the method of Eq. (6-17) if the univariate frequency distribution of both true scores were known for some population of examinees.

If test x and test y have been administered to separate random samples of examinees from the same population, their true-score distributions $g(\zeta)$ and $q(\eta)$ can be estimated by the methods of Chapter 16. The relation $\eta(\zeta)$ can then be estimated from $\hat{g}(\zeta)$ and $\hat{q}(\eta)$ using the equipercentile relationship [Eq. (6-17)]:

$$\int_{-\infty}^{\hat{\eta}(\zeta_o)} \hat{q}(\eta)\, d\eta \equiv \int_{-\infty}^{\zeta_o} \hat{g}(\zeta)\, d\zeta. \tag{17-6}$$

This equation asserts that ζ_o and $\hat{\eta}_o \equiv \hat{\eta}(\zeta_o)$ have identical percentile ranks in their respective distributions. Numerical values of the function $\hat{\eta}(\zeta_o)$ for given values of ζ_o are found in practice from (17-6) by numerical integration and inverse interpolation. The result is an estimated true-score equating of ζ and η. This method of equating does not make use of the responses of each examinee to each item, as do the methods of sections 13.5 and 13.6.

Figure 17.3.1 shows two estimates of the equating function $\eta(\zeta)$ relating true scores on two verbal tests, P and Q. Since P and Q are randomly parallel, being produced by randomly splitting a longer test, the relation $\eta(\zeta)$ should be nearly linear, but not precisely linear, as would be the case if P and Q were strictly parallel.

The relation $\eta(\zeta)$ was estimated by the method of this section from two different groups of examinees. Each curve in the figure runs from the first to the ninety-ninth percentile of the distribution of ζ for the corresponding group. The

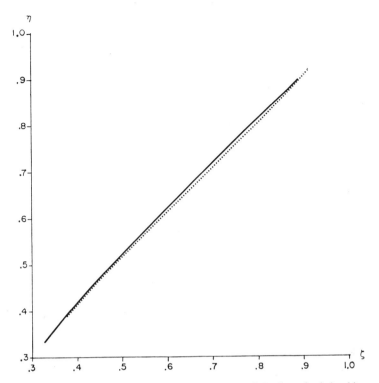

FIG. 17.3.1. Estimates from two different groups of the line of relationship equating true scores ζ and η for two randomly parallel tests, P and Q. (From F. M. Lord, A strong true-score theory, with applications. *Psychometrika*, 1965, *30*, 239–270.)

two estimated relations agree well with each other and are appropriately nearly linear.

17.4.   BIVARIATE DISTRIBUTION OF OBSERVED SCORES ON NONPARALLEL TESTS

Suppose $g(\zeta)$ and $q(\eta)$ have been independently estimated by the method of Chapter 16 and then $\eta(\zeta)$ has been estimated by the method of the preceding section. The bivariate distribution of number-right observed scores x and y can now be estimated from (17-4) by numerical integration.

An early version of this method was used[1] to predict 16 different bivariate

---

[1]The remainder of this section is taken by permission from F. M. Lord, A strong true-score theory, with applications. *Psychometrika*, 1965, *30*, 239–270.

frequency distributions involving three different groups of examinees and eight different vocabulary tests composed of five-choice items. The N's for the three groups were 1000, 2000, and 2523.

For one pair of tests, H and J, the four chi squares obtained were all significant at the 5% level. The writer's conclusion is that a difficult vocabulary test like H, which uses such unusual key words as *limnetic, eclogue, newel, sericeous,* measures something slightly different from an easy vocabulary test such as J, which includes such key words as *renegade, clemency, irritability*. This viewpoint, persuasive by itself, tends to be substantiated by the fact that for these four bivariate distributions the observed product-moment correlation was

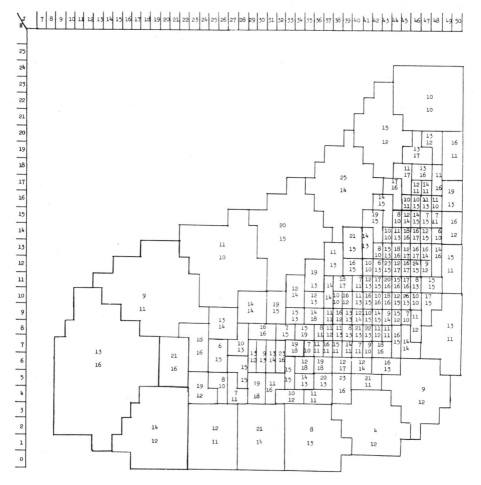

FIG. 17.4.1   Actual frequencies (upper) and predicted frequencies (lower) for Tests H and J.

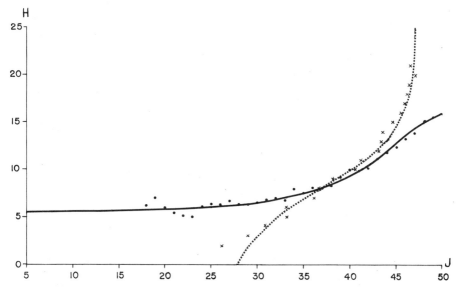

FIG. 17.4.2.   Theoretical regression of H on J (solid line) and J on H (dotted line) with actual column means (dots) and actual row means (crosses).

from .02 to .05 lower then the predicted correlation, whereas for the remaining 10 bivariate distributions the observed correlation was in every case a trifle higher than the predicted correlation.

Figure 17.4.1 compares predicted and observed bivariate distributions (N = 2000) for Tests H and J, the hard and easy vocabulary tests. Figure 17.4.2 shows for the same data the theoretical regressions of J on H and H on J, as well as those row means and column means of the observed distribution based on five or more cases. To the naked eye, the fit in these two figures seems rather good; the chi square is significant at the 5% level, however. If the two tests measure slightly different psychological traits, as suggested above, then significant chi squares are to be expected. The analysis carried out is in fact just the analysis that could be used to investigate whether the tests actually are or are not measuring the same dimension.

For the remaining 12 pairs of distributions studied, it is more plausible that both tests are measures of the same trait. For these, the model appears to be very effective: 11 of the 12 chi-squares are nonsignificant at the 5% level.

17.5.   CONSEQUENCES OF SELECTING ON OBSERVED SCORE

Table 17.5.1 shows the true-score distribution for a rejected group of examinees ($x \leq 38$), as discussed in Section 16.11. The estimated distribution of true scores

TABLE 17.5.1
Estimated Population Observed-Score (Noncumulative)
Distribution of Failing Students ($x \leqslant 38$) Compared with
Their Estimated True-Score Distribution and with Their
Estimated Observed-Score Distribution on Parallel Test y

Number-Right Score	Estimated Population Frequency* Distribution for		
	Test x	True Score	Test y
.	.	.	.
.	.	.	.
.	.	.	.
52	0	0	.1
51	0	0	.1
50	0	0	.1
49	0	0	.1
48	0	0	.3
47	0	0	.5
46	0	0	.6
45	0	.1	.7
44	0	.2	.9
43	0	.6	1.1
42	0	1.1	1.3
41	0	1.6	1.7
40	0	2.1	2.0
39	0	2.5	2.1
38	4.9	2.9	2.1
37	4.5	3.4	2.2
36	4.0	3.6	2.1
35	3.6	3.0	2.1
34	3.1	2.4	2.0
33	2.7	1.9	1.9
32	2.3	1.6	1.8
31	2.0	1.3	1.7
30	1.7	1.1	1.6
29	1.5	1.1	1.4
28	1.3	1.0	1.2
27	1.2	1.0	1.1
26	1.1	1.0	1.1
25	1.0	1.0	1.0
24	1.0	1.0	1.0
23	1.0	1.0	1.0
22	.9	1.0	1.0
21	.9	1.0	1.0
20	.9	1.0	.9
19	.9	1.0	.9
18	.9	1.0	.9
17	.8	1.0	.8
16	.8	1.0	.7

(continued)

TABLE 17.5.1
(*continued*)

Number-Right Score	Estimated Population Frequency* Distribution for		
	Test x	True Score	Test y
15	.7	1.0	.6
14	.6	1.0	.5
13	.5	0	.4
12	.4	0	.3
11	.2	0	.2
10	.2	0	.1
9	.1	0	.1
8	0	0	.1
7	0	0	.1
⋮	⋮	⋮	⋮
Total	45.5	45.5	998

*Number of students per 1000 students taking the test.

for rejected examinees ($x \leq x_0$) was found by the formula

$$\hat{g}_0(\zeta | x \leq x_0) = \frac{\hat{g}(\zeta) \sum_{x=0}^{x_0} \binom{n}{x} \zeta^x (1 - \zeta)^{n-x}}{\sum_{x=0}^{x_0} \phi(x)}, \tag{17-7}$$

$\hat{g}(\zeta)$ having been obtained by the methods of Chapter 16. A disadvantage of this result is that there is no way to check its validity.

From Table 17.2.1, we can write the estimated (noncumulative) observed-score distribution on form y for those examinees who are rejected by form x. The estimated distribution of form y observed scores for examinees rejected by test x is given by the formula

$$\hat{f}_0(y | x \leq x_0) = \frac{\sum_{x=0}^{x_0} \phi(x, y)}{\sum_{x=0}^{x_0} \sum_{y=0}^{n_y} \phi(x, y)}, \tag{17-8}$$

$\phi(x, y)$ having been estimated by substituting $\hat{g}(\zeta)$ into (17-5). This distribution is shown in Table 17.5.1 for comparison with the other distributions there. This distribution could be checked against actual test data if we could administer both form x and form y to the same examinees without practice effect.

Selection need not necessarily involve a cutting score. Given $f(x)$ examinees at observed score x, we can select a proportion p_x of these at random ($x = 0$, $1, \ldots , n$). The true-score distribution for the selected group will then be given by

$$g_p(\zeta) = g(\zeta) \sum_{x=0}^{n} p_x \binom{n}{x} \zeta^x (1 - \zeta)^{n-x} . \qquad (17\text{-}9)$$

The observed-score distribution on form y for the selected group will be given by

$$f_p(y) = \sum_{x=0}^{n} p_x \phi(x, y) \qquad (y = 0, 1, \ldots , n). \qquad (17\text{-}10)$$

Not only does this last equation allow us to estimate $f_p(y)$ when the selection procedure $\mathbf{p} \equiv \{p_x\}$ is given but it also can be used to find the selection procedure $\mathbf{p}$ that will produce a required distribution f_p of y. If the left-hand side of (17-10) is given for $y = 0, 1, \ldots , n$, we have $n + 1$ linear equations in the $n + 1$ unknowns $p_0, p_1, \ldots , p_n$. Since the matrix $\|\phi(x, y)\|$ will normally be nonsingular, values of $p_0, p_1, \ldots , p_n$ can be found satisfying (17-10) when the left-hand side is given.

To provide a meaningful solution to the problem stated, each value of p_x thus determined from (17-10) must satisfy the inequalities $0 \leqslant p_x \leqslant 1$. In practical work, it is likely that these inequalities will not always be satisfied, in which case some approximation will be required.

17.6. MATCHING GROUPS

Suppose two populations have distinctly different distributions of observed score $f(x)$. The *matching problem* is to select a subpopulation from each population so that the subpopulations are matched on ability (or true score).

Suppose subpopulations are chosen so as to have identical distributions of observed score x. This procedure ordinarily will *not* produce subpopulations that are matched on true score or ability, for the following reason.

Suppose that the unselected population A has considerably more ability than the unselected population B. If we match on observed score, we are mostly selecting the lower scoring people from group A and the higher scoring people from group B. Since observed score x equals true score plus error, when we select low values of x in group A, we tend to obtain a subgroup with negative errors of measurement. This means that the true scores of the subgroup selected from A are mostly higher than their observed scores. Similarly, the true scores of the subgroup selected from B are mostly lower than their observed scores. Thus selected subgroups matched on observed score are usually not matched on true score.

Since there is an infinite variety of possible true scores but only $n + 1$ different possible observed scores, it is, strictly speaking, theoretically impossible to select on observed score in such a way as to produce a subgroup having an arbitrary distribution of true scores. It may be possible, however, as we saw in the last section, to use (17-10) to select on observed score x so as to obtain a subgroup having a specified score distribution $f_p(y)$ on parallel test form y. If we can do this for both population A and population B, obtaining the same $f_p(y)$ for both subpopulations, then the subpopulations are matched with respect to y. This means that the true-score distributions of the two selected subpopulations must have identical moments up through order n. For all practical purposes, this would constitute a satisfactory matching on a true score.

This procedure will be effective if all the p_x found from (17-10) turn out to lie between 0 and 1. This is unlikely to happen for an arbitrary $f_p(y)$. In our problem, however, we are free to choose any $f_p(y)$ that we wish. Let us choose $f_p(y)$ so that the p_x found from (17-10) will lie between 0 and 1, both for population A and for population B.

The problem of finding such an $f_p(y)$ is simply the problem of finding a *feasible* point in a linear programming problem. If any $f_p(y)$ exists satisfying our requirements, it can be found in a finite number of steps by standard procedures for finding a starting point for the iterative solution of a linear programming problem.

Note that it is not necessary to find the optimal point or to solve the linear programming problem; it is only necessary to find a *feasible* point. If desired, however, we could proceed further, using linear programming to find the $f_p(y)$ for which $\sum_x p_x f(x)$, the size of the selected subpopulation, is as large as possible.

The procedure described in this section has not as yet been implemented. Thus no illustrative examples can be shown here. It would be desirable for some researcher to carry out the procedure and then actually administer test y to the selected subpopulations. This would provide a good check on the accuracy of the predictions made.

17.7. TEST NORMS

Suppose that a test publisher wishes to norm his test on a nationally representative norms group. If he selects a representative sample of schools and asks them to administer the test, he may receive many refusals. If so, any norms finally collected will be of doubtful value: the schools that finally agree to administer his test may be unrepresentative.

Suppose that the publisher can avoid refusals if he asks to administer only a 10-minute short form of the regular test. Our problem is then to estimate from their scores on the short form what the total norms sample would have done on the regular test.

Denote the short form by x and the regular form by y. We do not wish to go so far as to assume that y is simply a lengthened version of x; we assume only that both forms measure the same psychological dimension.

The relation $\eta(\zeta)$ between true score η on test y and true score ζ on test x can be found from (17-6). To find this relation, the publisher need only administer test y and test x separately to different random samples from any convenient population. The publisher does not need nationally representative samples for this purpose, since true-score equating is independent of the group tested (see Chapter 13).

In addition to determining the relation $\eta(\zeta)$ from some convenient sample, as just described, the publisher must estimate $g(\zeta)$, the true-score distribution for test x in the nationally representative sample by the methods of Chapter 16. The $\hat{\eta}(\zeta)$ from the convenient sample and the $\hat{g}(\zeta)$ from the national sample can then be substituted into (17-4) to estimate $\phi(x, y)$, the bivariate distribution of x and y for the national sample. The estimated national norms distribution $\hat{f}^*(y)$, say, for the full-length test y, is then obtained by summing on x across the estimated bivariate distribution:

$$\hat{f}^*(y) = \sum_{x=0}^{n} \hat{\phi}(x, y). \tag{17-11}$$

In any practical application of this procedure, x and y should be unspeeded (if they are speeded, they should be "equally" speeded, if this is possible). This requirement has discouraged but need not prevent practical application of this norming procedure. In some cases, this procedure may be the only way that a representative national group can be obtained for norming purposes.

Answers to Exercises

Chapter 4

1. .231, .296, .423, .6, .777, .904, .969.
2. .064, .288, .432, .216; 1.8; .8485; .6.
3. .050, .295, .459, .195; 1.8, .6, .8073.
5. 2.88, 3.26, 1.51.
6. .6 to 3.
7. Approximately −1 to +.5.
8. .050, .184, .075, .036, .275, .130, .054, .195.
9. .043, .092, .144, .125, .053, .013, .002.
11. −.69.

Chapter 5

1. .75, .95, 1.31, 1.8, 2.29, 2.65, 2.85.
2. .747, .795, .831, .807, .704, .540, .370.
4. .042, .143, .302, .415, .395, .264, .132.
7. .045, .105, .197, .25, .197, .105, .045.
9. 23.6, 7.0, 3.3, 2.4, 2.5, 3.8, 7.6.
10. .032, .122, .282, .406, .393, .264, .132.
12. .931, .833, .648.

Chapter 6

1. .022, .102, .306, .5, .440, .245, .107.
2. .135, .315, .590, .75, .590, .315, .135.
3. .51, .71, 1.01, 1.20, 1.11, .93, .81.

4.   3.2, 2.2, 2.0, 1.8, 1.5, 1.2, 1.0.
8.   .561, .649, .738, .72, .542, .308, .140.
9.   .069, .211, .367, .395, .330, .218, .110; 1.6, 1.5, 1.2, .95, .84, .83, .83.

Chapter 8

1.   .6, .4.
2.   .086, .351, .314, .249.

3.

$y = \frac{1}{2}$	1	$1\frac{1}{2}$	2
$\phi = .086$	.314	.351	.249

4.   .415, .585; .234, .293, .351, .123.

$y = \frac{1}{2}$	1	$1\frac{1}{2}$	2
$\phi = .234$	.351	.293	.123

Chapter 9

1. $-1.92, -.40, 0, .40, .84, 1.44.$
2.   1.83, .69, .64, .63, .66, .76.
3.

θ \ $x =$	0–1	2–3	4–5	6–7
2	0	0	.03	.97
0	.02	.27	.55	.16
-2	.46	.47	.06	0

Chapter 11

1.

$x \geqslant$	2	3	4	5
$\alpha =$	.69	.34	.10	.01
$\beta =$	.01	.07	.29	.70
$C =$	.70	.41	.39	.71

2.   24.1, 4.7, .91, .18, .03, .01;
     examinees scoring $x \geqslant 4$.
3.   .31, .26, .18.
4.   1.84, 1.64, 1.27.
5.   3.48, 3.12, 2.91; 3.
6.   .93, .83, .65.
7.   1.76, 1.58, 1.48; 1.5.

Chapter 12

1.   MLE for θ is $\theta = 0$.
2.   MLE for $\theta*$ is $\theta* = e^0 = 1$.
3.   BME for θ is $\theta = 0$.
4.   BME for $\theta*$ is $\theta* = e^{-5} = .0067$.

Author Index

Numbers in italics indicate the page on which the complete reference appears.

A

Aitchison, J., 12, *25*
Algina, J., 162, *176*
Amemiya, T., 12, *25*
Andersen, E. B., 12, *25*, 181, *191*
Anderson, M. R., 189, *191*
Angoff, W. H., 76, *80*, 207, *211*

B

Bennett, J. A., 12, *25*
Betz, N. E., 127, *127*, 146, *148*, *161*
Bianchini, J. C., 96, *105*
Birnbaum, A., 63, *64*, 65, 67, 72, *80*, 152,
   160, 162, 173, *176*, 186, *191*
Blot, W., 14, *25*
Bock, R. D., 12, 21, *25*, 189, *191*
Brogden, H. E., 12, *25*

C

Chambers, E. A., 14, *25*
Charles, J. W., 107, *112*

Christoffersson

Christoffersson, A., 21, *25*
Clark C., 157, *160*
Cleary, T. A., 146, *149*
Cliff, N., *160*
Collet, L., 227, *231*
Cox, D. R., 12, 14, *25*
Craven, P., 239, *253*
Cronbach, L. J., 6, *10*, 128, *148*
Cudeck, R. A., *160*

D

Dahm, P. A., 12, *25*
David, C. E., *160*, 162, *176*
Deal, R., 131, *148*
DeGraff, M. H., 107, *112*
DeWitt, L. J., *160*
Diamond, J., 227, *230*
Dyer, A. R., 14, *25*

E

Ebel, R. L., 107, 108, *112*, *113*, 227, *230*
Evans, W., 227, *230*

267

R

Rajaratnam, N., 6, *10*
Rasch, G., 182, 189, *191, 192*
Reckase, M. D., *160*
Rjabov, V. M., 239, *253*
Rock, D. A., 6, *10*, 146, *149*
Ruch, G. M., 107, *112*

S

Samejima, F., 12, 21, *25, 26*, 59, *64*, 153, *160*
Sax, G., 227, *231*
Schmidt, F. L., 207, *211*
Seder, A., 96, *105*
Seguin, S. P., 127, *127*
Shaw, C. B., Jr., *253*
Slakter, M. J., 227, *231*
Slinde, J. A., 5, *10*
Snijders, T., 166, *176*
Solomon, H., 12, *26*
Starbuck, R. R., 14, *26*
Stiehler, R. D., 69, *80*
Stocking, M., 92, 96, *105*, 136, *149*, 240, *253*
Stoddard, G. D., 107, *112*
Stone, M., 14, *26*
Stuart, A., 45, *64*, 71, *80*, 185, *191*, 197, *211*, 237, *253*
Subkoviak, M. J., 162, *176*
Susarla, V., 166, *176*
Swaminathan, H., 162, *176*
Sympson, J. B., 21, *26*

T

Thorndike, R. L., 207, *211*
Toops, H. A., 107, *113*
Traub, R. E., 227, *231*
Tversky, A., 107, *113*

UVW

Urry, V. W., 155, *160, 161*, 189, *192*
Vale, C. D., 96, *105*, 106, *113, 161*
van der Linden, W. J., 163, *176*
van der Ven, Ad H. G. S., 182, *192*
van Ryzin, J., 166, *176*
van Strik, R., 12, *26*
Varah, J. M., 239, *253*
Wahba, G., 239, *253*
Waters, L. K., 227, *231*
Weiss, D. J., 106, *113*, 127, *127*, 146, *148, 160, 161*
Werts, C. E., 6, *10*
Wiley, D. E., 207, *211*
Williams, B. J., 107, *113*
Wingersky, M. S., 92, 96, *105*, 189, *192*, 240, *253*
Wood, R. L., 189, *192*
Woods, E. M., 207, *211*
Wright, B. D., 58, *64*, 189, *192*

Subject Index